Inherited Silence

Inherited Silence

Listening to the Land,
Healing the Colonizer Mind

Louise Dunlap

New Village Press • New York

Published in the United States by New Village Press
bookorders@newvillagepress.net
www.newvillagepress.org

New Village Press is a public-benefit, nonprofit publisher

Distributed by NYU Press

Publication Date: July 2022

First Edition

Library of Congress Cataloging-in-Publication Data

Names: Dunlap, Louise, 1938– author.
Title: Inherited silence : listening to the land, healing the colonizer
    mind / Louise Dunlap.
Description: First edition. | New York : New Village Press, 2022. |
    Includes bibliographical references and index. | Summary: "An insightful
    look at the historical damages early colonizers of America caused and
    how their descendants may recognize and heal the harm done to the earth
    and Native peoples. Louise Dunlap tells the story of beloved land in
    California's Napa Valley: how the land fared during the onslaught of
    colonization and how it fares now in the drought, development, and
    wildfires that are the consequences. She looks to awaken others to
    consider their own ancestors' role in colonization and encourage them to
    begin reparations for the harmful actions of those who came before. More
    broadly, the book offers a way for readers to evaluate their own current
    life actions and the lasting impact they can have on society and the
    planet" —Provided by publisher.
Identifiers: LCCN 2021062315 (print) | LCCN 2021062316 (ebook) |
    ISBN 9781613321706 (paperback) | ISBN 9781613321720 (ebook) |
    ISBN 9781613321737 (ebook other)
Subjects: LCSH: Settler colonialism—California—Napa Valley—History. |
    Climatic changes—California—Napa Valley. | Indigenous
    peoples—California—Napa Valley—History. | Healing. | Reconciliation.
    | Napa Valley (Calif.)—History.
Classification: LCC F868.N2 D86 2022 (print) | LCC F868.N2 (ebook) |
    DDC 979.4/19—dc23
LC record available at https://lccn.loc.gov/2021062315
LC ebook record available at https://lccn.loc.gov/2021062316

Excerpted lyric p. 5: "Holy Ground" by Woody Guthrie
© Copyright Woody Guthrie Publications, Inc. (BMI)

Map artwork: Peter Soe
Author photo: Skip Schiel. *Photographs:* Louise Dunlap unless otherwise noted
Cover design: Kevin Stone
Cover photographs: Image in upper left by Skip Schiel; all others by Louise Dunlap
Interior design and composition: Leigh McLellan Design

To understand the storying of any place, I must also under-stand the storying of myself. Must follow traces beneath familiar surfaces to where ancestral structures lie.
  —LAURET SAVOY, *TRACE: MEMORY, HISTORY,*
    RACE, AND THE AMERICAN LANDSCAPE

As a nation, will you choose the path we have always traveled, a journey of silence that has benefited only a select group and oppressed others, or will you choose the road less traveled, a journey of racial reality that may be full of discomfort and pain, but offers benefits to all groups in our society?
  —DERALD WING SUE, *RACE TALK*
    AND THE CONSPIRACY OF SILENCE

Contents

Opening Words

The change we are facing is as deep as it gets.
　—LARRY WARD, "RESPONSE TO INSURRECTION"

Our task is to honor our ancestors, even those who caved beneath the weight of systematic destruction and became conquerors themselves. Our task is to remember that we are those beautiful Earth People.
　—LYLA JUNE JOHNSTON (DINÉ/EUROPEAN),
　　"RECLAIMING OUR INDIGENOUS EUROPEAN ROOTS"

Dear Readers,

THE WORLD IS CHANGING as I send out this book about my settler ancestors and the violent disruptions they brought here with colonization. No telling where things will be when the book reaches you. Powerful energies continue the ways of domination and control—over the Earth and all her creatures. Yet every day, new insights arise as whole communities struggle to understand and disengage from the harmful mind of colonization. New approaches, new ideas, new voices are being heard and acknowledged and the true story is at last coming clear. The work I send you is unfinished in so many ways.

Over a decade ago, I set out to look at a beloved place already suffering from climate change—an oak-studded hillside in what is now called the Napa Valley in Northern California. I'd felt deep intimacy and love for this piece of earth since early childhood, long before I understood that my great-great-grandfather had bought it in a time of what's now acknowledged as genocide. On its steep slopes are two year-round creeks in what I now know was a watershed tended by people we call the Wappo. I wanted to unearth the land's history and the roles my relatives had played in its colonization. I wanted to understand the wounding that must have taken place and how all of us—and the land—could heal.

I would learn that family history is America's second most popular hobby, but I was after more. I wanted to know my family's story in its full context, what had been left out of their tales and the genealogies available on Ancestry.com. I wanted to know the truth about my family's relationship to genocide. There are named methodologies and courses, now, for what I wanted to do: Critical Family History, Ethnoautobiography, Liberation Genealogy, Antiracist Genealogy, and probably more. Back then, I found my own way, with no real experience in historical research and many challenges. To provide missing information, for instance, I would have to use a classic tool of the colonizer—another settler-version of Native Californians' history, my own version. Though Indigenous friends have now read many parts of this book and said they are comfortable with my words, I know that no story I tell can touch their lived truths and may even deepen the problem.

My family's story also grew complicated as it led further back than California. People who settled the West had brought their mind-set with them from somewhere. My relatives had come from New England, where they were among the first to arrive from Europe to appropriate and rename the land. This was not just a California story but a national one.

As I followed clues back into our silenced history, other subjects required attention—enslavement, the supremacist ideas behind Manifest Destiny, restoration and repair, ancestor work from Indigenous cultures, climate disruption, grief, pandemic, decolonization, the healing of intergenerational trauma. It was a steep learning curve and I struggled with the discomfort of the true story, my complicit ancestors, and myself. I struggled with how to engage with the painful truth and hold it with love. I reached out for other white people to process our history, to do what somatic therapist Resmaa Menakem and others now call "metabolizing"—transforming our silence into a new culture that can look honestly at five hundred years of genocide and enslavement. There was a lot to learn, and much is still unfolding. I plan to stay open, keep learning and processing, and I welcome you to join me.

But please be warned. What you read may cause severe discomfort. Many of us have avoided that discomfort because our culture buried it in silence. Feeling it fully so we can move through it is our work now, and we need protective or spiritual practices as we open to the devastating facts. On a recent Harvard webinar I heard the Indigenous Wampanoag elders of that region caution against a merely academic approach to the university's treatment of their ancestors. "Our people do not discuss genocide without prayer and ceremony." This caution applies to all of us: Settler people experienced a different wounding in this terrible history. We, too, need healing practices to transform the shame and trauma we carry and continue to pass on. That shame is at the root of our silence. We need songs, poems, inspiration, spiritual practices, and affirmation that make it positive to acknowledge our history. As Larry Ward, author of *America's Racial Karma*, often reminds us, we need to reconnect with our essential goodness. For me this means forgiving our ancestors and ourselves, a deep process of change. Creating new practices for healing is challenging and sacred work. The land itself is part of this work. I hope you will find companionship for it and the energy to take part.

As I send this manuscript on its way, every day brings new resources, new ideas and websites, new teachers. Many others are taking up this quest to heal our history in unique and creative ways—to free ourselves for wiser action on the enormous challenges of climate, social systems, and our collective psyche that are calling out to us. This book is my small contribution.

CHAPTER I

Fires of Awakening

Months after the 2017 wildfire, new life springs from charred remains on Napa hillside.

I want you to act as if the house is on fire, because it is.
— GRETA THUNBERG, DAVOS, 2019

The internalized violence of many generations then was brought to Turtle Island, and that energy spread through the souls of the people like a forest fire that is out of control.
— EDUARDO DURAN, *HEALING THE SOUL WOUND*

Fire opens the door to the Spirit World and allows our psyche to communicate with other life present, past, and future.
— MALIDOMA SOMÉ, *THE HEALING WISDOM OF AFRICA*

I heard my fiery voice speak to me
This spot you're standing, it's holy ground
— WOODY GUTHRIE, "HOLY GROUND"

IN THE FALL OF 2017, an environmental disaster brewing for nearly two hundred years came to life late at night in the dry hills around California's Napa Valley, north of San Francisco. My family had been among the first Anglo settlers in this beautiful place, and I was just finishing a ten-year study of the land they'd passed down and the history they'd never told us. I was in the city that night and didn't know about the Napa fires until I choked on their smoke the next morning fifty miles to the south.

As if to remind us of something, those fires were world news on October 9, Columbus Day that year—the closest we come in this country to celebrating our roots in colonization. They followed an untimely heat wave and a desiccating north wind—called a Diablo wind by some reporters, the Santa Ana in Southern California, and *foehn* in Europe. Vegetation, including unusually tall grasses from the past winter's heavy rain, was dry as could be. Though ramped up by climate crisis, these conditions were essentially what the land had evolved with. Over half a century ago, in my childhood, dry winds would rise over faraway desert lands in the fall and roar down from the northeast. Flowing over hills like the ones east of Napa, they could pick up enormous speed downslope. Nowadays they came even faster. One climatologist clocked the 2017 winds at 120 mph, though most said 40 to 70—the force of a mild hurricane. With oceans heating up, our country had just seen the worst hurricanes ever off the Gulf of Mexico. The California winds brought wildfire, its magnitude the legacy of our colonial past.

Fires began simultaneously in several parts of Napa County that night, from electrical wires downed in the winds, a pattern that would be called "the new normal" as fires grew more intense in subsequent years. The worst 2017 fire followed a route from the northern part of the valley southwest into Sonoma County. Shortly after midnight, it reached the city of Santa Rosa, devastating broad suburban areas in a cousin's neighborhood and jumping a six-lane freeway. High winds carried flaming embers as far as a mile from their source. I'd been thinking about that corridor recently as I looked into the history of colonization. It was more or less the path vigilantes had taken in a deadly rampage to wipe out Wappo and

Pomo villages after the deaths of two brutal white settlers in 1849—the early phases of a terrible genocide that was never spoken of in my childhood. Later, I learned that big fires had burned through that route more than once since European settlement, but this one broke all records for speed and heat and threatened several Pomo communities still on their ancestral land.

News coverage was apocalyptic as I watched from Oakland, knowing that what I saw was being broadcast around the world as another major disaster. All our uneasiness about the Earth's ecosystem was now blowing up in our faces. Disaster had reached my own familiar ground—walls of flame, hillsides ablaze in the night, houses and trailer parks flattened like Hiroshima—closing in on the very place on Earth most like home to me. My screen showed a related fire in the hills east of Napa—"our" hills. This one also driven by high, gusting winds from the northeast, the Atlas Fire. I faced my screen short of breath, watching a familiar barn burn to the ground, the same fiery image over and over, like when we'd watched the twin towers fall years before.

The Coombsville area had been evacuated. Coombsville was the rural neighborhood up against the hills east of town and named for my family. Most of it was land my great-great-grandfather Nathan Coombs had bought from Cayetano Juárez in 1857. Before Juárez, it had been hunting, gathering, and tending land for the Wappo and Patwin peoples. It had come to Juárez as a land grant from the Mexican government, for his service in subduing these same people. That grant entitled him to use Patwin people living in villages there as his labor force. Nothing about this kind of enslavement or the brutality of the Spanish mission system that preceded it had been mentioned in my childhood, and it had been hard digging out the story.

Even with its painful racial karma, this land felt like part of my very being. Eighty acres of it, mostly in the hills, was still in my immediate family—owned by five of us in my generation and the next. I was the one who watched over it most closely and worked to maintain its natural beauty and harmony, as my parents had done before me. Over the past twenty years, I had been learning to listen to its needs. Online reports from the state fire agency now confirmed the Coombsville evacuation, but I wanted more detail than I could find on the net. These were hills I had known intimately all my life—the rocks, creeks, mosses, and oaks that had grounded me, even when I'd lived far away. I could feel their alarm in my bones and wanted to listen closely to them in this moment of crisis.

The only way was to go there in my mind. So, safe in my chair in Oakland, I calmed my breath and let my inner eye look out across Mother's field from under the big oak. Across the way, more live oaks would be standing dark green against the dry buff-colored field, with the hill sloping steeply up behind them to the "sunken rock," a boundary marker for the Coombs deed to the land. A compass would have indicated northeast, exactly the direction the winds were coming from—the direction I'd always known could bring fire. Old-timers, like Unc, who was Nathan Coombs's grandson, had pointed up that way when they talked of fire in the hills. I could remember fire up there in the 1940s, and farther north in the 1980s, when I'd visited burn sites with my mother to see the spring wildflowers that were always so amazing after a fire.

No one spoke of it in my youth, but the Wappo and Patwin peoples had used intentional smaller fires to tend the land, making sure things burned safely every few years to keep the brush down, the soil fertile and free of pests. The practice nourished the many plant species that had evolved with fire and was part of a ceremonial way of living that kept the earth healthy and in balance. Afterward, settlers had grazed cattle here until Unc's time, which at least kept the brush in check. Fires had been a regular thing in these hills before the Europeans arrived, but in my lifetime they had been suppressed as quickly as possible. The whole range of hills behind us was fire-prone, especially the parts that were brushy chaparral, but now they were also spotted with settlement. A private heliport we had just argued down before a county commission would have been right there in the riskiest part of the chaparral zone. A month earlier at public hearings, we had warned of fires—and now they were international news.

I thought of all the unnatural undergrowth on the hill above us—the tangle of poison oak, toyon, wild honeysuckle, the thickets of live oak seedlings that no longer had periodic fire or even grazing to keep them in check. A century's worth of dead branches on every shrub provided fuel "ladders" into the canopy. That tinder had grown denser and denser since my parents died—on my watch. I thought, now, of all the naturalists who'd shaken their heads and told me how much the land needed fire. I'd known they were right and yearned to try new forestry practices, like controlled burning, that were really old Indigenous practices. But I'd despaired of making it happen in these days of regulations and fire phobia. It looked like we'd let things go too long to use fire now. There was too much brush and dead wood on that hill to burn lightly, as it had for the Patwin and Wappo. A fire now could be so severe, I worried it would kill trees and sterilize soil, destroying the seed banks and all the magical hidden wildflower gardens on the hill. But at this moment, without any help from me, fire was happening—just as it had every ten years or so for all the millennia before we'd arrived. And this fire could be a cleansing force or a killing force. It could be both. I wouldn't know for a while.

Most on my mind were the huge, wonderful live oak trees around the house—the ones everyone saw as so peaceful—plus the little orchard my parents had planted and their simple, beautiful redwood house. The fireplace made of rocks Dad had carried down from the hill, Mother's native plant garden. The smooth brown arms of the manzanita, where I liked to sit and write on what we called the "quail bench." All of this lay in the path of those high winds from the northeast, off the hills where the Atlas Fire was making news. With embers flying out a mile beyond the fire, all could be gone in a moment in walls of flame—like what I was seeing on the internet. As I sat looking out from my chair, the possibilities unfolded before me.

Something came over me, then, that was like the feeling I hope I'll have when I'm ready to die—a feeling of acceptance, a kind of calm. I recalled something about climate disaster that I'd happened to read the night before—at about the same time the fires were starting miles away to the north—a talk by a Canadian First Nations elder. Like other Indigenous leaders who've stepped forward to help meet the fear and devastation of environmental chaos, Dave Courchene had urged his people not to beat themselves up trying to change parts of a system of exploitation that is determined to continue. He urged them to return "home" to traditional teachings that will ground them for taking right action in what lies ahead. He sounded like one of my Buddhist teachers. And he spoke of the power of Earth herself: "[I]t will be the power of the earth that will stop the invasion of the earth . . . the forces of nature herself that will stop the abuse that is inflicted on her."

That morning as I contemplated the terrifying fires and the overdevelopment and climate disruption that lay behind them, Courchene's words floated back to me, taking the fear out of the fire. I knew he didn't mean we should give up. We would have to do our part. But I felt a deep confidence in this idea that the Earth could take action against the abuse. That was what this fire was doing. Would we as a community, as a society, hear the message of the fire, recognize the destruction as a call to wake up to its real causes? Could we see that this fire—and climate change itself—traced directly from our ancestors' colonizing mind-set, our disrespect for what Indigenous peoples call the Original Instructions and our continuing failure to care for the Earth and one another? Politicians were, in that very moment, threatening to replace an international climate agreement with coal and fracking and to use the poison fire of nuclear weapons. We were experiencing what I'd once seen in one of those dreams that stays with you for a lifetime so you can finally get its message. Years ago, I'd dreamed of fire on this same dry hillside, a beautiful fire that burned without destroying—until my fear turned it lethal.

How to deal with that fear? As I listened long-distance to the land, a calmness came over me, releasing me from anxiety about the fire and its apocalyptic threat. I didn't need a particular outcome. I could let go of my parents' house and even the huge, wonderful trees surrounding it if that was what the Earth needed to do her healing work, to awaken us to better relationship with the forces of nature. I sent this thought out to friends around the world who would be worrying about me as they heard the news. Fifty miles from the fires, the city around me struggled with terrible fumes carrying the toxins of burning homes. Whirling through a day of emails, calls, and messages from relatives and Napa people, I was strangely at peace.

In the early 2000s, not long before her death, my youngest sister, Susan, and I had joined a fire ceremony in Boston led by West African shaman-scholar Malidoma Somé. The one other person in my family drawn to Indigenous thinking, Susie was on what turned out to be her last independent sister visit from rural Maine. My other sister, Sarah, also still living on the East Coast, joined us later for a meeting about the Napa ranch, which had just recently come to us through inheritance.

It was awesome to be with Susie in a situation so unlike what we knew from our proper white California upbringing. We'd both read Malidoma's book and begun to understand about ancestors and the unbalance he says our Western mind has with fire. This ceremony—dangerous to Western-ers who aren't well aligned with water and grieving—aimed to strengthen community, connect us with ancestral energies, and help us relate to fire as a force of transformation, not destruction or incineration.

The heart of the ceremony was an altar with candles we approached one at a time, so the energy of fire could burn away our obstructions. Afterward, each of us was received back into the "village." I saw my sister's face light up with joy as she received a loving embrace from an African American woman—something I was sure was new for her. In retrospect, I see this was part of a much larger healing for our entire family. Perhaps Susan had met some of our problematic ancestors in this ritual, or fire had opened a path for her to the Spirit World. For whatever reason, that night I had intense dreams that helped me not long after to deal with this beloved sister's untimely illness and death.

Years later, at the end of that first day waiting in the city, I learned by email that "the fire is on the ranch" but not near the house, where we'd always mowed for fire protection. Mother and Dad had been on the right track. They weren't aware of the First People's burning practices, but they knew how grazing had kept the woods free of brush when we first knew the land and they understood enough to plan for fire safety. Since then, whoever was caretaker had mowed the nearby woods every year—most recently, Robert and his son Clark. As the fire roared past on the hillside, those two dear men worked all day with tractor, fire hose, and portable water tank filled from the pool—putting out spot fires that started up from cinders blowing into the mowed area. After spraying around the house, they put the whole thing to bed and went home to give us a call. Would more winds come up in the night, blowing embers? There would be no way to know. For days, those strong winds would threaten to return. For days, stumps smoldered and the risk remained.

The second day, I heard no word about whether the house had survived the night—and knew there was no way to find out. Many times I felt my chest tighten, the muscles of my arms and hands trying to "do something." I tried to note these feelings and honor them to help them pass. And I waited, my heart slowly returning to peace. I knew the hill was in good hands—not just Robert's and Clark's. The energies of earth and fire, wind and water were playing their role, too, caring for the land in the ancient ways once again.

In the city, there was a run on N95 masks, the kind that cover your nose and mouth to protect you from industrial fumes. For a week, the air felt terrible, with regional alerts warning people my age to stay inside. I became expert at finding fire-related information on the internet. But then on the seventh day, the Coombsville evacuation order was lifted, and another kind of wind came up, which blew the air clear and fresh. With a friend, I headed up to the ranch—just for a few hours. I had to see for myself and touch the earth.

I'd made the trip a thousand times since childhood, but never with such turmoil in my heart. The first scorched limbs and blackened earth took my breath away as we turned into my father's road. As in my mental picture, the fire had swept south, consuming the entire steep hillside of the ranch, most of its eighty acres. With a few exceptions, it hadn't come down into the mowed area near the house. Except for some browned leaves at ground level, the oaks around the field were still a healthy dark green and heavy with acorns. But behind them, and all along the hillside, trees stood scorched or blackened, a few green ones remaining here and there. Underbrush was completely gone and you could see far upslope among the bare, charred stalks of toyon, bay, and young oaks. The ground was a mosaic of ash and charcoal alternating with patches of unburned oak leaves. I didn't go up on the hill that visit, but from below it looked like what I had hoped for, that this had been a fire of mixed severity, a healing fire, very close to what the land had been waiting so long for.

That first time back after the fire, I walked quietly out into Mother's field—in direct touch at last with this piece of earth I had visualized from the city. I moved slowly, feeling the ground under my feet, listening with all my senses, and taking everything in. I remembered what Robert had said on the phone—how he'd seen the fire enter the field and creep southwest toward the house—a tiny, low line of flame. He'd stood there watching it slowly cross the open expanse and die out midway. Now I could see how that gentle flame had charred everything in the far half of the field. That surface was black, spotted with a few pale oak leaves blown far from their trees by the fierce winds.

Two small rainstorms since the fire, just a sprinkling, were enough. Now where the field had burned, small circular green bursts of the native bunchgrasses with deep roots were coming back from dormancy. Thin green blades shooting out to form delicate mandalas of life against the blackened earth. *Stipa pulchra* and *Danthonia californica*, the field's original bunchgrasses—the ones that had almost been displaced by European oats and thistles—had responded well to the fire. Small mounds made by voles and gophers had risen up all over the field. The little creatures had survived underground and were turning over the burned soil, burying carbon, slowing its release into the atmosphere, and fertilizing the earth with minerals from the fire.

A week later, I was back to learn more. The air remained crystal clear but acrid and hard on the lungs in or close to the burn zone. Even with the N95 mask, I felt weak climbing the hill, but did so, though I wasn't sure my heart could take it. Step by step up through the mosaic of ash and charred grasses overlaid with oak leaves, toasted brown in the fire's sudden heat. The earth strangely brittle underfoot. Familiar landmarks missing or transformed, burned-away roots leaving dark tunnels in the soil, a huge stump still smoking. The two-and-a-half-inch black pipeline that had brought creek water to the house, now a thin ribbon of wrinkled plastic stretched tight against the earth. Being in this landscape was hard on the emotions. My mind read each sight as death and destruction. But here and there a vibrant live oak, unharmed by fire, reached out leafy green limbs to shade the strange ground. A few bunchgrasses coming back. Buckeye trees—already leafless and dormant before the fire—looked alive and well under their thin bark. How amazing that each species has its way of coping with this old evolutionary friend. And some places were still alive and green. The water looked cool in the little dam on the smaller creek. And, along the big one, acres of invasive blackberry had burned to the ground, leaving the natural contours of the land visible again after at least a century. Nearby huge trees had crashed in a tangle of monster trunks and limbs.

It was hard to think how to move forward. We'd have to replace the water tank on the big creek, carry a new one up there somehow, through the maze of fallen oaks. We'd have to clean the air system in the house, which was still full of toxic fumes from the fires. Everything outside was covered in dust and ash. And how would we handle all the burned limbs and downed trees so they could hold what was left of their carbon load as long as possible? Trees sequestering carbon have been our bulwark against climate change, but some say these fires have already released more carbon into the atmosphere than Californians have saved from all our conservation measures. Others say the vibrant regrowth expected after such a fire will pull significant carbon from the atmosphere.

What we faced at our place was minor. So many others lost everything they held dear in that fire. Some of the valley's artists lost their entire life's work along with their homes. The nightmare of returning to a toxic heap of ash and the brutal labyrinth of insurance, banks, and labor to replace even a shadow of what you loved. And the fires hit many with no access to these resources, including farmworkers who didn't have documents to be in this country. With government personnel overseeing everything, it's said they understood their peril and moved west, in groups, to the coastline for safety. Now, perhaps for the second time, they were climate refugees.

The ecological roots of this disaster had troubled me during the tense days before we knew what would happen at the ranch. The unusual triggers for this fire—desiccating heat, wind speeds, eerie multiple origins in sparking electrical wires. The painful irony that the fire added to global warming by releasing so much stored carbon. The extreme toxicity in incinerated urban areas, along with loss of homes and human suffering. These were the local face of a mounting range of disasters afflicting the Earth, and they would return. As if for emphasis now, a second untimely heat wave set in during the recovery period—and it was stifling hot even in bayside Oakland. All of it seemed to say loud and clear that we had crossed a line.

In those strange days of late October heat and bad air, I felt in my bones what I'd only acknowledged in my worst moments. My work on our history had shown that the roots of today's environmental unraveling lay in a consciousness that Californians—and many Americans—have harbored since settlement and before. What was normal to the people who'd come from Europe—deforestation, soil abuse, extraction of water, and general disregard for a diverse ecosystem, including its human members—had laid the groundwork for the disaster of climate disruption. A good part of the mix was our arrogance about how European ways were better. The Coombs family and their pioneer cohort had brought with them a worldview and a lifestyle that had led to this moment and become the hallmark of affluent America. We could not "fix" the disaster of this fire by going back to the way we'd lived before, to more houses built of toxic materials and a fossil fuel mentality that resulted in electrical wires strung through the vulnerable landscape. Those things were part of what I have come to call "colonizer mind". Einstein had put it very clearly: "A problem cannot be solved from the consciousness that created it."

That consciousness had included lethal disregard for the Indigenous peoples and their worldview, fellow humans who'd evolved with the land and knew its ways. Our first governor had openly called for exterminating them, and the new state's first legislators had criminalized the setting of modest fires that the First People relied on to keep the land fruitful and in balance. Fires that would have mitigated catastrophic ones like these. The new white Californians had feared fire, did not understand its relationship to the land, and arrogantly thought they knew best. Now we are beginning to see our perilous relationship with fire energy—fossil fuels, AK rifles, nuclear fire—the deranged fire mentality that West African teacher Malidoma Somé had warned industrial cultures about.

This fire—in a year of hurricanes, heat waves, and human madness— seemed a disaster so huge, it might wake us up to the hell realm we'd created. How many of us realize we can't go back to things as they were? A new awareness could be the real healing of this fire. Could it open our eyes to a way of living in reciprocity with the Earth and one another?

Could it help us listen to those who lived here before the Europeans, who had found a balanced relationship with fire and with water, soil, and the other creatures?

I thought constantly about birds during the fire. Fall migration had begun a few weeks earlier, and in Napa there had been flocks of robins and a few quiet hermit thrushes flying in for the ripening toyon berries on the hill. The big oaks had been alive with warblers, titmice, and other small birds passing through. What had happened to all of them roosting in local trees at night when the fire hit? What were their ancient instincts in times of fire?

When I first returned to the ranch, bird life was much subdued, even in trees that hadn't burned. In the parched, smoky air, I filled the bird-baths, which were crucial water sources, and immediately saw robins visit them. They, at least, were still here. My third visit, the air was cleaner, and I sat under the manzanita, writing near the pool—a special nook that almost always surprises me with bird life. As I wrote, I began to hear familiar voices—those of the acorn woodpecker, rufous-sided towhee, black phoebe, and a flock of band-tailed pigeons descending into the high oaks for the year's enormous acorn crop.

Then a small commotion made me look up into the manzanita—a mass of tiny birds swooping and foraging in the twiggy branches over-head. Were they bushtits, the tiniest of our birds, which travel in flocks? I didn't think so. One came very close, dropping down into the dry leaves near my feet, then lifting up and fluttering just above the ground a few inches away. A bushtit would never do that. Another stopped foraging to approach me at eye level. Cocking its head just slightly, inviting me into a strange eye contact. Only one bird I knew did this—the ruby-crowned kinglet, black eye with white eye ring. But they are usually solitary, and here at least a dozen were darting back and forth across the pool, hovering like flycatchers after tiny insects. Chasing one another around the manza-nita like kids in a playground. None of them seemed to have the red crest that marks the males when they're excited—I remembered my mother showing me. So I wondered if maybe they were young ones, summer nest-lings migrating together. I remembered that ruby-crowns move down to these elevations from the Sierra, and flocks also migrate longer distances from north to south. Even without the red crests, these little acrobats were elegant, with their delicate wing bars and lovely olive green backs—and those soulful eyes. For a long time I watched them feeding and playing.

Later, I found on the internet that young ruby-crowns migrate separately from their parents, and earlier. They're sent out first. What an amazing thing to find their way without elders through places they've never been, and such hostile ones as this fire zone. This little band must have been thanking themselves for locating such a perfect resting place, so beautiful here, with water and everything they needed for their journey on through the burned hills.

In the months after that fire, I attended forums where environmentalists and wise people sought to change our consciousness about fire. The only ones with a truly different vision were Indigenous leaders. Despite the brutal treatment I'd learned about in my research, some California tribes still knew their ancient teachings about fire and had thriving programs, using them on the little land still in their hands. Standard mainstream forestry practices now acknowledged the value of intentional burning, which was used in some parts of the state. But Indigenous peoples had evolved with the land, and their resilience came from deep spiritual roots. For them, fire was not so much a management tool as a sacred practice of reciprocity with Earth forces—a medicine for keeping things in balance. Mostly, the environmentalists still carried some of our European arrogance and were not tuned to the medicine. To change our consciousness about fire, we'd have to change our consciousness about colonization.

Meanwhile, I continued to watch and listen as the land I'd been close to since childhood began to recover. I watched strange mosses grow in over the deepest burns. Toyon, bay, and madrone sprouted from the roots of charred stalks. Globe lilies and manzanita seedlings rose from bare earth in once-impassable thickets. Some big oaks outside the mow zone had sustained such deep wounds that they continued to fall more than a year later. I grieved half-burned valley oaks with trunks four feet across that died in the next summer's heat. From nutrients the fire had left in the soil, the wild oat grass that Europeans had brought into the ecosystem—

which had long ago crowded out native fire-resistant grasses in most of the state—grew three times as tall as I'd ever seen it, posing yet another fire risk.

I kept thinking about the time two centuries back, before these invasive plants, when Wappo people worked together to care for this land—about the gentle ways they had handled fire to make the land safe. And I chafed at the laws that now placed ownership in the hands of people like us, who didn't listen to what the land needed. The fire confirmed for me a sense that had touched me gently in childhood and grown stronger as I'd cared for our family's place and learned its history. A sense that the land did not really belong to us, but we—myself anyway—belonged to the land. My sister Susan would have understood, but it might be a leap for the others in my family.

It was time for me to pull together the story of this land and its history—in our family's time and before. What earlier events on the continent had led to the disaster in California? I wanted others to see what I had come to understand. Very great wrongs had been buried in our silences; a worldview we had seen as normal had led us to a deranged climate and a country warped with hatred for darker-skinned people. There was no way to heal without looking back at what we had not told ourselves.

Most of it is painful to speak and hard to hear. The story starts with my childhood in the mid-twentieth century and the view of our history told in my settler family. I follow with the brutal counterstory of what really happened to the land and its Original People in this part of California—also the key to our present climate crisis. The next three chapters look at my immediate family—how we came to care for the land and how our consciousness of its history slowly began to change. After that, three chapters dig back into earlier generations. First those who lived here during and immediately after the genocide—playing their role in clearing and changing the landscape. To understand their silences, I then look further back into the generations preceding them—all the way back to those on the *Mayflower*—and the mind-set that came with the ones who made their way to California.

I am the twelfth generation on this continent and my sister's grandchildren are the fourteenth. Like so many others, we have ignored our problematic past and, without acknowledging it, we carry wounds and obstructions from that past. The final chapter looks toward healing what Indigenous people call the "soul wound," an injury that affects all touched by this history. Woven throughout are passages in a different voice, passages where I listen to the earth and the wisdom in my heart. These are the voices that keep me going.

On that hard October day back in the city when the Atlas Fire raged and there'd been no news from the ranch, I lay down on my floor to do some movements that help me let go of fear and tension. As I melted into those movements, the words of a Woody Guthrie song came to me, a song not known to the world until after the great American folk musician's death.: "Take off, take off your shoes / This place you're standing, it's holy ground . . . / Take off your shoes and pray . . ." Woody's song was about Moses and the burning bush, but it reaches farther: "Every spot on earth I trapse around / Every spot I walk it's holy ground . . ." It was the truth I had been learning in my lifetime—that all land is sacred, even when we have violated it. I wanted to sing this song to the Napa land, but it was still too risky for me to go there. So once again—this time lying on the floor with Woody's song in my heart—I sent my mind out to that spot under the big oak.

There I felt myself standing shoeless in the circle of wood chips we'd put down to protect the big tree from climate-driven blight. The place we'd held a four-generation picnic during a June heat wave. I stood there looking out at the smoking hillside, feeling the sharpness of wood chips against my feet and a slight dampness, maybe from things being watered down for the night. I felt the earth exchange energy with my feet.

What helped me stand there was an outpouring of love—from and for the big oaks. For the little cluster of deer Clark told me he'd seen sheltering there and browsing the early acorn drop, even with the fire raging so near. Love for the pair of Cooper's hawks calling as they hunted in the margins of the fire. For the field itself, at last feeling the loving touch of fire, denied for so very long. The field ready to heal at last.

That same love went out to the ancestors I'd uncovered in my research—who now came to stand behind me—my mother and father, who built the house and tried to keep the land "natural," my sister Susan. And all the colonizer and bystander ancestors I had struggled so hard to love as I learned about their lives. Malidoma Somé had said they actually yearn to support us in healing the harm they caused.

Love comes when you're all in something together, like we were in this moment with the oak trees. All my relatives were here now. Sophie Roper, with her love of manzanita trees. Foster, with his asthma—at great risk in the smoke of these fires. Aunt Ella and six generations of East Coast Ropers finally able to grieve the wounds of conquest. Unc, uneasy about his avocado trees. His grandfather Nathan Coombs—the first to buy this land—stood with us, dumbfounded but sharing our concerns. And his wife, Isabel, her mother a Lucero among six generations of Spanish and mestizo settlers in the Southwest. These blood ancestors stood behind me, and I could feel what Buddhists call the "land ancestors" creeping in—Cayetano and Maria Juárez and some of the Wappo and Patwin people who belonged here before and still do—forming a strong circle around us all.

We stood together here, not so much protecting the house as inviting the winds of the world into balance. Undoing these hundreds of years of fossil fuel abuse, the hotter heat, the speeded-up winds—all of it working to tear apart the beautiful system Mother Earth and the First People had put together, the system I'd faintly sensed as a child and my mother had begun to understand. That system was reasserting itself through the fire. With this love, I could feel the peace of the earth—wise and solid-holding this terrifying excrescence of wind and dryness, heat and fire, longtime human error and amnesia.

CHAPTER 2

Beyond the View
from Unc's Deck

Road through the woods to Mother and Dad's house.

*Euro-Americans used stories and histories . . . to construct
an imagined community where they were manifestly destined
to rule California and where the Californios and California
Indians who preceded them . . . were unworthy of self-rule.*

—LINDA HEIDENREICH, *THIS LAND WAS MEXICAN ONCE*

*Stories are among our most potent tools for restoring the land
as well as our relationship to land. We need to unearth the old
stories that live in a place and begin to create new ones.*

—ROBIN WALL KIMMERER, *BRAIDING SWEETGRASS*

Watching Sunsets with My Family

IT'S A HOT AUGUST EVENING, intense bone-drying California heat, but cooling off as the sun drops toward the western hills. I take my supper out to the deck of the small redwood house my parents built in their last years on land they inherited. I pull up a chair and look out through the weave of trunks. A wave of gratitude moves through me even with all I've learned about this place. Acorn woodpeckers still swoop back and forth among the oaks, calling to one another as they settle in for the night. Golden light spills north along the dark skyline across the valley. That skyline always pulls at my heart like family.

I watch as the sun goes down—tans and purples of the western hills darkening into navy blue. Golden sky turning pale peach, then rose and vivid scarlet. My sister Susan, when she lived for many years in the Maine woods, missed western sunsets most. A few clouds flare into wild shapes that shift and change as I watch. An hour from now, it will all die down to a rusty color of red, like old blood.

In the 1940s, when I was just seven or eight years old, we used to watch the sun set over this same skyline from the deck of an older house that's gone now. It stood a quarter mile to the south, on the bigger piece of land we called "Unc's ranch" or just "the ranch"—640 acres in the Napa Valley, passed down in the family from some of the earliest Anglo settlers. That acreage seems huge today, especially in the high-end real estate of the Napa wine country, but it was just a small piece of what our settler family had once owned. "Unc" was Nathan Coombs, their descendant and my father's uncle—a lawyer and politician and a kind, quaint-looking "old-timer." Unc's deck jutted out over the hillside above big coastal live oaks and a unique cherry orchard; it had a wide roofed-over porch wrapped around three sides of a brown shingle house. And the porch faced west into what we all knew was the best view in the world.

On a clear evening, beyond low hills and pastures, we could see out in three of the four directions: west across the valley to an unforgettable skyline; south to Mount Tamalpais and the San Francisco Bay; north to

Mount Saint Helena. These landmarks positioned us—an hour's drive north of San Francisco on the rim of a fertile and beautiful valley draining into the bay. A much sought-after location, then and now. Some evenings we watched white sea fog pour in over that skyline from the Pacific. I can't speak for the adults, but we children didn't realize, then, that back in settler times there was violence all across this panorama, that no part of the land before us was free of terrible pain and the need for healing.

Night after night we'd look out on the view while the grown-ups had their Manhattans and highballs with dips and crackers. Unc and our family and maybe other relatives, sitting together through the long sunsets into the dark, watching the stars come out, eating our dinners on square metal picnic plates with paper inserts—simple 1940s California dinners of macaroni and cheese, meat loaf, salad made with iceberg lettuce, and peaches or cherries that Mother had canned from Unc's orchard. The air was mostly clear and beautiful in those days. Smog hadn't come to this part of California yet, nor the particulates of catastrophic wildfires. We had no idea what was ahead or how our bubble of a world had come about. We did not know the true story of our past.

I was the eldest of the children on that deck, awkward in my plaid shirts and blue jeans, but at home in the woods and quietly taking in my elders' views about our place in the world. My sense of family took shape on that porch as we looked for the evening star or commented on the sunset. "Allus sets in the west," Unc would say in his funny, old-fashioned way. He had a sort of high-pitched voice, almost incongruous in a stocky, large-bellied man who was a politician, and he'd take his wet cigar out of his mouth and hold it when he spoke. Some raised their eyebrows, but no one commented. Sitting there in the sunset, we talked about deer caught in the headlights or skunks hurrying ahead of the car at night. We didn't discuss politics, past or present, though Unc would soon become a state senator, with views most of us had problems with. Never any open controversy. And we didn't talk about vintage wines—as people do nowadays on beautiful evenings in the valley.

Unc had built this country house in the early twentieth century—a bachelor's retreat near his home in Napa, a base for his fruit-growing projects and weekend barbecues with political buddies. After World War II, he offered the place to my parents when we had nowhere else to live. And later, when we moved away for Dad's job in the city, he welcomed us back on weekends to hike the steep hills and oak-studded pasturelands that he rented out to dairy farms before the vineyard boom made Napa famous for wines and tourism. I had no idea, then, how just being on this land meant a kind of status and privilege few could dream of. And no idea at all of the loss and trauma that had opened the way for our ancestors to settle here. All I knew was that we loved this place and felt a deep belonging.

If we'd been ready to think about it, we would have known that long before our people came here—before the Spanish priests or the Mexican ranchers—other families sat out on these slopes in the evenings, watching the sunset. Families that came up the creeks from home villages in the valley to gather food and medicine or harvest acorn crops in the fall. For them, belonging meant taking care of the place year-round, including burning the landscape even up here in the hills. The First People knew what they were doing in ways that astound today's scientists. Their fire fertilized the soil, encouraged new growth for deer and elk, and killed off pests that could hurt the big trees or ruin an acorn crop. It balanced things and even kept the water cycle healthy and the creeks flowing. Their first time in the valley, Europeans noted the burned fields. After that, settlers tried to stop the burning. They didn't understand how it kept the land healthy and controlled underbrush that could fuel wildfires. In those evenings on Unc's deck, we didn't understand, either.

Pioneer Stories

The school I moved to in Berkeley taught the 1940s standard fourth-grade California history—the glamour of the Spanish missions and the forty-niners' gold rush, with very little about the tribal people who lived here before. I remember memorizing that their diet of acorns made them slow and passive. It would be nearly half a century before I learned how much more nourishing that diet had been than our macaroni and cheese. And it would take me that long to learn the names of the people who had lived on the Napa land—the Patwin and the Wappo—whose territories had met somewhere near here shortly before the first Coombs arrived. When I interviewed Unc for my fourth-grade essay about California history, I remember he expressed concern for those who were here before us—Mexican ranchers and Indians, whom he lumped together as a weaker people, "natives" we had taken advantage of with our sharper Yankee wits. "Poor devils," he called them. I wasn't sure whether this was compassion or something else. It was the same expression he used for deer hit by a car or gophers mangled in one of his traps. But, for these, he'd usually add, "Oughta cut its neck." "Poor devils" was the only way I ever heard him acknowledge harm done to the people we'd displaced.

Except for the "poor devils" part, most of my interview has slipped from memory, probably because Unc tended to drone on in words I'd heard over and over about family history. I would have different questions for him now. At eight years old, I knew only that "we" were the Americans, the exceptional people, though I don't remember Unc giving us any ethnic label. You don't need one when your people are at the center of things. Unc told our story in the Napa Valley, starting with his grandfather, my great- great-grandfather, also named Nathan Coombs. Nathan the pioneer had come west as a youth from Cape Cod, in Massachusetts. He'd reached California in 1843—when Mexican settlers, known in history books as Californios, were establishing big cattle ranches in the region—and he'd married a rancher's daughter. There was no mention of Indians in Unc's story. The young Nathan somehow got hold of a good bit of land—Unc did not say how—and used a piece of it to found the town of Napa. The ranch we were so attached to was the only part of his holdings still in family hands.

Exactly one hundred years before I wrote my fourth-grade paper, this first Nathan Coombs had joined other early pioneers in the Bear Flag Revolt of 1846. Every school taught this episode of California history: the Yankee capture of a Mexican outpost in Sonoma, less than a day's ride over those very hills we could see from Unc's deck. A flag made from a petticoat with the rough drawing of a grizzly bear was its signature and later became our state flag. Unc described the Bear Flaggers as patriotic men seizing California from the Mexicans to turn it over to the United States. Other historians would see a drunken brawl by rowdy frontiersmen or a power play by then U.S. Army captain John C. Frémont, who didn't participate in person. Even Anglo historians didn't agree, and schoolbooks in my day didn't give the views of "natives" on the Bear Flaggers—only the story told by the victors. The Mexican-American War and Treaty of Guadalupe Hidalgo followed. In 1848, California and huge segments of the West that had already been colonized by Spain, then Mexico, became part of the United States.

Other big dates in his story were the gold rush in 1849 and California statehood in 1850. But our family had a presence in the region years earlier, while it was still part of Mexico, thanks to the first Nathan's wife, Isabel. I remember Unc taking me to see her family's gravestones an hour's drive east on Cache Creek, in Yolo County, on a hot spring day under huge valley oaks. Her parents, Will Gordon—"Gran'pap Gordon"—and his wife, María Juana Lucero Gordon, were our earliest ancestors in California, five generations back from me. They had arrived in 1841 from another Mexican colonial holding—Taos, in what's now New Mexico—and qualified for their own land grant, since María Lucero was a Mexican citizen. Unc always said her family was "pure Castilian." We all remember how often he repeated this phrase, and later I would figure out why.

Most of my paper was the litany of leadership that Unc recounted with such pride. My great-great-grandfather had served twice in the new state's legislature, setting the tone for his descendants. His son Frank—Unc's father—was speaker of the California State Assembly, U. S. minister to Japan, U. S. district attorney, and a one-term U. S. congressman. In his spare time, he wrote an unpublished novel celebrating Manifest Destiny and the early days of conquest—where flowery sunsets glorified the golden West. Unc followed his lead as district attorney, state senator (on California's Un-American Activities Committee during the Communist purges), and a member of the Native Sons of the Golden West. Back then, this organization required descent from gold rush–era settlers, promoted settler history, and played a major role in stigmatizing Japanese Americans during and after World War II. Two of Dad's brothers would later hold public office in Napa. All but one were Republicans who believed that pioneer values—Yankee ways from the East Coast—were best for the land

and all of us. It's uncomfortable, now, to realize how normal it seemed to me then—the mind of the colonizer as I learned it on Unc's deck.

My paper itself is long gone, so I don't remember whether I questioned Unc's version of history in any way. For a fourth grader, it was exciting to be related to one of the Bear Flaggers, who were being celebrated statewide that year. I probably wrote exactly what Unc told me, including all his pride in the conquest of California. At that point, I was absorbing the family legacy. And Unc was a likable kind of guy. Who else would take me to a patriotic parade or a hearing in the state capitol? Who else would enlist a little girl to help irrigate his unique avocado and kumquat trees? I had no idea there might be things he didn't talk about, other points of view on this land, my father's family, the history of settlement in California, and the nation we were part of.

In my immediate family, we were taught not to mention family status. My fourth-grade paper focused on Unc and his prestigious ancestors, but when conversation among school friends turned to whose father or grandfather did what, my sisters and I were trained to keep quiet. Kids at our all-white grammar school didn't have landed pioneer ancestors, even though most were well-off and probaby looked down on us, since we had only one car, made lots of our own clothes, and had no "maid" to do the housework. Our standing in the world didn't come from financial success.

Part of the reticence came from my mother. Her own landed settler roots in the U.S. South went back generations further than my Dad's in the West. But she didn't speak much about her family's history, either. I'm guessing she wasn't comfortable with her people's role in enslavement and didn't want that talked about. We got the message that it was bad manners to speak of our ancestors. And, because we somehow believed that ours were "better" than even the rich kids' ancestors, to mention them at all would have been to brag. Much later, I realized that these "manners" protected us somehow, kept us from standing out above the crowd, where we might have had to face challenges. Our silences also kept us from repairing the harm and from facing inward to recognize our own arrogance.

But I complied and didn't speak about my California forebearers after writing my fourth-grade paper. I didn't think much about them, either, for many years. The Coombses and the Dunlaps, the Gordons, the Ropers, and the Strongs were faces in yellowed sepia portraits. Men with mustaches in stiff collars and women with tightly coiffed hair, wearing brocaded silk—even way out here on the California frontier. Sometimes I found these images in crumbling leather books in Unc's old house in town—where we'd lived during part of World War II—or hanging framed on walls in dark corners of elderly relatives' homes. These people were part of a musty past that carried no interest for me then, and for which I even felt a kind of aversion I didn't want to explore.

The Hills Speak to Me

The land they'd settled was another story. It had stirred me from the very beginning. As the first grandchild, I was taken on Sunday drives through the valley. Unc and my grandparents were passing on something they loved. And the land was truly beautiful—each hill and pasture green or golden with the season, tall valley oaks draping their branches over spring streams, wildflowers flashing color on the slopes, and elegant dark blue hills shaping the skyline. It would be half a lifetime before I understood how this land had become "ours" and what it meant to own even a small piece of it.

Then after the war—when I was seven—our family got to live at Unc's ranch for a year. Dad taught my two sisters and me how to duck under barbed-wire fences without ripping our shirts, Mother and I learned names for the plants that grew on the hill, and Unc taught me to find the road by going downhill if I got lost. Then they let me roam. Unc's ranch was a mile square—some of it steep, with creeks, cliffs, and canyons, and some of it gentle hills—classic cow pastures crisscrossed with barbed-wire fencing and occasional stone walls from early days. As an openhearted child, I got to know most of it—and all the different, beautiful ways it looked from month to month throughout the year.

I can still remember what it felt like to hug a big oak trunk soft with a two-inch shag of moss in the rainy green winters, and how the slope behind the house got steeper as you climbed over stumps of old buckeye trees to see the first ferns in a shaft of sunlight. I can still remember places where the woods opened up just enough for patches of wild strawberry plants. In early June, you could pick enough tiny berries for a child-size feast. And in a certain place, at just the right time in March, you'd find a couple of trilliums with their three broad leaves surrounding a small three-petaled wine-colored flower. When my parents called me in for dinner by honking the horn on our old blue Ford, I never felt like I'd had enough time on the hill.

Unc was part of my affection for the ranch. We could always tell his car coming up the lane, a big Ford sedan with dust billowing out behind, even though he drove very slowly, as people did in those days to keep the dust down on dirt roads. Unc would park in the deep oak shade and emerge already comfortable in his ranch clothes—soft brown colors that wouldn't show the dust. His old felt ranch hat was a softer, more battered version of the one he wore to the office with his three-piece suits. He'd say hello to whoever was around, then disappear into all the chores he did to maintain his special trees. He moved slowly, carrying fertilizer, traps for gophers, clippers, or a shovel. We hardly saw him once he headed for the orchard, unless we went with him to help.

Unc's specialty trees grew on a steep piece of land recently cut from the woods and surrounded by a high deer fence. Inside were grapefruit, blood orange, kumquat, and avocado trees at least three stories tall—their fruits delicious in fall and winter. I would help by tromping around to check the deer fence where animals had dug their way under to get at the greenery, or dragging the irrigation hose to each tree so water could pool around the base. That water came from a small dam on one of the creeks, which also served the house for washing and bathing. With cattle grazing above, it wasn't clean enough to drink. Later, Unc had a well drilled, but walking up the steep hillside with him to check the pipeline from the dam remained a favorite chore. The hard labor of pruning, plowing, and picking the cherry orchard, Unc hired out to seasonal workers.

Mother made us stand back when Unc got up on a chair to reach the top shelf of the kitchen cupboard, where he kept his stash of strychnine-laced carrots for killing gophers. Somewhere nearby he also kept a shot-gun for shooting the "poor devils" to put them out of their misery when he found them in the pain of dying from his traps.

That's how it all started. For the next six or eight years, when we came back for weekends, Unc's wild hillside was my special place. As soon as we got there, I'd melt up into the woods, my refuge during all the years when young people feel isolated and misunderstood.

New Landowners, Darkening Skies

In my teens and during college, my love of the outdoors expanded into California's high mountains, which I explored with my family and the Sierra Club whenever I could. But the Napa oaks and creeks were always home base. Meanwhile, the old people had started to pass on. My grandmother Amy Louise died in 1960, and Unc a few years later. At that point, Unc's ranch—the square mile I had loved as a seven-year-old—was broken up into parcels for sale. Our branch of the pioneer Coombses was gone. My father and Uncle John—both Dunlaps—each kept a corner of the land to build their dream houses. The rest of the acreage quickly filled with big, elegant homes surrounded by new vineyards in the former pastureland. The look and feel of the land around us had changed. By this time—Prohibition long over—the wine industry had made a comeback, and the Napa Valley was attracting businesses, gourmets, and wealthy people from all over the world.

I wonder what my parents—and Unc—would think about environmental quality and global climate disruption today. The local weather wasn't consistent or the air pure in their time, either. Environmental historians say California's climate has always been extreme—with wet winters and dry, hot summers, varying dramatically each year in length and intensity, not to mention periodic drought going back way before settlement. Winter and spring storms could be violent, bringing mud slides and flooding rivers. Every seven years, Unc would say, you would see snow on the peaks around the Valley. He had stories, too, about the dry north winds that would come at the end of a hot summer, the ones that have grown to nightmare strength with climate change. The grown-ups used to debate endlessly on the porch: Were we looking at fog or cloud, haze, mist, or smoke? There were also "low fogs" and "high fogs," "low clouds" and "high clouds," and all kinds of hybrids. It would be another ten years before the word *smog* entered our vocabulary in this part of California. And we had no way of knowing about the toxic-air alerts of the twenty-first century.

The skyline hasn't changed since my childhood. But the sunsets seem more intense. Starting in the 1990s, the dry season brought smoke from wildfires roiling the sky, along with dense air from cities, automobiles, and industry in Asia. The valley adds its share. With vineyards everywhere instead of pastures, there's more pruning and the growers burn their waste. On a legal burn day in spring, a day without much wind, you can see the air thickening with bluish smoke, releasing sequestered carbon. Sometimes you can hardly see across to the western hills. Now the skies carry a dense load of particulates. Is this what's making the sunsets so red? Some of them stay vivid for forty minutes—beautiful but ominous.

After World War II and my dad's short tour of duty in New York, our family drove home to California in our first car, a prewar Plymouth bought secondhand to carry us back to the Napa Valley. I remember how the skies darkened when we drove through Pittsburgh, Pennsylvania, then famous for active steel mills. There the air was so dense with industrial smoke that the streetlights stayed on all day, so we could find our way in the time before freeways. That eerie dark air stirred fear in me—fear that I wouldn't be able to breathe, that the end of the world would be like this. That feeling has come back more than once, and sometimes on these evenings of deep reds and scarlet. Aren't we supposed to pay attention to what the sunsets are telling us?

Unc was pretty much pro-development and was buddies with people in Napa who were selling real estate and building along the highway. I would learn that his Coombs grandfather had also been absorbed in land sales and development. But my immediate family watched with dismay as field after field went over to spread-out housing and roadside shopping plazas in the postwar boom—all of it adding cars and eating away at air quality. We loved the clean air of the high mountains, which we considered wilderness. We also knew the economics of development. We often heard about one of Dad's law clients gradually selling off his land, until all that was left was just one corner of a field jammed between two highways but worth millions. That didn't seem to be what land was for.

It was wrenching to move away from California in the 1960s for marriage and work on the East Coast. But in some ways it was a relief from the feeling of loss. I couldn't bear to see bulldozers and new parking lots every time we drove to Napa. I couldn't bear to see another meadow of blue lupine and goldfields gone over to parking lots. Already I felt a sense of desecration in the earth around me. Rachel Carson had written her *Silent Spring,* but I couldn't bear to read about what I already felt so keenly in my bones. The comfort of the world I'd grown up in also seemed to dissolve as the social movements of 1960s taught me more about what held things together. I'd begun to have arguments with my parents about the Vietnam War and to question earlier wars. Dad and Mother both thought the atom bombs dropped on Hiroshima and Nagasaki had been necessary to prevent a longer war that might have cost our uncles' lives. Now we know that Japan was ready to surrender and public opinion was carefully orchestrated by Hollywood and the president's office. Many military leaders have repudiated the decision.

Like so many others in the sixties, I was stirred by the freedom movement in the U. S. South, where Mother's relatives still lived. During graduate school, I learned new ways of thinking from fellow students in the Berkeley Free Speech Movement with roots in the civil rights struggle. About that time, I had a prophetic dream of a young Black child behind bars in a courtroom, fearful and lonely. I didn't understand much about dreams then, but this one was so moving, I knew it held guidance for my life. I was waking up to the realities of race and injustice, sensing that many wrongs were related in a way it was hard to articulate. I did want passionately to contribute to a more just world. Moving east in the late 1960s, my first job was teaching writing at Boston University, where Martin Luther King, Jr., had gotten his doctorate. I was there outside the chapel where he had preached, keeping vigil and sobbing with hundreds of others when we got the news that this man who'd stirred our hopes so deeply had died from the shot fired in Memphis.

Indigenous Voices Change the Narrative

Since I loved the natural world and the California landscape, my family had hoped I would find a career in botany or the new field of ecology and settle down nearby. Instead, I studied literature and lived far away in New England as a writing teacher for over forty years, loving my work but always homesick for the California oak woodlands. In the 1970s, I lived in one of Boston's neglected Black neighborhoods—with toxic weed lots for greenery and city trees stunted by lead from auto exhaust. I remember a shortcut along train tracks through the former meatpacking district, which still smelled of suet, as I walked to my second job teaching writing at a new campus of the University of Massachusetts.

We were supposed to be an affordable, "people's" Harvard, so this meant our students came from every ethnicity and neighborhood in the city. Very few had parents who'd gone to college, and I'm sure none had family with acres of land on the West Coast. Writing was a struggle for those students and for me, too, even with all the privileges I was learning to recognize—educated parents, access to an elite university, free time for self-enrichment. But the struggle gave us something in common. I found myself listening to my students more deeply than had happened in my own education, engaging in authentic contact across differences of class and culture. I was learning to see the entitlement I'd been raised with and taking next steps on the long path that would lift the silence and change the family narrative—the pioneer narrative—for me.

Other white people have asked where I got the courage to look at the hard truth of our history. I can't think of a particular moment that empowered me or set me on this path. No ghosts rattled furniture; no dire illness turned my heart in this direction; no teacher or healer sent me on a vision quest. No vision or letter from the deep past called me. But the times were right—the books and the people who came my way—individually and in groups—all of them helped with a shift in my consciousness that was huge and is ongoing.

One of the books I read with my students was *Black Elk Speaks*. The point of view Unc had passed down, which I had echoed in my fourth-grade paper, began to change in this first experience with a Native author.

My students and I pored eagerly through *Black Elk Speaks* in our temporary classroom in a former insurance company building downtown. It was the late 1960s, and minds were opening to information about our nation's past that had not been part of the dominant narrative.

Telling his story to white Nebraskan John Neihardt in the early 1930s, an elderly Lakota holy man looks back at a life that coincided with U.S. settlers moving into his homeland and destroying its way of life. Black Elk describes the vision given him by Spirit World grandfathers around 1870, when he was only nine years old. Then, the Lakota (the Sioux of our schoolbooks) were still living "in the circle," their beliefs reflected in circular tepees set in a communal circle under the great round arc of the open sky. Their way of seeing the land reminded me of my love for the California mountains and Unc's ranch. The Lakota held a huge segment of the West by tradition and also by treaty with the expanding United States. But gold and settler demands threatened those treaties and the world they knew. Black Elk saw that his people would have to travel "the black road," a terrible path toward starvation and dissolution of their lifeways.

Still a young child, Black Elk had received this vision to heal his world in its time of destruction. But the vision was so powerful, and the child still so young, that he could not speak of it for many years, much less find support to begin his work. And not long after the vision, things got much worse for the Lakota. To make way for railroads, farming, and extraction, U. S. policy came down hard on the Native population—exterminating the great buffalo herds on which they depended and breaking treaties to set up smaller reservations. Many tribal people had to move into towns, where they were made to live in square houses on government rations that rarely came through as promised. Fear and hatred from settlers only grew stronger, culminating in the massacre of hundreds of women and children in an unarmed camp at Wounded Knee Creek, in South Dakota, on December 29, 1890. Our schoolbooks had called it a battle in the "Indian wars" that built our country. Looking back forty years later, Black Elk told Neihardt, "A people's dream died there."

Critics have questioned Neihardt's role. As a white writer with an agenda, he'd left his subject's later-life Catholicism out of the story. Yet

Black Elk's insight had told him this writer could help him share his message with the world. However imperfect the vehicle, a message got through, opening my mind and many others. I was devastated by what had happened to the Lakota, and upset by this firsthand account of lies and deception by white settlers and the military. I'd grown up among people of privilege with pioneer values, but I thought we'd believed in honesty, respect, and justice. The dissonance was painful. Black Elk's story became a generative one that I returned to year after year, in part for his visionary connection with the land he belonged to—its plants and landforms.

As my class read *Black Elk Speaks,* other white Americans were beginning to recognize the atrocities in our history. Alongside the civil rights and American Indian movements, awakenings from the Vietnam War and books like *Bury My Heart at Wounded Knee* (written by a white librarian) were changing long-standing stereotypes. But what had happened in California was not yet part of that awarenes, and white historians generally shied away from the word *genocide.* It would take many more years for me to learn that my home territory had experienced its own terrible period of slaughter some forty years before Wounded Knee—during the very period my ancestor Nathan Coombs was making his fortune here.

Black Elk had opened my eyes, but I wanted more than books. As I read about the First People, I looked for those living and active in the world around me. By this time, I'd become a peace activist alongside my academic work, joining local groups focused on racial justice. In 1990, through my work in a graduate program at MIT, I joined a circle of Indian activists and supporters we called the Massachusetts Solidarity Committee. (They preferred the term *Indian* to *Native American,* which was in vogue at the time; I was learning to listen, not think I knew best as a white person.) Our first project was fund-raising for a remarkable event taking place in 1990 for the centennial of the Wounded Knee Massacre. One of our group members was Lakota, like Black Elk. At her invitation, a friend and I joined her on the reservation in late December, one hundred years after the massacre. In the bitter depths of winter, Lakota elders organized a sacred overland horseback ride, a ceremony to "wipe away the tears and mend the sacred hoop." A time to return to the circle, to nourish the resilience of a people violated a century earlier.

With my friend Skip, I volunteered support for three hundred horse-back riders traveling through the deep cold on the route taken by a band of Lakota seeking sanctuary but headed for the great tragedy at Wounded Knee. Besides serving meals, support meant pitching our little blue mountain tent in a circle of majestic tepees, listening in talking circles, where descendants of survivors told stories of their ancestors' and their own suffering, seeking to heal. On the final day, I experienced the profound energy of prayer. I walked the frozen roads to the massacre site with a Buddhist nun and Lakota people whose ancestors had made the original journey on foot with Spotted Elk (Chief Big Foot in the history books).

At our backs was what Black Elk had called the "cleansing" cold of the north wind—a windchill factor of seventy degrees below zero. Tears froze on eyelashes. Surrounded by sage smoke and ceremony in a culture much older than my own, I opened myself to feelings of grief, anger, and shame that most white Americans probably had not tried to face. Here in this place that had seen such atrocity—now a sacred place—I choked up with sobs as the impact of our history washed through me. Our people had done this. How could I live with the knowledge of it?

Back in Boston, my Indian friends helped me see that shame was a miserable trap I could get stuck in. The Solidarity Committee said, "Get out there and do something!" Skip and I spent the next two years sharing the story of the ride to counter the triumphalist narrative of Columbus that would envelop the country in 1992. Our solidarity group continued to raise money, share culture, and support tribes local to our area. Taking action with them began to transform the shame into healing energy.

For years after, I thought about it. My pioneer ancestors were not present at the Wounded Knee Massacre. They didn't handle the rapid-firing Hotchkiss guns or shoot down fleeing women and children in the bloody gullies. But they could have been there. They were part of the political consensus that sponsored the killing; they benefited from the railroad, the mines, the ethnic cleansing of the continent.

Unc was born in 1881, so he was nine at the time of the massacre and most certainly heard the news as passed on by many Anglo reporters. His father's appointment to Japan two years later came from Benjamin

Harrison, the same president who'd broken up the Great Sioux Reservation and appointed the Indian agent now blamed for what happened to the Lakota. The massacre at Wounded Knee was another chapter of the pioneer legend Unc had told with such pride. My relatives likely saw it as a necessary step in securing the West, making it a safe place for nieces and grandchildren, not so different from how my own parents saw the atrocities of Hiroshima and Nagasaki. Wars of conquest were in our blood. Later, I would find that six generations of my family had fought "Indian wars" on this continent—never spoken about on Unc's deck, but surely known in our deep consciousness, our dreams, our DNA.

An odd thing struck me as I spent that week with the people of Wounded Knee in 1990. Elders are greatly revered among the Lakota. Among the older people I served in the food lines or sat with at honoring ceremonies, many reminded me of Unc and my Coombs relatives. Not Unc in his three-piece suit, but Unc in his soft brown shirt and faded tan pants, dragging hoses out under the avocado trees or sitting on the porch after supper with the relatives. Was it the pointed nose and sagging cheeks, the thin, wispy hair and watery, elder eyes that still twinkled at certain moments?

Painful stories from the ride confirmed that many Lakota had Yankee blood in their veins. Was that it, or was I noticing a kind of shyness, a sweetness and reticence, that made these old-timers of the tiny towns of Kyle and Manderson and Porcupine seem familiar to me? For reasons I didn't understand, they touched a tender place in my own childhood memories, a place where the old ones gathered on the porch and talked about the past. In addition to all the feelings that came at Wounded Knee, I also felt among family there, alongside my friend from the Solidarity Committee. When ceremonies ended with *Mitakuye Oyasin!*—the Lakota affirmation of peace, translated as "All My Relations"—I joined in with a passion that came from somewhere very deep. I knew we were all related—the wronged and the perpetrators. And I knew my life was about learning the fuller story and seeking to heal.

The time at Wounded Knee had shown me what it feels like to be welcomed into an older culture and how important it would be for me—a

white woman who'd grown up with entitlement and now taught in a prestigious university—to value Indigenous leadership and not assume that
my ways were "right." Undoing the mind-set I'd inherited remains a lifelong process. After Wounded Knee, I deepened this work and also my
Indigenous friendships. I became a devoted reader of *News from Native
California*, a wonderful magazine about California Indian culture and
its resurgence. As I continued to learn and stay active, I would begin to
untangle our family's history on the Napa land.

On the deck in 2005. A half-moon hangs in the cool, dark sky to the
east. To the west, another redder-than-red sunset, topped by a layer of
hot pink, perhaps from fog. Its epicenter is deep in the Southwest; we're
only two weeks from the December solstice. But a tiny space in the oaks
throbs with elemental red more brilliant than any lipstick or paint—the
most intense sky color I can remember. The prickly-leafed branches of live
oaks lace their black against the bright color, which lasts and lasts as I get
out my notebook and sit down to write about a new journey I have just
made with Indigenous friends whose roots are in this California region.

My time with them will be another turning point. Like the ride to
Wounded Knee, this first of the Shellmound Peace Walks has been a healing journey—walking through desecrated but still-beautiful land to find
the sites of villages torn apart by colonialism, and sacred burial places in
once-huge mounds of shell, now hidden under malls and parking lots
around the San Francisco Bay. Together, we laid down prayers for those
harmed by this history—Indigenous prayers, Buddhist prayers from the
Lotus Sutra, prayers of the many nations we represented. To heal this great
wound of the soul, we built a community that has lasted and grown strong.
The leaders called all of us to focus on our ancestors—whatever their role
in the trauma of settlement. We were asked to love and honor them for
their own healing and that of our society and the land. My ancestors need
this healing and I am ready to do my part.

Caring for the Land

When my parents died just a few years after my time at Wounded Knee,
the house they'd built and eighty acres of mostly steep hillside at the north-

east corner of what had been Unc's ranch passed to me and my sisters—all three of us living on the East Coast then. With all the new vineyards and elegant residences springing up in Napa, the open, rural nature of the land we'd known as children had deep meaning for all of us. We agreed to keep the place more or less as Mother and Dad had done—"natural," as we saw it, though that idea would change for me as I learned more about its ecological history. Even then in the 1990s, it was hard to know what "natural" land meant, since whatever was left of it was fast disappearing around the valley. As best we could, we carved out an agreement with the local land trust that would protect what we loved from development forever, no matter who in the future would own the place. And, from three thousand miles away, we organized ourselves to keep things going. It was not a solution to the history we'd inherited, but for me it was a step in that direction.

I was the plant person. Even though I'd lived in a third-floor apartment in the East for almost forty years, I still remembered where the wild strawberries grew. To my amazement, I still knew the names of plants I'd collected in my college botany course and drawn, photographed, or written poems about. On Mother's Day in 1992, two weeks before she died, my mother had talked to me long-distance from the hospital. She was lying there worrying about the garden she'd been creating around the Napa house, with plants she'd brought down from the hillside. It was a unique garden, especially in the days before native plants became a gardening trend in water-dry California. Mother was anxious to transplant a certain yellow-flowered shrub called sticky monkeyflower, a variant she knew would drape gracefully over the stone wall near the pool. Her voice was dreamy, perhaps with morphine, but there was also an edge of urgency: "I've been lying here wondering what's going to happen to it all, to the garden," she confided. Probably she knew better than I did, then, how little time she had left. "So I thought about you, Louise. You understand these things. You'll know how to keep it going."

I was a continent away, reading a stack of final papers at MIT, but my heart said yes without hesitation. "Yes, of course, Mother. I will do whatever it takes." I knew she was asking for more than just transplanting the sticky monkeyflower. The two of us had shared our way of loving the land for a long time. And she was right—I would know how to keep her garden going and visit the special places she knew on the hill. At the time, I had no idea how much would unfold from this moment. But after that painful spring of her dying, I had a mandate. I would take over her membership in the California Native Plant Society and get myself out west periodically to do what she was asking. It felt like a sacred promise to her and the land—and still does. I could continue what she had begun and return to my old love at the same time. Now I would have a reason to spend time in this beautiful place during all the seasons as I remembered them from my girlhood, and I could learn its hidden history.

In my late fifties and sixties, with all that had changed for me, I could roam the hillsides that had been the love of my earliest years. I could make friends again with the creeks and the oaks and those magical little microgardens of California native plants hidden away on the steep hillside. A good part of this book comes from what I wrote in my journal as I got to know the land again, sitting on the deck or inside by a wood fire, reflecting on what I'd seen on the hill. I was a naturalist again, relearning how to listen to the land—returning to a direction I might have taken in my youth but did not. From clues in the books on Mother's shelf, I began to learn how the First People had cared for the plants here—the people my Buddhist teachers called the "land ancestors." Slowly finding sources in an era still wrapped in silence, I pieced together what had really happened when settler colonizers from the East Coast arrived—including my blood ancestors. Especially as white historians grew willing to talk directly about genocide, I began to understand the violence that had been left out of Unc's stories.

As the years went by, I came as often as I could and eventually moved west again to live closer to the land and its history. Every time I drove up the dirt road Dad had laid out among the big live oaks, I could feel a peace filtering into me. Was it the trickle of the creek, the slanting light through the trees, cricket song in the evenings? The smell of the land cooling off after a summer day? Some wholesomeness of the land itself? Everyone who came here felt this peacefulness in their different ways. They marveled at the statuesque oaks around the house or the hum of native bees in Mother's wildflower garden. You could see their faces relax and open to it all—faces of my nieces and nephew, our cousins, family friends, even Indigenous friends who knew about my ancestors and the complications of this land. I began to trust that, no matter how bad the true history of this place turned out to be, something in this land was more powerful than that history, something my parents had sensed and nurtured that could lead to healing.

During these years, the world was also changing. All Americans, including descendants of colonizers, now lived with wildfire, hurricanes, pandemic, and racial hatred that recalled Black Elk's vision of the black road. The Lakota visionary had seen "the winds of the world ... fighting ... like rapid gunfire and like whirling smoke ... women and children wailing." I saw poverty deepening in the cities, summers growing hotter and storms more extreme as forest fires raged and skies grew denser with smoke and industrial soot—government in denial. Chemicals—worse than those Rachel Carson had known—poisoned air and water, affecting the health of all living beings. I tracked hot particles from nuclear disasters in Russia, the United States, and Japan. I watched our government—the one my ancestors served and my parents revered—grow more openly hostile to darker-skinned people, more supportive of companies exploiting the land.

For those who knew the history, it was nothing new. But the problems intensified as we approached 2020. I watched as people took more refuge in possessions, grew quicker to attack one another, ignoring the looming problems of climate and racism. I stayed active but sought the grounding of the Buddhist practice I'd begun when my mother died, the guidance I continued to seek from Indigenous wisdom, and the inspiration of the Napa land. That support helped me dig into this history.

I'm alone on the deck with the sunset. But I can feel their presence—cousins, uncles, grandchildren, great-aunts, and maybe some of the very Ancient Ones. We're here under the oaks at tables with baskets of wildflowers from the hill, the kind of ceremony our relatives understood. Mother and Dad built this place with family in mind. Dad carved out massive limbs for a view of the skyline, so their house could echo that other one we'd all loved a half century earlier. With this place, they passed on their love of the land to their daughters and grandchildren and to great-grandchildren they never knew but who are here now. It's over seven generations since our first relatives came to California. That's the number my Indigenous friends plan for in their traditional teachings. It's time for us to look back at how we got here and what it means that we're on this land. Like Unc's place in my childhood, this house carries the complexity of our history—all that needs healing and all that offers healing. And many more of us are ready, now, for the full story.

CHAPTER 3

Facing Our Silenced History

The likely "sunken rock" at the northeast boundary of the Tulucay land grant (1837), Nathan Coombs's purchase (1857), and our family's eighty acres of land.

The Earth was subjected to monumentally huge insult during the time of colonization.

—EDUARDO DURAN, *HEALING THE SOUL WOUND*

It's a terrifying thing to face the blood and the genocide and the suffering and the theft and the lies. . . .
It's terrifying to Americans to face that.

—ROBERTO GONZALEZ, FROM ESTELLA ACOSTA,
BLOOD, GOLD & MEDICINE: HEALING MAIDU COUNTRY

Who Lived Here Before?

WAKING EARLY on the sleeping porch into ethereal birdsong, I am blown away by spring. These long, sweet warbles and trills of first light touch something deep. I think I know the daytime cheeps and calls of these birds, but not these otherworldly morning voices weaving through the canopy of fog and live oaks. I want to record it, fix it in my consciousness, replay it when I need a dose of awe. But my Japanese Buddhist friend would say, "You cannot hold it," and she is right. It's that residue of settler mind in me, wanting it for my own. This is a moment to experience in the beautiful present, not to collect or possess.

My mother slept many nights on this porch, and I imagine her waking like this on a March morning, hearing the ancestors of these same birds. She must have known this special spring music of theirs. I wonder if she thought about the earlier people who slept here in this zone of oaks at the base of the hills—the ones whose names we didn't know. The ones who belonged here for millennia but got left out of our family's story. They came this way for their acorn camps, to harvest medicine plants and burn underbrush. They tended this land. They must have slept here and known this music of the dawn.

A century before my birth, they were still coming up into this hilly country from villages along the river to harvest and care for the land, sometimes with their children for extended campouts. I wish I could tell you more about them, but it hasn't been easy to find their story or how the takeover happened. I'm not even sure what they called themselves. So many were killed or driven out of this place. Only as I finished this book was I able to meet some who still carry the knowledge of their culture. Settlers here were so eager to possess and change the land that none of the First People's villages is left in the valley. No ongoing presence like at Wounded Knee and other parts of the country. No Black Elk reaching out to children of colonizers. But that didn't mean they had "vanished," as some books said.

Anthropologists and early settlers had written about the First People before they were fully dispersed, but their maps and tales didn't agree and I didn't trust their ways of seeing things. The tribal name on maps was Wappo—but that was the Anglicized version of the Spanish word *guapo* (brave), given by the first settlers for their fierce fighting spirit. Already we were ignoring what the First People called themselves. Pushed off ancestral lands into the next county, today's Wappo tribal historian explained to another writer that three peoples had lived in the valley, speaking the same language—the Meyahkmah, the Mutistul, and the Mishewal. I cannot presume to tell their story. The whole history of our country has been one white version of "Indians" after another. Not wanting to add yet another version but needing to show what my ancestors left out, I've tried to use the information I could find without shaping my words from the mind-set I inherited.

So far as we know, the whole valley was Wappo ancestral land way back in human memory. But anthropologists' maps show another people, the Patwin, in the southern parts of the valley at the time of colonial settlement. Some call them the Wintu. The line on the old maps runs right through the middle of what was Unc's ranch, near the southern edge of our place. Native boundaries followed ridgelines rather than the streambeds that marked European boundaries. So the Indigenous way included entire watersheds. We don't know, but sometime not long before the Europeans arrived, and maybe in reponse to their presence farther south, the Southern Patwin, relatives of the Wintu people in the Central Valley and north to Mount Shasta, moved into the tidal reaches of the Napa River. Maybe this was contentious, but their villages were well established by the time European soldiers and settlers got here. Like the Wappo, the Patwin tended land beyond their villages and came up into the hills often.

In collaboration, land and people held a balance, each species playing a role like relatives in a family—elk, grizzlies, beaver, and salmon, some gone now, though some starting to return. California's diverse ecosystems were so rich that Indigenous populations here were the densest on the continent—and this was still true in the the North Bay as the colonial presence moved up from Mexico in the 1800s. Both Wappo and Patwin had all they needed—game, harvests of acorn in the fall stored for the rest of the year, seeds for pinole, bulbs to roast, feasts of clover in spring, plants for medicine, basketry, and cordage, clean and plentiful water. Anthropologists say the Wappo bathed daily, and men gathered twice a day in sweat lodges centering each village.

Their year was rich with ceremony for the well-being of people and land. Those in the first Spanish expedition to the valley, in 1823, witnessed Indigenous land care—a recently burned field—without understanding its ecological or cultural meaning. And the whole beautiful network of environmental wisdom, mutually supporting species, and sacred sites that had made this place home was soon pulled apart by European disease, massacre, enslavement, and ecosystem disturbance. It was a terrible time of collapse, but it was not the end.

Thirty years and three waves of colonization after first contact, early settler George Yount, who had taken over much Wappo land, told the editor of his memoirs that "almost all distinction of tribe and nation is gone. The remnants wander up and down the valley together, or sit broken hearted and disconsolate along the streams under the oaks." By 1905, Napa census takers found no Wappo at all in the city, and in 1910, the year my father was born, only seventy-three in Napa and Sonoma Counties. In 1924, anthropologist Alfred Kroeber—who studied the Patwin and had a summer place in the valley—said there were no longer any Patwin here and as few as twenty-four in the entire state. Most white Americans of the time thought that "Indians" were more or less dying out, "vanishing."

But that was not what happened. Yount's and Kroeber's observations were misleading, and Kroeber's damaging to the future of California tribes seeking federal recognition. Now we know of amazing survival and resilience, thanks to people like Corrina Gould, Lisjan Ohlone spokesperson in the East Bay, who traces some of her lineage to one of Napa's Patwin villages. Not long ago, I heard her explain the region's history to an international crowd. "We were colonized three times in a matter of decades," she told them, "the Spanish missions, the Mexican ranchos, and the Anglo Americans." Each wave of colonization brought different forms of violence to land and people.

Like many who grew up in California—or anywhere in North America—I knew on some level that the taking of land must have been violent. But I hadn't really looked at that violence. I'd been raised on stories that made settlement a noble enterprise or at least not a brutal one, stories like Unc's that celebrated the idea of a gifted people taking over. The dominant narrative gave the impression that Indigenous peoples either died from epidemics of European disease (which were indeed terrible) or went quietly elsewhere. It was painful to look at the reality. The sobbing and grief I'd experienced at Wounded Knee came up often as I worked—and intensified as I wrote this chapter about the genocide in our region's history.

Since I was not in ceremony but studying on my own through books, I also had what were probably somatic reactions to the material—allergies, digestive problems, concussions, and even a heart attack. I heard one white historian who studied the California genocide tell how he burst into tears at his dissertation defense, and another describe how he choked back sobs on leaving the library. I've heard Indigenous people say we need to begin with prayer if the subject is genocide. All of this speaks to the intense pain in looking directly at what really happened. I emerged from my research convinced that Americans must face this pain if we want to heal ourselves and our country. I hope I can tell the story in such a way that—whoever you are—you are supported in listening.

When I began to look in the 1990s, Native writers were publishing the truth and mainstream consciousness was slowly starting to change. By the end of the twentieth century, scholars and writers of all ethnicities were addressing the trauma of colonization. Genocide—a term I didn't hear in my college years except in regard to the Jewish Holocaust—became a recognized field of study. As I pulled together what had happened on the land near Unc's ranch, some excellent histories came out, all documenting a California genocide during the Anglo wave of conquest from 1846 to 1873—the very years my ancestor Nathan Coombs was establishing himself in Napa County. Events in the valley would turn out to be pivotal. To understand our own family history and the wounds to the Napa land, we needed to know the whole truth of settlement in this place, no matter how grim.

The First Wave:
Fourth Graders Still Study the Missions

SIXTY-PLUS YEARS after my own fourth-grade class, I visited Mission San Rafael Arcángel, north of San Francisco, at the foot of imposing Mount Tamalpais. It was one of the places Indigenous people from the Napa Valley had been taken as "converts" to do hard labor. A mother and daughter were visiting at the same time, planning a fourth-grade "Mission Project." It was hard to believe such a thing was still in the curriculum of California schoolchildren. In 2013, the gift shop was selling items to help today's kids build a mission replica. I recalled the awe that stirred my own fourth-grade soul when I was told that Franciscan missionaries brought God to Indians and launched the state's history. The volunteer at the desk still seemed to see missions as holy places. This one, she said, was a place of healing, built in a sunny spot as a hospital for Indians who grew sick working at fogbound Mission Dolores in San Francisco.

I stood there wondering if I should speak up. Why not share what I was reading about whole villages—men, women, and children—coerced into the missions? About the real roots of disease there—not fog, but grueling work, whippings, and lack of healthy foods. Why not tell of brokenheartedness, of separation from parents and family, from oak trees and hot, open hillsides, from elders and medicine people who had held the community together? Separated from all they had known. Why not tell today's children how crowding in the missions had worsened the epidemics of new European diseases—sometimes killing 90 percent of a mission's population, leaving young ones completely on their own in a strange and changing world. Why not tell of children raped by soldiers, of despair-driven abortions, plummeting birth rates, and child mortality as high as nine out of ten? Could I say something to help today's children see and feel the pain of these early ones?

Ten years later, in the era of toppling statues and a heightened sense of history, I could have done it, but in that moment, I couldn't muster a voice that was kind enough. My heart was still full of righteous anger that would work against what I had to say. I wanted this mother and daughter to open up to what I was learning, in all its dissonance. In this very diocese just a few years back, a bishop had apologized for the mission system. Why was a gift shop still promoting the whitewashed story I'd learned as a child?

I'm on the quail bench with my computer and a cup of tea. It's warm in the morning sun as I write and remember how my mother used to rest here after a bout of active gardening. This redwood bench carved with the image of a California quail was one of her refuges. A large manzanita has grown up since her time to offer shade.

I hear a rustling in the low branches behind me—a tangle of undergrowth I've wanted to trim out. I'll rethink that now because it's filled with clucking sounds, a collective of subtle voices. Who's there? I turn my spine as slowly and silently as I can, like the great horned owl turning her long neck. There are quail all through the brush behind me. The Wappo called them *pipi*—the perfect name for the sounds they are making. I can't see how many are there. But I sense them nestled in the shaded dry grass. And just over my shoulder on low horizontal branches, two males are keeping watch, jaunty black topknots bobbing. The Patwin name for quail was *saka kay*, exactly the call these males make to warn the others of danger. I keep writing. Any other move will upset them. The *puck, puck, puck* of my keyboard merges with their quail chatter, as if we are sharing language. I wonder if they enjoy this sound, find it companionable. They are such sociable birds. I'm happy they seem to accept me here.

They continue resting in their special places, chattering softly, rattling the dry leaves. I continue typing, turning my neck carefully once in a while for a look. Eventually, with a little commotion, the whole covey starts to move. One at a time—elegant males in the lead, with feathered topknots bobbing—they make the run past the quail bench and across the open slope at my feet. I keep on typing as they settle into new resting places.

By 1776, the drive to establish Franciscan missions along the California coast had worked its way north to the San Francisco Bay along with the Spanish military. With three missions and later five, thousands of Native people from the Bay Area and further inland were driven from their villages into huge farming workforces. Recruitment was supposed to be voluntary but wasn't really. Anthropologist Kent Lightfoot unpacks the hard survival choices First People had to make as their food sources came under threat from European uses of the land. An Ohlone source says women's thumbs were tied together in a cluster as they were herded to captivity. Military expeditions set out to capture whole villages or retrieve converts who tried to escape to the world they'd known before. Precontact warfare had been largely symbolic for the First People. But at this point, historians say, they learned to fight in new ways—sometimes against relatives from the missions who helped their captors in raids. Violence—once seen as the lowest form of power—became a survival technique that tore away at traditional ties.

I've found no one study of mission recruitment in Napa's villages, but we know Wappo and Patwin were taken to Mission San José in the South Bay, as well as to San Rafael Arcángel and the last of the missions built in 1820 over the western hills in Sonoma. Meanwhile, the region churned with vicious warfare to defend the European presence. The early 1800s saw a series of fierce battles along the big Sacramento River, which flows into the North Bay from the Central Valley. In 1817, Lt. José Sanchez and "a small army" burned an entire village near present-day Benicia, where nearly all perished. Sanchez wrote that the chief sang his death song, triggering mass suicide, while his own men tried to save lives. Others say the Spanish set the fires. Maps told me the people in this area were Southern Patwin, relatives of those in our southern end of the Napa Valley, cousins and aunties of the people who gathered acorn on what would become Unc's ranch.

The same year I visited Mission San Rafael Arcángel, *News from Native California* carried Vincent Medina's story of a fourth-grade project on Mission San José—from a boy whose Ohlone ancestors had been forced labor there. Instead of modeling the mission with a purchased kit, he showed it under attack by the rebel Estanislao in 1829. In my own school days, all figures of resistance had been erased from the narrative, but by now I knew of Estanislao and his intertribal force of one thousand dissidents. The military had counterattacked, under a young officer whose name I knew well. Mariano Vallejo, later a general, was given 66,000 acres of land grants in the North Bay and became the most powerful man in our region as the mission phase ended and the second wave of colonization began.

Violence in the Rancho Period

When the Mexican government of California took over mission lands in 1833–1834, the idea was to return them to the Indigenous peoples. But instead, most became land grants to former soldiers for cattle raising. Through land-grant ranchos, Vallejo and other regional strongmen surrounded themselves with loyal countrymen who would Europeanize the landscape and participate in its defense. In Napa, one of them was Cayetano Juárez, who later sold part of his grant to my great-great-grandfather—including the piece passed down to us. In this phase, Native villages included in the land grants were considered part of the deal, a source of labor. Their residents worked like serfs on the European feudal model, caring for alien crops and cattle as they watched the loss of their traditional food sources and an ecosystem going into crisis. Invasive European grasses and thistles spread by cattle took over the wildflower meadows that had provided diverse nutrients in seeds and bulbs. Domestic animals fouled water and competed for key foods like acorn. Without the careful use of fire, soil nutrients, vegetation, and waterways lost their balance and familiar species began to disappear. The devastation would grow as settlement intensified.

Sociologist Kari Norgaard and the Karuk people she works with in the far north of California call this ecological destruction a "leading edge" of the genocide. For them, it is still happening now as traditional food species succumb to government mismanagement and the salmon in their river are at risk. Karuk people fear that without the foods and practices that anchor their way of life, they will disappear as a people.

In the North Bay, Vallejo built strong military campaigns against resistant tribes, keeping his eye on a Russian outpost up the coast. In the early 1830s, he fought the Patwin in the southern part of the valley, much of which he soon "owned" through one of his land grants. One site was a large village called Suscol, downstream from present-day Napa, in an area we could see from Unc's deck. There, Vallejo defeated the Patwin but formed a strong alliance and friendship with their leader Sem Yeto, whom he renamed Chief Solano, a common controlling strategy of colonization. From then on, the Patwin had allies against traditional enemies like the Wappo, and turned their fighting strength against tribes targeted in Vallejo's campaigns. Solano's name was later given to the county just east of Napa, where his image on the seal is still seen on all police cars.

A few years after the alliance, an especially vicious battle took place at the Suscol site, against tribes from the Central Valley. Supposedly, they had planned to sweep west over all settlement in their path—two thousand strong. Vallejo, with Solano's help, responded. Known for exaggeration, George Yount tells the story in his memoirs, as if it were a Hollywood script. Six hundred Patwin allies rise up from the long grasses to surprise the attackers, while mounted troops circle from behind. In the end, Yount says, "the field presented one immense harvest of death." Other sources say Vallejo's forces dragged 150 Native dead to mass graves in a tidewater ravine of Suscol Creek.

With Patwin assistance in 1834, Vallejo turned his attention west and north, attacking a group of Wappo known as the Satiyomi, killing two hundred, and taking three hundred captive. In 1836, he attacked more Wappo, killing twenty. In 1843, his brother Salvador attacked the Pomo near Fort Bragg, on the coast, killing 170. The numbers come from Sherburne Cook, a twentieth-century physiologist who found ways to look back and count the dead in these battles as he tracked the steep decline in the Native population. He says these were not skirmishes, but major preemptive campaigns with large troops of white soldiers and Indian auxiliaries. Cook says the Wappo population dropped by 40 percent during this period; the Pomo by 10 percent. Cook had managed to look directly at the relentless violence I had only guessed at—and it grew worse.

The same period saw vicious epidemics of European diseases in Northern California. Ordinary sicknesses like measles, diptheria, typhoid, and the flu became pandemic mass killers among a people with no historical immunity and spread like wildfire along Native trade routes. Later, when I traced my Coombs ancestry back to the *Mayflower*, I saw the role of disease in this earlier phase of conquest. A three-year pandemic of European diseases had wiped out 90 percent of the local population, enabling a Pilgrim takeover. All across the continent, epidemics preceded settlement—as if a tool of conquest—weakening Indigenous populations and throwing entire ecosystems into disarray when the keystone being—the resident human—was no longer in charge.

It's hard to imagine the relentless violence of the smallpox pandemic that struck the North Bay in 1838–1839. Mexican soldiers and settlers were vaccinated and survived, along with Vallejo's privileged Patwin ally Solano. But for the main Indian population, Vallejo merely quarantined them and wrote that "they died daily like bugs." Cook says half of the general's personal Indian guard and half the Indians in the Sonoma Valley died in this epidemic, along with an estimated two thousand Native people in the region.

Rancho economy relied on Indigenous labor, and there are some stories of decent treatment on the ranchos. But already in this period, settler violence against the First People was on the rise. George Yount arrived in the valley in 1831, twelve years before Nathan Coombs. His "told to" memoir is a major source for the period. Becoming a Mexican citizen, he wangled the first local land grant given to an "American" and had a reputation among settlers for good relations with the Wappo. He supported Vallejo's battles and also attacked Indians on his own, in a way that would become common in the next wave of settlement. One of his tales has him pursuing supposed Native cattle raiders into the mountains east of Napa. There his people destroy a village, kill "many," scalp some, and fight off a counterattack as they head homeward, leaving the ground soaked in blood. Indigenous cattle raiding grew as European uses of the land ate into traditonal food sources and left communities malnourished and starving. More and more frequently, supposed thefts of free-range cattle—termed *depredations*—became a pretext for grassroots citizen violence that revealed the vicious feelings that fed genocide.

Sweat Lodge Massacres

An especially painful story has survived in some detail in only one version I've found. An early chronicler of the Napa Valley, C. A. Menefee, recorded it in 1871, some thirty years after it took place. He says a large Wappo village stood where the town of Oakville is now, north of Yount's place in the valley and likely also part of his grant. Settlers across the hills in Sonoma claimed these particular Wappo had stolen their cattle, so they rode over the mountains one night in the early 1840s to retaliate. Since Wappo men gathered morning and evening for purification in the village sweat lodge, they were inside when the vigilantes arrived. Menefee says the settlers "surrounded the 'sweat house,' in which about 300 Indians were assembled. The whole number were slaughtered, man by man, as they passed out and the tribe thus almost exterminated at a blow." Generally a pioneer booster, Menefee is shocked at the "wholesale massacre" but doesn't note the special horror of a sweat lodge attack.

It's likely he didn't know that for Indigenous Americans, a sweat house is sacred space, a place of refuge and renewal, with practices varying by tribe. Later in his book, Menefee pronounces Napa Indians incapable of religious sentiment and also quotes an Anglo informant who derides the Wappo sweat house as a bizarre health practice. We know very little about Wappo sweat ceremonies except that they were important. One Wappo story places the very moment of human creation in a sweat house.

I cannot speak for the Wappo, but since my time at Wounded Knee, I've been invited into sweats with ceremonial leaders from other tribes. Held in the close, dark space by drumming, deep heat, sage smoke, prayer, and a grounded community, I've felt my body grow passive and receptive as my heart opens. Friends who are of the culture experience ancestral presences and spirit guides. In this altered state, "fight or flight" seems unimaginable. It's painful to think of pure terror interrupting a moment when one felt safely held in ceremony. Like being shot down in prayer or meditation today.

I was appalled by Menefee's story. But as I worked on this chapter, I found that sweat lodge attacks were common, a regular strategy of the colonizers. Accounts of them came from all over Northern California, including at least four others in our immediate area. One in 1841 was conducted by General Vallejo himself, just north of Napa, in what is now Lake County. In 1843, his brother Salvador set fire to a sweat lodge full of Pomo, who'd invited him inside for negotiations. Whatever Menefee understood, the attackers must have realized that sweat lodges were places of prayer, where people were physically and emotionally vulnerable, not able to fight back. The perpetrators must have seen that mass killings in the sacred space of a sweat lodge—like killings in churches, synagogues, or mosques today—would mean a heightened form of terror. The pattern suggests conscious intent—not just to kill many "at a blow" but to traumatize, to destroy the web of spiritual connection that gives a people the will and strength to survive. It suggests a hatefulness so intense, it is hard to acknowledge.

These massacres weren't highlighted in other histories. No research monographs or school curricula that I have found take note that tactics this barbaric were routine in settler history here. No poems, no days of mourning commemorate. No formal apologies to previous generations. And yet this story carries the full burden of hate and fear that charged the mind of early settlers. Perhaps, like Menefee, people in the Coombs family expressed shock upon hearing of the Oakville incident when they arrived in the valley. But they accepted it as normal and silently passed on that acceptance to their descendants. If we can look at the enormity, feel the pain—grieve—I would like to think we can begin to lift the heavy burden of silence we carry and transform the residue of hate and violence that remain today.

The Third Wave: Textbook Genocide

Between the missions and the ranchos, the twenty years and more of Spanish-speaking settlement in the North Bay were devastating. But modern historians agree that the third phase, Anglo-American settlement— the time of squatting, land grabs, scalp bounties, militias, and the gold rush—was the most violent and murderous of all. That was our family's time. Nathan Coombs and his father-in-law, Will Gordon, arrived among the first of the Yankees filtering into California during the rancho period, moving easily into territory that was already under European control. Gordon, whose wife was a Mexican citizen, received a land grant east of the Napa area in 1841. Coombs arrived as a visitor there in 1843, moving on to Napa two years later with young Isabel Gordon as his bride.

Most Americans have no idea of the deep, deliberate violence of colonization. Indigenous historian Roxanne Dunbar-Ortiz describes shattering military tactics for destroying noncombatants and food supplies that Americans brought to this continent from European wars and carried west. Until I read the new books about California's genocide, I didn't realize that our story here was in many ways more violent than in other parts of the country. What had taken two hundred years in New England took only twenty in California. White authors like Menefee had recorded a few of the worst attacks and epidemics, lamenting their brutality even though siding with the settlers. But the new scholarship was rich in detail that turned the abstract word *genocide* into something that made your skin crawl. Simply because of the timing, my ancestors were part of it. Possibly they had taken up weapons against the Original People. With one exception, I would never know for sure. But even if they had not used guns, they had accepted, stood by. We had all benefited from the violence. Our way of life was built on it.

Nathan Coombs, age twenty, had been in California just three years when he joined the action in 1846 that would lead to the end of the rancho period. Writing my paper as an eight-year-old, we had celebrated the centennial of the Bear Flag Revolt. In the 1950s, Unc had traveled throughout the region, made the rounds as an "old-timer" and descendant promoting the heroic mythology of brave pioneers standing up to supposed Mexican tyranny. Later, I realized the takeover was part of a pattern common in the Latin borderlands throughout the nineteenth century, where Anglo settler bands known as "filibusters" forced their way into Spanish settlements and declared themselves a republic. Some accounts belittle the Bear Flag incident as a drunken brawl, but serious harm came of it. A twenty-first-century study, *This Land Was Mexican Once,* convinced me that even the brawl angle was a colonizer's cover-up. The Bear Flag action was more than "just" drunken young men acting out. Author Linda Heidenreich, who is Latina and was raised in Napa herself, shows how stories differ depending on who tells them. She gives Californio versions alongside swaggering Bear Flagger tales.

Reading both sets of stories, a sick feeling came over me. This was not the benign, near-bloodless "rebellion" I had been led to imagine, and it was certainly not the high-principled republicanism of Coombs family stories. The Bear Flag period was messy, disorganized, violent, and racist. The imprisonment and poor treatment of Vallejo (who actually favored joining the United States) was bad enough, but worse were the bands of armed gringos who roamed the region, looting from the ranchos, stealing, and intimidating—riding into Indigenous villages and raping women. What had I thought? This is what happens in wars of conquest.

Heidenreich shows how Bear Flagger violence targeted women and darker-skinned people. The more European-looking Californios mostly survived, but darker-skinned families like the Berryessas (who were classified "mestizo") attracted special violence. Three unarmed Berryessa men were shot on sight by Frémont's troops near San Rafael after the Bear Flag incident, with five other family members killed by Anglos as the war progressed. Stories masking the violence quickly formed among the victors, demeaning women as sexy senoritas, attracted—so it was said—to Anglo men with blue eyes. Californios of all social classes were dehumanized as "greasers," a slur targeting people of Mexican descent that hung on in California until at least my teenage years. Among laws the new state enacted was one actually called the "Greaser Act," passed in 1855 during one of Nathan Coombs's terms in the legislature. Meanwhile, around Napa and Sonoma, Bear Flaggers were a focus of public adulation, writing for newspapers, creating celebrations, and spreading their version of the hostilities as Unc had done later on. I remember hearing some of the residue and feeling distrust of "greasers."

Gringo violence continued to afflict Napa in the new period. Shortly after the Bear Flag event but prior to statehood, while California was under U.S. military rule, another mass killing struck near Yountville. By this time, my great-great-grandfather had begun to acquire land in and around Napa, though it was not affected, so far as I can tell. This time, a Robert "Growling" Smith led an attack on ranches in the valley, slaughtering Native farmworkers, no reason given. The attackers moved east toward Sacramento, killing more Native workers and kidnapping others to sell for slave labor—another atrocity that would become a pattern. Though brought to trial for murder and enslavement under the interim government, the "Growling" Smith trio was acquitted by judges who were former kidnappers themselves. The brutality would soon intensify as the discovery of gold in 1848 brought 100,000 new settlers to California in one year's time and "extermination" became an explicit goal in the new state.

1850: Bloody Island in Lake County

I learned about Bloody Island after returning from Wounded Knee full of questions about Napa's story. At the back of my parents' bookshelf, bundled into a plastic bag, was a tattered copy of *The History of Napa and Lake Counties*—four inches thick, bound in frayed brown leather, a volume I'd explored as a child in Unc's house. A compendium of settler history, agriculture, mining, and business, it was written the year Unc was born. I'd quickly lost interest in it as a child. But now, amid all the data, I found a drama that raised the hair on my arms. Years later, Benjamin Madley would focus a pivotal chapter of his book on Bloody Island—including repercussions in the Napa Valley itself—showing how these events set a pattern for the genocide that would follow in the rest of the state.

The story began with two Anglo settlers, Charles Stone and Andrew Kelsey, leasing land north of the valley, near Clear Lake, in the 1840s. Cattle and the Pomo people who still lived on the land were included in the deal. Stone and Kelsey worked the people hard, withheld food, impounded all bows and arrows (preventing both resistance and subsistence hunting), and took the headman's wife as their servant and sex slave. To show off for visitors, they hanged starving Pomos and whipped or shot them dead. Early author Lyman Palmer calls it "slave labor of the worst kind" (though elsewhere he refers to the two men as "brave frontiersmen.") He says they "took Indians down to the lower valleys and sold them like cattle or other stock." In the winter of 1849, months before statehood, the starving Pomos rose up and killed these two men who had been so cruel. Palmer accepts this.

But retaliation followed—killing at least one thousand Indians from multiple tribes across several counties. Immediately, a U.S. military reconnaisance detail set out for Clear Lake, mowing down dozens of Indian villagers and farmworkers along its route through the upper Napa Valley. Madley quotes settler accounts of troops riding into a Wappo village near Calistoga, opening fire, and killing thirty-five, then moving on to a ranch to slaughter farmworkers, telling the protesting rancher to "shut up." This party deemed all four Pomo tribes at Clear Lake complicit, proposing a campaign to "cut them to pieces." Behind this decision, Madley says, were two premises that would inspire twenty more years of massacres—"collective Indian guilt" (entire tribes bore responsibility for an individual's act) and "pedagogic violence" (indiscrimate punishment would teach all Indians a lesson). Dunbar-Ortiz describes similar "exemplary violence" in New Mexico. When weather permitted the next spring, seventy-five soldiers hauling three boats headed to Clear Lake with military orders to "exterminate" all tribal people there.

When they arrived, villages were empty. People had fled to the mountains or a large island at the north end of the lake. No evidence connected families on that island with those who had worked for Stone and Kelsey. Some say the group had come for a ceremony at a sweat lodge—but orders were to attack without negotiation, without taking prisoners. What happened there on May 15, 1850, shocks Palmer. A few Pomo swam to shore, but soldiers killed women and children, following them into the water, shooting and clubbing them. Some say one hundred died there; some say as many as eight hundred—which, by Madley's calculations, would make this one of the most lethal massacres in all of U.S. settlement. Members of the expedition continued to kill indiscriminately as they headed west, wiping out whole villages. The mountainous country beyond iconic Mount Saint Helena at the head of the valley was now a killing field for the Pomo. The next decade there would see the Mendocino War, an all-out effort by tax-supported local militias to destroy a Native population that was beleaguered and starving.

The Bloody Island story still affects many lives. I've heard Pomo leaders tell the story from their oral tradition. One told of his ancestor Lucy Moore, who took refuge in the water as a young girl, surviving undetected below the surface by breathing through a hollow tule reed, so the bubbles of her breath would not betray her location. Hiding underwater had been Pomo children's hide-and-seek—a play strategy that became a means of survival. Later, *News from Native California* featured eighth-grade Pomo Jayden Lim's telling of the story. The young historian places herself in a lake "red with the blood of her family," taking "deep breathes" through the tule reed that saves her life.

I watch the Napa land changing. The seasons were never regular, so it's hard to say that patterns are new, but something doesn't feel right. European thistles and grasses that got their start with colonization thrive in the present chaos, and new pathogens like sudden oak death. I think there are fewer insects and birds.

The changes weigh on me. A bird's flight can lift my heart for the moment, but the heaviness returns. I cultivate the long view—we cannot be sure what's coming next or hold on to the world we've known. The earth of my childhood wasn't the starting point; the Napa land had an earlier life under Wappo and Patwin care. How did they feel when the earth they knew began to fall apart? Frank Lake, a Karuk tribal member up north along the Klamath, speaks of emotional pain living with a degraded river as "enduring an assault on one's relatives yet being powerless to fully stop it." I feel a double dose of grief for what the First People lost and for the changes I see now in these hills.

Trying to face the horror of the sweat lodge massacres, I learn about the Tibetan Buddhist "charnel ground practice"—a meditation with open heart in a terrifying place of death. For Tibetans, a charnel ground is the place where bodies of the dead are placed in the open air to decompose—a place of stench and terror. For us, it could be Oakville in the 1840s, the filthy air of hot weather gone off the charts, the browned leaves of sudden oak death, or our own intense personal pain. Teacher Pema Chodrun shows how to sit in this pain, completely open to our feelings—no theories, no excuses, no elaborating stories, just the raw feelings. Start with a brief dose—just a few seconds—however long we can accept the pain fully. It will change in some way. A war veteran with PTSD says it's the only thing that helps him. A man sentenced to life imprisonment says over time it has healed his fear. I am just a beginner, but they say when you can find relief in the charnel ground, the place of pain becomes "the pure land"—holy ground.

Clear Lake was especially remote for Europeans. But the more "civ-ilized" Napa and Sonoma Valleys also experienced waves of vigilante violence after the Stone and Kelsey deaths. Racial fear and hatred surfaced in many settlers' minds. During the winter, while the army prepared its attack on Bloody Island, Sonoma men, including Benjamin and Samuel Kelsey, brothers of Andrew, mobilized vigilante action to hunt down all Indians in Napa and Sonoma and kill or drive them into the mountains. They targeted three very different tribes, living up to seventy miles from the killing, most of them working on Anglo and Mexican ranches that were still organized on the feudal model of the earlier era. Madley specu-lates that envy of the wealth landed settlers could gain from Indian labor was part of the angry mix that drove vigilante action.

In February 1850, twenty-four armed men rode through Yount's and another ranch, killing Indian workers and burning their homes and sup-plies, then veering west to wreak havoc in Santa Rosa and Sonoma. In early March, a group of forty or fifty rampaged through the Napa Val-ley, led by one of the Kelsey brothers. They headed for Suscol, near the mouth of the Napa River, where there had been so much killing a decade earlier. There was still a large Indian village there, a good fifty miles from Clear Lake. Menefee says this group was "turned back by another party of white men at Napa" but then went north and "murdered in cold blood eleven innocent Indians" as they "came out of their 'sweat house.'" Madley mentions other white opposition to the vigilantes—people complained to the governor and wrote of their horror. The closest newspapers in San Francisco reacted strongly. But, though arrested, the murderers from Sonoma—including both surviving Kelsey brothers—were able to avoid trial, and went on with their lives.

I was grateful some Napa people resisted the cycle of violence—re-lieved to find this crack in the genocidal mind. I wanted to know their names, honor them with a statue, find their descendants. But I also wanted names of the ones who met to plan the violence and rode on the murder-ous hunts. New arrivals had tried gold mining and failed. The towns must have been full of them, hanging around, miserable and frustrated, ready to blame their troubles on Indians and envious of landowning ranchers. What about Nathan Coombs? At this point, he was doing well, prospering from land deals in the gold rush boom. Probably too well-off to join a crowd like this. But what about his friends and drinking buddies? The men in his business life? Coombs had known the Kelsey family since arriving in California. They had settled in the same area and at least two brothers had been with him in the Bear Flag Revolt four years back—comrades in arms. Coombses and Kelseys were part of the same cohort of early settlers. People tend to stick by their friends even when they don't join up. The atrocities of Stone and Kelsey and the murderous reprisals that followed their deaths were not simply the work of "bad eggs." The mindset behind theses acts was part of a culture Nathan Coombs shared. If my great-great-grandfather did not actually ride with the vigilantes, he was certainly not likely to have opposed them.

The settler colonial mind-set was full of contradictions. Writing in the 1870s, Menefee's shock at the massacres went hand in hand with fulsome praise of the settlement enterprise. He dedicates his book to the pioneers of California, "the purest nobility, the vanguard of civilization." The people they displaced are "wretched," "hideous," "loathsome" "savages" and those in Napa County "lower in the scale of intelligence than any other upon the continent." My stomach churns at his words. His attitude was commonplace in my ancestors' world. And it was the bedrock of genocide.

Intention, "Extermination," Enslavement

The Bloody Island story from the old book on my parents' shelf stayed with me like a nightmare. The rough, dark house of Stone and Kelsey remained a shadowy presence as I returned to my research. Years earlier, never realizing I would have to apply it to the land around Unc's ranch, I had studied the UN definition of genocide from 1948. A key factor is intention. In California, intention to destroy the Native population could not have been more explicit, with the state's first governor calling for "a war of extermination" and policy after policy that followed.

The new state immediately passed a law called the Act for the Government and Protection of Indians. It sounded benign, if paternalistic, but it was not. Besides promoting enslavement, the act made explicit what would later be listed in the UN definition. To provide forced Indian labor for Anglo ranchers, it set rules for indenture—called "adoption" or "apprenticeship." This policy separated Native children from their parents, placing them "under the care" of farm families to work until they supposedly came of age.

The UN Convention on the Rights of the Child recognizes separation of children from families as a "means" of genocide, and this tears at the heart. Menefee mentions that indentured children seldom lived more than two or three years. Labor historian Richard Steven Street estimates one in four Northern California farms held kidnapped Indian children. There was supposed to be parental agreement, but loopholes supported a profitable child kidnapping industry, strengthened by a measure passed in 1860, during Nathan Coombs's second term in the legislature. Some of this was repealed in 1866, after the Thirteenth Amendment outlawed slavery, but historians think the practices likely continued.

The same law linked vagrancy to forced labor. Any Indigenous person without means of support in the white economy—which included most Native people—was labeled a "vagrant," rounded up, and sold to the highest bidder for a four-month term of unpaid labor. Modern prison-justice advocates will tell you similar practices still afflict "vagrants" of marginalized ethnicities. California ranchers returned workers after four months to booze-friendly neighborhoods with a few coins in their pockets—so they could be arrested again for drunkenness and another term of work. As Horace Bell put it, "Los Angeles had its slave mart, as well as New Orleans . . . only the slave at Los Angeles was sold fifty-two times a year as long as he lived." Another malignant practice was to pay workers in cheap liquor, fueling addiction and dependency.

The 1850 Act for the Government and Protection of Indians also spelled out whipping penalties for Indians and criminalized the cultural burning of open land that was essential to ecosystem balance and Indigenous food production. Destroying a people's means of subsistence is another means of genocide recognized in the UN Convention on the Prevention and Punishment of the Crime of Genocide. A Native writer posting the act on an Ohlone website commented, "It is surreal, as a native, to transcribe such a document. It is a challenge to work for redemption and healing when this part of history is forgotten or hidden."

Lest we think these practices showed an especially warped California mentality, they were also common in Puritan New England two hundred years earlier. With the touching title *Brethren by Nature*, a book by Margaret Newell documents enslavement of Native children, payment in alcohol, and "vagrancy" leading to forced servitude. The same definition of vagrancy would become part of the so-called Black Codes in southern states after the Civil War—criminalizing emancipated Black Americans and essentially returning them to slavery in prison labor.

In the hills behind Unc's ranch and a little north was a small valley where we used to go for picnics until it was dammed to become Lake Berryessa, named for a Californio settler family and now flanked by protected wilderness in a new national monument. Madley links the name Berryessa to a kidnapping gang focused on local Indian children. They weren't the only kidnappers: Sherburne Cook estimates that between three and four thousand children were stolen from families in Northern California between 1852 and 1867, with one hundred moved through Lake County in just the summer of 1862. A century later, sitting on Unc's deck, we had no idea that faraway diplomats in the United Nations were defining separation of children from parents as part of something called genocide or that, ten miles away, kids like us had been torn from their relatives in a beautiful valley that would be underwater by the time we were grown.

"Only a White Population"

The years following statehood saw a frenzy of extermination as "Americans" poured into the new state, claiming land and mining rights. By this time, the Napa Valley was nearly clear of what were called "wild Indians" living on the land. In 1851, the cavalry removed many by force. In a few villages or rancherias, Native people still lived and worked on the remaining land grant ranchos, though some moved north, trying to avoid white settlement. Even the remoter counties were now filling up with would-be ranchers, settlers, and miners, and these settlers began clearance campaigns that chill the heart.

Historian Brendan Lindsay writes, "It was as though 100,000 white men appeared out of nowhere in twelve months." The newcomers wanted "only a white population in California," as *Californian* magazine proclaimed in 1848. Lindsay says white Californians used the tools of democracy they had learned in the East—petitions, citizen meetings, and pressure on elected officials—to get what they wanted. California's genocide came from the grass roots, not from a Hitler figure. Along with the act supposedly protecting Indians, the new state passed a Militia Act: At citizen request, the state would fund "volunteer" armies for limited campaigns. Indians were the only enemies. Petitions and citizen demands poured in for military action to "punish," "chastise," "clean out," or "totally annihilate" Native people living on land white Americans wanted for grazing and agriculture. Volunteers earned five dollars a day plus expenses, far better than the average three dollars per day in the mines. Drinking, a numbing practice in other genocides, was common, and the militias destroyed whole villages along with the coming winter's food supply. Within four years, the state paid out $924,259 to militias. Overextended, it then issued war savings bonds—like those I bought with dimes and nickels as a patriotic child during World War II, but these state bonds supported so-called Indian wars. People who invested in them—who most likely included my relatives—earned 7 percent interest from genocide.

When citizens weren't satisfied with what the state could do, they funded their own militias through subscriptions. This form of crowd sourcing also raised money for bounties—when towns and counties did not offer them—for scalps and severed heads. In one county, scalps brought fifty cents each and heads five dollars. I'd heard of these bounties and wondered if they were exaggerated—it was hard to realize white Californians had been this vicious. But Lindsay documents their existence with records, testimony, and newspapers. During my great-great-grandfather's second term in the state legislature, one of its committees investigated the Mendocino War against the Pomo northwest of us—not the rightness or wrongness of the war but why it had cost the state so much. Legislators heard remorseless testimony from militiamen: "[At dawn] we attacked and killed 20 consisting of Bucks, Squaws and children and also took 2 squaws and one child prisoner. Those killed were all killed in about three minutes. . . . We found . . . no sign of any depredation having been committed by these Indians." In this case, the militia had acted beyond its mandate, which was to punish Indians for specific thefts of cattle or "depredations."

After statehood, federal negotiators worked out eighteen treaties with California tribes to establish reservations, as in other parts of the country. Some one hundred tribes in the early 1850s signed these treaties, expecting reservation land and other benefits in exchange for beloved homelands they had been persuaded to give up. So much is said these days about the shame of broken treaties, but in California, these treaties were not even ratified by the government. A groundswell of settler sentiment persuaded the U.S. Senate to place them under an injunction of secrecy for the next half century. Eventually, other smaller reservations, often called rancherias, were established. Some were like prisons headed by the military.

The atmosphere that allowed this to happen was fed by local newspapers statewide spewing the hateful, dehumanizing language that made deception and murder of fellow humans possible: "bucks" and "squaws" (both terms were negative sexual slurs), their animal-like nature, and "depredations." One slur unique to California—though rhyming with the n-word—was the term *digger,* demeaning California tribes who dug bulbs for food. With grotesque racial cartoons and jokes, the newspapers whipped up fear, hatred, and greed. One called for strychnine-laced watermelons and other foods to be left out for starving Native people. Small wonder the Wintu word for white settlers was *yapaitu wintun,* "poison people."

Media, politicians, and ordinary letter writers of this period all seem to have convinced themselves that extinction of "the Indian" was a corollary of Manifest Destiny. "Humanity may forbid," one said, "but the interest of the white man demands their extinction." Some said the more quickly this happened, the more humane it would be. Sickened by reading these words from the founders of my state, I thought of Unc's comments about gophers who had eaten his strychnine-poisoned carrots—"Poor devil. Oughta cut its neck"—and how he'd expressed what I'd thought was sympathy for the First People by calling them "poor devils." Now his expression seemed more likely the residue of murderous ideas that had been in the air since before his childhood.

It's been extinct here since 1929. The California grizzly—Ursus arctos horribilis to the scientists who named it—was one of those species forced out of balance by European settlement. These bears had been part of the web of life in Wappo and Patwin times. Many California tribes have stories of their likeness to humans, of bear–shamans with powers to harm and to heal. Ecohistorians say the way they clawed up the soil helped shape our ecosystem. But before Anglos took over the valley, the grizzly population had skyrocketed. George Yount claimed he'd killed as many as five or six in a day and seen fifty or sixty in a twenty-four-hour period. Historians of the great bear say two human causes tipped the balance. Removal from their lands and their staggering death rate in the mission period meant the people who were ecosystem caretakers for millennia—the "keystone species"—could no longer play their role in keeping the balance. Plus, the bears' diet got a boost from the ranchos. Cattle were easy prey, but even easier were the huge piles of meat left to rot after mass slaughter for hides and tallow. Grizzly scholars say the population peaked from around 2,500 at first contact to 10,000 in 1848, the year California became part of the United States—one for every twelve humans.

These numbers did not hold once Yankees began to pour into California for gold and entrepreneurs hunted down animals to sell as meat to miners. Profit aside, hunting grizzlies became a badge of courage. My family tells a story of Nathan Coombs mauled in such a hunt. Reading what happened to the bears brought me to tears. It was the same story I was painfully uncovering about human genocide in California. When not poisoned with strychnine or attacked and slaughtered outright, grizzlies were captured and enslaved—serving as pets, performers, dancers, flute players, beasts of burden, and even collaborators in hunting other grizzlies. Like Indians, they were sent on entertainment tours around the world with entrepreneurs like P. T. Barnum. In San Francisco, one was kept caged in public view for twenty-two years, as its peers in the woods were killed off. The press used the same disparaging words—*brutality* and *depredations*—perhaps rooted in the same unreasoning fear. One hunter advertised his services as a premier Indian and grizzly killer all in one. Such was the collective mind of my ancestors' world.

I'm not a numbers person, so I marvel at the demographics others have assembled about this disastrous time. California's varied ecosystem and rich food sources had made its original population the densest per square mile on the continent. Scholars think the First People numbered as many as 300,000 in 1769, when the mission enterprise began. If, as some think, European diseases had been causing havoc even earlier, then true precontact figures could have been much higher. In any case, by 1860 the total had dropped by 90 percent, to a shocking thirty thousand. According to Sherburne Cook, by 1880, the year before Unc was born and shortly after the period of genocide, the Native population statewide stood at 12,500, less than 5 percent of the original number. Cook and others who sought to record and document the losses would have rejoiced to learn that by now the numbers have risen from those low points and many tribes are regaining their languages, culture, and respect in the world.

One hundred years after California's gold rush and just after World War II—during the years when our family gathered on Unc's deck—a United Nations convention recognized the new term *genocide,* but the convention was not ratified by the United States for another forty years. The UN definition fit well in California, where there had been clear intent to destroy or exterminate all or a substantial part of a national or ethnic group. California had also followed the means outlined in the UN definition. Along with killing Native people outright, we had destroyed the conditions of life—the ecosystems—that supported them. And we had intentionally separated Native children from their parents to labor in settler households and later separated them from families and their culture by placing them in boarding schools. Though few spoke of it when the term *genocide* was coined, California history matched the definition all too well.

As I learned the grim story, the beautiful skyline we'd enjoyed from Unc's deck became a panorama of death. If we'd sat on that deck with full knowledge of the silenced history, we could have pointed to at least twenty sites of mass killing in the decades just before and after Unc's grandfather bought the land. Starting out behind the dark hills at the valley's mouth, where the earliest battles had taken place, and moving west to the bayside flatlands, where Vallejo had fought the Patwin. Then sweeping our gaze across to the western skyline, which blocked the view of his other battles. Tracing north up the valley, behind the low hills near Yountville to that first terrible sweat lodge massacre and so many vigilante attacks on Wappos working on the ranches. Reaching the beautiful wedge-shaped Mount Saint Helena at the northern end of the valley, gateway to Lake County, where U.S. troops had tried to exterminate all Indians. Beyond that—there was no way we could see far enough—lay county after county, scene of the vicious slave raids and massacres in Madley's and Lindsay's books. And back around behind us—over the hills that separated us from the Central Valley—were more atrocities: the unspeakable violence of the gold rush in Maidu, Nisenan, and other Sierra foothill country, a death march of starving tribes to Round Valley, villages decimated by epidemics, babies thrown in the fire, vigilantes tying men to stakes and shooting them. More than a panorama—an entire zone of genocide had encircled us at Unc's ranch. That's how bad it was, and no one had told us a word of it.

Learning from the Survivors

As I learned these things, I looked for ways to change the silence surrounding our history and the seeds of a genocidal mind in ourselves. On visits to California in the mid-2000s, I joined four yearly journeys called the Shellmound Peace Walks. They were hosted by Ohlone people (again, not the name they had called themselves), who'd lived in small tribal bands throughout the Bay Area. With them, a group from five continents walked the circuit of the bay, supported by the same Japanese Buddhists I had met at Wounded Knee. We visited village and burial sites—most known only to a few and obscured by twentieth-century development. I learned about the shell mounds, once huge rounded hills of discarded shells, some massive enough to be seen from ships outside the bay. Far from being merely middens or garbage dumping sites as early settlers thought them, these mounds were the Ohlone people's revered monuments, holding buried ancestors and ceremonial objects along with shells. A different idea of what is sacred lay behind them. Some were dismantled as pavement for roads, their spaces now covered in malls and tract homes. Today's Californians live and shop on the sacred places of the Ohlone people.

We had shuttled through commuter traffic to the southern tip of the bay on the outskirts of San Jose. From earlier Shellmound Peace Walks, I knew these wide expanses of salt marsh, morning mists, and the bare rounded hills rising up behind Silicon Valley to the east. Our Ohlone friend Corrina Gould welcomed us to a circle fragrant with burning sage. She told us she always felt good coming to this stretch of land. "There was a cluster of villages here and several shell mounds," she said. "Some of my own people came from these villages. This was our place. Everything we needed was here—all the foods we loved. We harvested salt from the bay and tules for building houses and making clothing." In the morning light and lingering sage smoke, the picture seemed very real.

"But when they opened Mission San José," she continued, gesturing up toward the hills, "this was the first village they came to, to take my people up there to work in the fields, to be enslaved for life, with no chance of returning." She paused and we all felt the emotion. "We're going to walk there today, just about the same route my ancestors took." Suddenly, those hills looked very far away, even in the fresh morning air. Patwin and Wappo people had also been marched to this mission all the way from Napa. I saw how it might feel to lose your home and be taken there for life.

Then Corrina looked up in silence. Circling high above us were a dozen huge white birds with neat black markings on their wide wings. I knew they were white pelicans because my mother's notebook had mentioned these amazing beings with nine-foot wingspans circling at the Napa place, and I'd once seen them myself high up in the golden eagle's airspace. These pelicans fly long distances inland to remote desert lakes— always in flocks that circle and circle before moving on. Looking up at this auspicious sight, Corrina thanked them for blessing our journey and this work of learning and healing.

The Shellmound Walks sought to educate the public and stop the bulldozers. But their deeper purpose was ceremonial—healing the trauma of genocide, like the ride to Wounded Knee years before. Here again were sage smoke and prayer offered by Indigenous people. Here again, a mandate to revisit the hidden history of violence and suffering. But this journey hit close to home for me, walking through familiar landscapes, along roads I had known in the morning fogs and hot fall afternoons of my childhood. What had been the most ancient shell mound on the bay had once stood tall in the town where I grew up, but it was now under a parking lot. Standing on that lot in the company of people whose ancestors lay below the cracked pavement touched me deeply. By now, I knew something about my own family history and our complicity. And I had learned to listen to the land—even disturbed, paved-over land. As the weeks of this first walk went by, I could feel a shift in my relationship to colonial settlement. I came alive at a deeper place in my heart, and found myself speaking out at gatherings along the way about my ancestors and the healing we, too, needed to do. One of the Native leaders called us all "Earth People," regardless of ethnicity. It felt good to be included.

The walks were a rare chance to engage in daily life with First People who are still here in Northern California, reviving their culture against all odds. People like Corrina, strongly built, passionate, dedicated to re-learning her language. Corrina's distant grandfather was José Guzmán, the last fluent speaker of their language, forced to labor at Mission San José—which Estanislao had tried to liberate—not far from what's now Silicon Valley. I will not forget her words when the walk stopped at that mission. Looking at us with brave, dark eyes, she shared her family's painful history and her connection to the sacred places under the strip malls and highways we had walked that day, her determination to honor her ancestors. Sitting under the twisted Spanish olive trees that still stand before the whitewashed adobe building—now a tourist site that has erased her family's story—Corrina's eloquence broke my heart open once again.

The walks took us past places where some of my own relatives had lived—remnants of fruit orchards like those my father and grandfather had worked, now crowded out by housing or car dealerships. So my mind was ready when Corrina encouraged us to honor our ancestors—not just Native walkers but Earth People from settler backgrounds, too. "Honor thy father and thy mother" had been part of the training in my childhood, but I knew now how far it was from simple. Our ancestors were flawed and problematic. Some had taken part in genocide or stood by during it. Even though I didn't think mine were directly involved in mass killings or gold rush–era bounties, I knew they shared the interests and the hateful mind-set I was learning about. Some had been policy makers. All had happily received the benefits. Honoring them was going to be difficult as I learned their stories.

I would have to move beyond the idea of ancestry that I was born into—ancestors as figureheads in family trees, divorced from history, important for their genes, property, and status. The Shellmound Walkers and the Asian Buddhist and African-lineage people who joined us had a larger view. Ancestors pass on habits of mind, wounds, and silences that come from the historical context they inhabited. But in the larger, more Indigenous view, they also pass on love and support from a place that is deeper than that history. Much of the world believes that once the old ones enter the Spirit World, they see with true vision. They recognize harm they've done and are appalled. No longer able to undo their mistakes, they look to their descendants to clean up after them. And ancestors can offer us energy to powerfully assist in this. The wider view helped me realize that even my most culpable ancestors are more than bad guys. They, too, have a role to play in healing our genocidal history and the land. To change the legacy of the pioneer Coombses, to clean up their messes, I would need to know them better, to open my heart to their help—as people do in other cultures. This would take enormous effort but was essential to healing.

It had taken many years to get beyond Unc's stories to the facts of genocide, so I knew our settler wounds were buried deep and not visible to most of us. Would I be able to tell that story in a way that could be heard by the children, great-grandchildren, and beneficiaries of those who once wanted "only a white population in California"? Would I find anyone among my ancestors who had taken steps—even small ones—to acknowledge the great wrongs, to heal their consequences? Had any of them begun to experience the consciousness shifts that were leading me out of the silence? Would I be able to forgive their silence and the mind-set they had shared as part of their culture? To honor them as the Shell-mound Walkers had urged? And could my efforts bring healing to these ancestors, too—in ways they wouldn't have understood in their lifetimes?

I decided to begin with the family members I knew best and move back into the history of the more distant ones. My mother was a good starting place. It was easy to see her as an Earth Person who had acknowledged some of her own racial history and formed a bond with the Napa land that went beyond ownership. My father, too, had moved beyond some of the attitudes he was raised with. Starting with these stories, I could look back at the more problematic generations who had settled here during the genocide and brought the colonizer mind with them. I would need to look further back, too, to our first coming to this continent.

We live in a precarious moment as the climate of our planet—its biological and social systems—unravels while we watch. Even before the challenges of the year 2020, a favorite writer, Joanna Macy, called this crisis unique in human history. Naomi Klein had also said there'd been no other "crisis for the human species . . . of this depth and scale." But when you look deeply at the times I've described, the crisis of California's First People had many similarities to the environmental disaster and social collapse we face now.

For Indigenous people in California, the network of plant and animal species they had evolved with lost its coherence in a single lifetime. Species that were like relatives to them went extinct—elk, antelope, and more. Alien cattle and pigs trampled their gardens of edible bulbs and seeds and devoured their acorn crops. Invasive plants took over. The very shape of the land was changed by plowing, damming, and dredging. Cultural practices—like burning to clear brush or enhance an acorn harvest—became criminal acts. Food sources were fenced off with barbed wire. Water and air grew toxic. Diseases from other parts of the world ran rampant, killing as much as 90 percent of a community at once. Trusted medicines no longer worked. Community leaders and healers died like everyone else, leaving just a few people to carry on in a world that had fallen apart. Alongside that destruction had come mass slaughter, kidnapping, rape, enslavement, and separation of children from parents—children who would be raised as servants by settler families or sent to boarding schools guided by the saying "Kill the Indian, save the man."

Those were the terrible times the Lakota holy man saw in his boyhood vision about the same time they were unfolding in the Napa Valley. And now my own culture was facing our version of what he had called "the black road," our own disastrous unraveling. Among my Native friends, I saw that the very people who'd survived the terrible third ascent of Black Elk's vision have ancestral experience facing pandemic, unstable climate, species extinction, and social chaos. They are the ones with inherited memory of surviving rapid ecosystem and cultural collapse—the ones with what my Mohawk friend Patricia St. Onge calls "the anti-bodies." Many have worked through deep trauma to heal with grace and compassion, urging love and forgiveness as we face the crises together. If we are entering that terrible period of destruction, we who are still blinded by a colonial mind-set need the true stories of what led us here. And we need the help of those who bore the brunt of that history. We need right relationship with Indigenous people, the land, and ourselves.

With all the disruptions in our seasons, a beautiful thing is happening that I don't remember from other Januaries. Usually, birds from farther north winter over in the shelter of the oak canopy. Robins, hermit thrushes, and varied thrushes—a strange, shy bird. Smaller than a robin, they have similar colors in a different pattern, splashes of red, with sharp black lines near the eyes, like markings on a Navajo rug. This year's migrating flocks are larger than I remember. Ten hermit thrushes near the house. Varied thrushes all over the field. The hillside crop of toyon berries gobbled up before Christmas. Why so many birds this year? Did conditions up north in the deep forests cause their populations to expand? What brought so many to our woods for the winter? Is it a sign of imbalance or return to an ancient balance? I only know that these birds have an evening ritual that brings awe and joy each time I hear it.

At dusk, when the last golden light hits the hill and the treetops, these birds settle down in the branches to roost for the night. Tractors and chain saws across the fence line are quiet now, but thousands of birds make subtle noises, shifting to the best branch and calling softly. The robins' definitive *chirk, chirk* and a magnificent collective clucking fill the trees. A few late ones fly in quietly. Behind and above the settling sounds is a sweet, high-pitched, whistling kind of music. Perhaps it's made by the varied thrush. If I step outside at this magical hour, the music overwhelms me. Sound waves pouring golden out of trees still in sunlight on the hill—chorusing, singing their simple plainsong to the setting sun. Was this the soundscape of the Patwin and Wappo during the winter months? Or is this something new—winged ones from the north adapting to changes, finding refuge in this small piece of oak forest that remains more or less as it was?

CHAPTER 4

Mother's Legacy
Reciprocity and the Pansy Field

My mother, Elizabeth Farrell Dunlap, at the "old stone wall," with the Pansy Field behind her, April 1991.

Standing in the pure needlegrass was like being back in time, the culms reaching thigh-high and so dense as to mostly obscure the bunches beneath them. The wind blew the stems, making a loud, rustling noise.
    —LAURA CUNNINGHAM, STATE OF CHANGE

Restoration is imperative for healing the earth, but reciprocity is imperative for long-lasting, successful restoration. Like other mindful practices, ecological restoration can be viewed as an act of reciprocity in which humans exercise their caregiving responsibility . . . We restore the land and the land restores us.
    —ROBIN WALL KIMMERER, *BRAIDING SWEETGRASS*

In Love with the Pansy Field

NEARLY CIRCULAR and partly enclosed by a mysterious "old stone wall," what we called the Pansy Field spread out over ten or twelve acres in the southwest corner of Unc's square mile. Every year in April this field glowed with small golden wild pansies (*Viola pedunculata*) that Unc called Johnny-jump-ups. Walking out into that field as children, we entered the world of winds and light and grass and little golden pansies with dark brown markings on their faces. All kinds of other wildflowers grew there, too—tiny white popcorn flowers coiled like forget-me-nots, short spikes of pink owl's clover alongside silky orange California poppies and heavenly smelling blue lupine. Wild larkspur—hard to spot because their rangy flower spikes are deep violet, almost black, a magical color you can't see unless you're really looking. Under the oaks were buttercups and delicate magenta shooting stars in the early spring. And always the common brodiaea, a modest purple lily whose bulbs were food for the First People here.

A true wildflower meadow is more than a field in springtime. More than seeds, sun, weather, or soil. There's an energy in these places that humans can sometimes feel when we walk there, the Earth's natural qi. In my youth, we called it "wildness" and didn't realize that humans had helped shape it. Long after the family walks of our childhood, environmental historians explained what Indigenous people knew all along: The remarkable flower-meadow ecosystems that delighted early California settlers did not happen by chance. They evolved over thousands of years of tending with controlled fire, the digging stick, and ceremony as the First People groomed the land to encourage bulbs and seeds for food and plants for basketry. These meadows were a collaboration between plants, weather, humans, and more. Centuries of human intention sanctify them, and Earth speaks directly to us in such a place—if we can hear—linking us to all our relatives in what we call the ecosystem. The Pansy Field we knew as children had this special magic back then—and some of it was still there when I began to write.

My mother, Elizabeth Farrell Dunlap, felt the call of the Pansy Field immediately. As early as World War II, she organized springtime children's walks there for our city cousins and friends. In half a mile of pleasant walking, you could reach the perfect picnic spot—a little meandering creek just beyond the field and the old stone wall. We kids would strip down to our undies and play in the water, shrieking with joy, making dams out of rocks, sometimes falling in and getting covered with mud. Our picnics consisted of cheese and crackers, carrot sticks, and milk sealed with corks into old-fashioned blue glass Coke bottles that you could return for a deposit. At the end of the day, we'd trudge home through the field, cleansed by the vastness of sun, wind, and wide expanses of grassland—never having seen another soul.

We had no idea then that fields like this had been the mainstay landscape of California before our settler ancestors got here and changed everything. We didn't know about the Indigenous women who'd tended these fields or dug bulbs while their children played nearby. We didn't know about the violence that had destroyed their way of life. As children, we knew only our own times and how happy we felt on this stretch of land. But it may have been our love for the Pansy Field that began to wake my family up.

As the years went by, the field became a center of interest for Mother. Though her own roots were far away in a southern state, something spoke to her in this landscape where her husband's family had so much history. Whenever she could, she would visit with binoculars and flower books— just to watch what happened from year to year. Maybe she began to learn a little of the land's history. On her shelf was an early study of Indigenous uses of plants in the California landscape. The current studies on genocide hadn't been written yet. I gave her the first book that came out on the Ohlone people in the 1970s and told her a little about the Wounded Knee Massacre, but I don't think she had any idea how brutal the takeover had been. She did have a healthy skepticism about Unc's old-timer stories and had moved away from views about slavery in her own southern family. But—so far as I know—she never looked directly at what had happened to the Wappo and the Patwin in the area where she lived for years. I'm not sure she even knew their names—and I was just learning them myself in her lifetime. For white people back then, this information was not easy to find.

Even without knowing much about the First People, Mother had a feeling for indigenous ways of being on the land. In those days, she was spry and active in jeans, long-sleeved blue shirts, a small backpack, and a knitted hat holding back wisps of light brown hair. Years later, I would find her penciled notes: "Solo wildflower walk—lay down on *Orthocarpus* in middle of pansy field. Lark sparrow nest on ground near vireo tree." I could picture her there. *Orthocarpus* was one of her favorite wildflowers, a little spike of pinkish purple. Owl's clover to most of us—no relation to real clover. Lying on the ground in the flowers, she connected with every-thing we loved in that place—a state of mind where human thoughts fade and the land speaks directly. More than once, I shared these experiences, lying near her on the Napa earth in deep silence. She had taught me to feel that connection.

But Mother also approached the land with a keen university-trained mind. Here in the Pansy Field, she began cataloging the plants that grew on Unc's square mile. Eventually, her list became a card file in the kitchen drawer near where she drank her morning coffee. There were nearly three hundred species in the file, all named in Latin, complete with her unique place names for where they grew—Quail Hill, Pink Rock, Lily Falls. A mythic realm I've pieced together from remembered hikes with her. Always a gardener, in the 1960s Mother became interested in California native plants. Studying them was perfect for her. She had a master's degree in Latin and Greek when few women went beyond a bachelor's degree, but she put it aside to start a family. Now she could use Latin again to proclaim the genus and species of any local plant—as named by Euro-peans generations ago. And if not, she would go to work with a hand lens and botanical keys to figure it out.

After Unc died in the 1970s, Mother and Dad built their own place in the northeast corner of what had been his ranch. Now she could spend most of her time with the Napa land. Besides visiting the Pansy Field, now owned by others, she roamed the hillside behind the new house, especially in the wet winter months, when she could transplant things. Her idea was to bring her favorite hillside plants down near the house, where she could enjoy them when she was too old to get around. It must have been a dream come true—to create a garden of indigenous plants around a house in the woods. How many people who love plants get to do something like this? At first, she had the entitled style of many gardeners—she could decide what to plant and where. But Mother took notice when the land had other ideas. She gave up on a bed of exotic raspberries because the local birds (which she also loved) ate every one of them. She was learning to listen for what the land wanted, to watch where the wild strawberries liked to grow and plant them around the walkways in her garden. I remember her showing me how to guide their long rosy tendrils so they could spread into the places they felt at home.

She brought shrubs down from the hill to sculpt the spaces around the house—manzanita, toyon, and cream bush. *Heteromeles* and *Holodiscus* she would tell me, just to be sure I still remembered the Latin from my own botany courses a couple of decades earlier—and probably because her friends glazed over when she used her beloved scientifc language. She found other California native plants in nurseries—*Ceanothus,* the blue California wild lilac with spicy-smelling foliage, and the pale gold Douglas iris, which has now naturalized into huge clumps along the road. Native plants were starting to appeal to gardeners then, as people learned how perfectly they matched a climate of periodic drought. Mother was experimenting and learning what the land wanted—collaborating, not just imposing her will. This was the garden she would ask me to care for— something she and the land had created together—the task that would bring me back to the West Coast after her death and set me to work exploring how the land, like its people, had been colonized.

It's near sundown and I'm heading home so Dad won't worry. The high slopes are awesome in the green of January—with all the new plants coming up that Mother knew so well. This is the first year she isn't up here with me—talking, happy to be with her daughter, digging up plants for her garden, and planning.

Her plans continue even without her. Today in her garden, I found rooted shoots of shrubs I'm sure she started with a method called layering—scraping the bark off a small branch still attached to the parent plant and covering it with soil. In cool, moist, root-forming weather, roots grow from the wound and a clone of the parent plant makes a start. I'm sure the First People knew this way of collaborating with plants. Did Mother forsee how I would discover these plants she'd started? *Ceanothus* and wild currant to transplant to other parts of the garden? I remember her talking about layering. I think she did it whenever she saw a low-lying branch, and I've started to do it, too. I won't know for months if my layering will take. But if the rains last through spring, I may find a dozen new plants when I get back to see Dad again. These gifts from Mother are a message from the afterworld and an affirmation that I can carry on her work.

Wild Oats and Settlement Change the Land

Mother dreamed of a wildflower meadow like the Pansy Field near the house in the two-acre open field we could see through the great arms of the live oaks. It was perfect for baseball games with grandchildren, and I'd seen her run around it solo, flying a kite—a joyous woman in her seventies on one of her breaks from gardening. But the field was what you might call degraded in a botanical way. Even before our Yankee ancestors, weedy plants from Europe had come with the Spanish colonizers. Now in late spring, wild oats rose chest-high if the rains were heavy—*Avena barbata*, an annual grass from the Mediterranean that had long ago choked out the wildflower carpets and unique native bunchgrasses over most of the state. As the oats dried to golden straw and bent to the ground in summer, a crop of yellow star thistle *(Centaurea solstitialis)* would take over, another vigorous plant from the Mediterranean. We knew these thistles from roadside patches: grayish stringy plants with small bright yellow thistle heads and ivory spines that dug wounds in your skin, leaving toxic irritants, or ripped tough denim clothing. Author John Muir Laws says a single plant produces 100,000 seeds a year and the species has infested 22 million acres of grassland in California. With these two invasives in the field, wildflowers and the bunchgrasses that were their natural companions had no chance.

As a child, I loved the tall, graceful wild oats and made whistles in springtime from their sweet-tasting tubular stems. It was years before I realized how these grasses told the colonization story we hadn't learned in fourth grade. Seeds of the wild oat entered our ecosystem with the first Spanish missions along the coast and the military outposts protecting them. They came invisibly—in the hooves of cattle and the straw of adobe bricks. Wildly successful in this new place, they spread quickly around the missions. Their range expanded dramatically after secularization and land grants devoted to Spanish livestock. By the 1830s, a single California rancho might have had fifteen thousand head of cattle producing hides and tallow for international markets, plus sheep, horses, mules, and pigs. All grazed far afield into the Coast Range hills, carrying the seeds of *Avena barbata*. This European plant was a rapid colonizer.

The wild oats spread so much faster than settlement that early settlers found the First People using them for food and thought they were the original vegetation. By 1860, an estimated two million cattle in California had spread invasive grasses, thistles, and other European plants that essentially changed the landscape. The competitive, quick-growing oats robbed moisture and nutrients and blocked the sun, so native perennial bunchgrasses could not set seed or offer space for young seedlings. And cattle went out of their way to chew down the native grasses, which they found delicious. The sheer volume of grazing destroyed topsoil and cut deep erosion gullies, dirtying the water, changing ecosystems along creeks, and making survival even harder for indigenous plants and the people who had evolved with them.

While directly degrading the landscape, settlement also broke apart the Indigenous culture that had helped to form it. Careful tending of the ecosystem through fire, pruning, seed gathering, selective bulb harvesting, and ceremony came to an end in this part of California. Destruction accelerated in the 1840s, when Anglo settlers like my great-great-grandfather pushed into the Californios' land. Ranching acreage expanded. Mega wheat fields replaced wildflower meadows, though fortunately not the Pansy Field. By 1900, 40 percent of California's 31 million acres of old-growth forest had been logged, and the vegetation on our hillsides had changed dramatically. At that point, ethnobotanist Kat Anderson says, "the conversion of much of the state's perennial grassland to annual exotic grasses was complete." Along with the early grasslands went the statewide carpets of seasonal wildflowers, remaining only in isolated patches like the Pansy Field.

With conversion of the grasslands, many plant species that had coexisted before settlement were lost or became what political scientist Stephen Meyer calls "relic species"—plants that remain in smaller and smaller segments of their original range. Becoming so isolated, they no longer share a wide-enough gene pool to adapt to disturbances like climate change. Other "ghost species" survive only in special preserves or zoos. In his chilling book *End of the Wild*, Meyer classifies most species on the continent as either relics or "weed species" that thrive among human-caused disturbances. He says there is no longer anything else. In 2010, British scientists said 22 percent of plant species worldwide (more than one-fifth) were threatened with extinction, 80 percent due to human destruction of the places they've adapted to in order to live and grow. Ten years later, the figure had doubled. I wanted to grieve these losses with my mother.

Unc, who was born in 1881 and could remember the earlier period, had mentioned the "old-fashioned bunchgrasses," but I don't remember seeing any in the 1950s. Throughout his time, Unc's entire square mile, except for the orchards, was rented out as pasture for dairy cattle—even the steep hillside and the magical Pansy Field. Cattle had ranged through here since the 1800s, keeping underbrush in check and chewing down what remained of the original grasses. Even though I'd roamed everywhere as a child, and thought I knew every plant by sight, I had never seen bunchgrasses on the hill, not in childhood and not on walks with Mother in the 1980s.

Then, the summer after her death, hiking up to check one of the pipelines, Dad and I found a whole slope of *Festuca californica*—a dramatically handsome native bunchgrass. Its eighteen- to twenty-four-inch clumps, like elegant cushions with seed heads three to four feet high, still showed some green in the dappled shade of the dry hillside. Dad thought these grasses had started up a few years earlier when the pipe above them had sprung a leak, giving them more water than usual. Old seeds in the soil, still viable after many years, must have germinated. Later, I found other stands of *Festuca,* some older and denser—with wildflowers like purple Chinese houses and yellow globe lilies growing elegantly among the clumps. There's a special beauty about places where the bunchgrasses have returned—no longer the summer tangle of dry, scratchy annual grasses from Europe, but a spread of harmonious mounds, a hillside refuge. Once, I found a quail's nest under the little canopy made by one of those mounds, a perfectly spherical hidden space—lined with fluffy, delicate feathers and piled with dozens of spotted eggs. *Festuca* was returning to our hillside some twenty-five years after the last of the cattle, and I knew my mother would have been overjoyed.

Restoring the Field Near the House

Mother did all in her power to restore the magic of the Pansy Field to the field near the house. She dreamed of pansies there, scattered among bunchgrasses and their graceful flock of companion flowers. Her notes show that she gathered seed from across the road to plant in the field— *Orthocarpus,* tidy tips, poppies, and the blue lupine she called "my lupine." Her seeds would bloom the first year but didn't reseed or sustain themselves. Still, at one edge of the field now, you can find a few pansy plants she brought there, a species that's notoriously hard to transplant. The original Pansy Field was no longer in the family, but the people who owned it asked Mother to teach them enough botany to name what grew on their land. She took the job seriously, thinking their understanding would preserve the plants she loved.

To pursue her dream for the home field, Mother consulted early restoration experts in the 1980s. Struggling to survive in different parts of the field were isolated clumps of purple needlegrass, Latin name *Stipa pulchra.* "Remember," she'd cue me, "*pulchra* means 'beautiful.'" This elegant grass—also California's official state grass—is a delicate mound of green, with graceful two-foot purplish seed heads spraying out to ripen in May. To thrive in the field, it needed its own sun and space, as in the old days, before the wild oats began to compete. Mowing cleared the oats temporarily so *Stipa pulchra* could grow more freely. With less interference, its seeds could germinate in the wet season at the end of the year. Mother planned several rounds of mowing—as the oats sprouted but before the bunchgrasses produced seed and after *Stipa*'s seeds had ripened but before the summer heat. Her schedule varied with rainfall and temperature each year. Since mowing also protected the house from wildfire, it became part of Dad's fire-control plan. By this time—without the burning of the Original People or the grazing of early settlers—underbrush and tinder on the hillside had become a problem.

Native grasses began to respond to the mowing. But the star thistles called for more. The wiry little plants were survivors, coming back strongly after the last mowing in May or June, when everything else went dormant for the summer. So Mother started a "thistle patrol," with her three grandchildren or anyone else who came to visit in summer. Each week, she'd walk us slowly back and forth through the field in a line, scanning right and left for the slightest hint of gray-green foliage in the pale mowed stubble of grasses. When you sensed a thistle—perhaps just a single short stalk with one tiny blossom not even showing its yellow yet—you'd stoop to the bone-dry ground and pull it out. Star thistles had a root system that didn't put up much resistance. The trick was to get every single one of them so they couldn't reseed, and that's where the grandchildren came in. I can picture her out there in the cool of morning, flanked by three small children, perhaps holding the hand of the youngest, moving slowly through the field, eyes sweeping from side to side. "Here's one, Grandma!" a little voice would call—and she would be there with her shovel.

I joined the thistle patrol on summer visits and watched how each year there were fewer to pull. In what seemed like a short time, there were no more yellow star thistles in that field. Later, after Mother's death, when I talked to restorationists myself, they were amazed at her accomplishment. These days, invasive plant–control activists struggle to remove star thistles. Mother's vision of restoring the land was ahead of its time.

Just once in the year 2010, a good twenty years after the field had been cleared of thistles, I found three isolated plants in the far northwest corner. They hadn't set seed yet. Two were only a couple inches tall. I could practically feel Mother beside me, gasping "Oh no!!!!" And I reached down to pull them out that very moment.

But restoring the field to a wildflower meadow was much harder than anyone realized. Mowings had to match erratic weather shifts. Today, there are patches of needlegrass but not the profuse wildflowers of Mother's dream or the magic of the Pansy Field. In one corner, poppies reseed themselves, but they don't spread. There's one beautiful clump of purple milkweed *(Aesclepias cordifolia)*—a magenta-veined plant with slightly fragrant tassels of dark wine-colored flowers. The First People used the tough strands of its stems for cordage. One year, I saw a single spear of owl's clover—which would have made Mother happy—but no further signs. A few purple brodiaea grow here and there, the plant Kat Anderson says is stimulated by selective digging. Indigenous women harvested the bulbs for food, leaving the "mother" bulbs and the very small ones to grow for the following year. Their digging aerated heavy clay soils, shook mature seeds down into the loosened earth, and buried them to assure germination. It's probably time for us to use the digging stick.

Nearly thirty years since her death, I still hold Mother's dream of restoring the field, especially with climate disruption setting in. Deep-rooted perennial grasses store significant amounts of carbon in the soil for the long term. Restoring native vegetation has become a promising way to sequester carbon. We flex Mother's mowing schedule as the seasons grow more unpredictable. This year is part of a long-term drought, so we haven't mowed yet in March. But way on the other side of the field, a grassy presence looks thick and healthy, moving silvery in the wind. I walk out—and sure enough, the whole north end of the field is purple needlegrass, a soft, airy lawn of *Stipa pulchra.* From just a few clumps five years ago, it's spread and spread. Thick, bushy older clumps and small newer ones—all of them lush and green with the little rain we had earlier. And for once there are no competitors. The European wild oats, scratchy foxtail, and clover that usually shade the bunchgrasses this time of year are struggling with the drought. But not deep-rooted *Stipa pulchra.* It is thriving in the field again, especially in the dryness. After millennia of fluctuating weather, this plant knows how to survive extremes. My mother would rejoice to see it here at last—making seed for the future.

Its ripening seed heads catch the late-afternoon light as I walk through, collecting—like the early Wappo aunties must have done with their burden baskets and scooplike sticks. Indigenous friends have taught me about harvesting—ask permission, don't take it all, scatter some seed near the mother plant. I take my fistful of ripe seeds to the southern end of the field, where feral pigs rooted everything up last winter and the soil is still crumbly, bare, and receptive. Even now in my mind's eye I see the restored grasses—laced with wildflowers—*Stipa pulchra* holding space for the return of poppies, lupine, tidy tips, owl's clover. The whole beautiful tapestry of the wildflower meadow.

Hillside Restoration

Though she was a very sociable person who loved having guests, Mother also loved her solitude, especially after moving to Napa, with Dad in the city during the week. She seemed as happy then as I'd ever known her, ranging up every gully and onto every slope of the steep hillside that was the bulk of their eighty acres. Observing, transplanting, and cataloging plants, naming her favorite places. With her feeling for language, Mother loved giving names. Hawk Creek and Pink Rock Lookout were as real to her as anything on a map. Looking back, I wonder if this was a way of exerting ownership, a vestige of the colonizer. Or did it honor her growing intimacy with the land, her way of belonging? Was it her way of sanctifying these places? Mother was full of complexities.

She liked taking people to spots where the shelter of the canyons and the rock and soil structure created unique microclimates and wild-flower mixes. Mimulus Falls—not too far from the house on a seasonal creek—was perfect for grandchildren or friends easily winded by steep slopes. She could be prescriptive about routes. But when I visited from the East Coast, she took me on more intuitive walks to remote places, like the miraculous Lily Falls. We'd pull on our boots and long-sleeved shirts to protect against poison oak. She'd don her orange knitted hat and a belted leather sheath with clippers for thick underbrush. We'd take her little shovel and a plastic bucket if it was winter, when we might find iris or fern to transplant. Her small backpack hung ready near the door. She might have had a route in mind, but she was open to suggestions from the land itself.

I've learned her ways. All these years, I've worn her same orange hat and carried her bucket and shovel. A tree, a shaft of light, a new wildflower, a bird's movement, a game trail—or the memory of a walk with her—can lead me up and off in a new direction. And from there, one place leads to another. Sometimes my camera urges me to linger, to catch a drop of moisture on a spiderweb or get down on my belly in the mud. And I've used her shovel for restoration work, especially on patches of the notorious French broom, a tough, woody shrub from Europe that easily colonizes the steep woods and drove Mother crazy in her lifetime.

Soon after moving into their house, she and Dad found a sinister thicket of broom along their trail to Lily Falls. Bright yellow flowers in spring and green leaves in summer, when other things are dry. If you know the indigenous look of this land, broom is always out of place. It looks lovely on dry Mediterranean hillsides, but in our ecosystem it's a feared invasive. (Our family called it "Scotch broom," a related European plant.) Well-meaning gardeners choose broom for its easy growth and cheerful flowers. But once planted—as on the local golf course—broom goes feral, spraying a wide area with tiny black seeds, viable in the ground for decades, ready to sprout at any time. Hundreds of woody broom plants can quickly choke out other vegetation, creating dense growths hostile to wildlife and stockpiling more of those long-lived seeds year after year. A rich woodland glade becomes an impenetrable thicket—a monoculture where nothing else can live—and a true fire hazard. It's a legendary eyesore along rural roads where open woodlands with a mix of ferns and special wildflowers are now dense broom thickets. Finding just one patch of broom on her precious wild hillside, Mother took serious steps.

I didn't see that first patch, but she hinted that she and Dad had done something risky there. She and I always stopped at this place to pull new shoots that showed up even in the dry season—spotting their tender cloverlike leaves (they're in the pea family) and upright woody stems. Once in a while, we'd find one missed on previous visits, now six or eight feet tall—with bright yellow flowers or ominous tough pealike pods with silvery hairs. We'd count the seedlings we pulled—sometimes several hundred in just this one spot—and announce the number proudly to my father. I noticed the soil in that place was crumbly and disturbed, with little else growing there. It was only after Mother died that Dad told me they'd sprayed poison, trying to wipe out that broom.

For all her earth consciousness, Mother was also a product of her times. She'd gardened with chemicals ever since I could remember, using toxic substances on snails, roses, even lawns where we children wrestled and played every day. I'm pretty sure she used DDT before it was banned. At the Napa place, I recall her decked out in an unwieldy old canister backpack with a spray gun but no mask—eradicating poison oak with Roundup, a product of the Monsanto company, now Bayer, that would later become notorious. The stuff in her canister was powerful enough to destroy an entire stand of poison oak on contact. Vigorous as a plant can be, poison oak is a native plant that can behave invasively. Mother courted death in those woods—to keep the place as safe as she knew for family members. Cleaning out the shed after her death, we piled up one rusty, scary-looking tin after another for the toxic-waste dump, finding them shrouded in cobwebs and old mouse nests, their labels ominously corroded. Mother died from lymphoma, a more and more common cancer of the lymph system. No one spoke of it then, but surely the poison from those rusty tins had harmed the system that filters toxins from the human body. Research and successful lawsuits now confirm the connection.

I head up the creek, hoping to see the beautiful wild azalea that should be blooming now in late May—but keeping an eye out for broom as I move into the steepness. Something tells me it's not far away.

Even so, I'm shocked to find its tiny seedlings and soft, succulent plants choking up the path ahead and the spaciousness of this place. So far, indigenous plant life is holding on—ferns and yellow globe lilies sparkle in the dappled light. I throw down my pack and begin pulling broom with both hands, grabbing and yanking the larger plants as I slide the tiny tender ones easily out of the ground. A crazed state of mind takes over, and I look down toward the creek, where water tumbles below a rocky escarpment. Things are worse down there. Not one but many mature, woody, blooming plants, a small forest with seeds ripe and ready to spray. These plants got their start during Mother's lifetime. A patch she missed. I plunge down and spend two more hours there, clipping the silvery seed pods so I can cart them away and using Mother's little shovel to pry out the sturdy roots. The trunks are two inches thick, and there are too many seedlings to count. I work feverishly, losing my favorite hair clip, heedless of poison oak.

Somewhere in the frenzy, an intense, magical fragrance shifts everything for me—calming, surrounding, and blessing me in this work. It is the California wild azalea (*Rhododendron occidentale*)—the very plant I set out to find on this hike. Not just the slight musky scent of its foliage but also big clusters of delicate white blooms with golden centers, unfurling ten feet above me in the sunlight. Its otherworldly odor—sweet, with a hint of faraway places, a hint of spice—always stirs a mysterious energy. Now it carries the memory of my mother and so many of our walks. Did she know I'd taken a spray of it to the hospital on her last morning and spoken its name, hoping she could still hear me. Here on the hill, I feel affirmed. I am continuing the work of stewardship that she began, and I feel her support.

I wish Mother could have known about M. Kat Anderson, the ethnobotanist whose work has helped me think about restoring what the land has lost. Anderson started publishing around the time Mother died, in 1992—short articles on the horticultural practices of Indigenous Californians. By 2005, she had pulled her work into a five-hundred-page book called *Tending the Wild: Native American Knowledge and the Management of California's Natural Resources*. Using histories dating back to the eighteenth century, field notes from early observers, interviews with Native informants, and hands-on plant research, Anderson pieces together the untold story of how the First People tended the plant and animal world going back at least twelve thousand years. She shows how California's tribes had shaped what settlers thought was wilderness by cultivating, pruning, burning, seeding, and transplanting to improve habitat for game, control disease, and nourish plant sources of food, basketry, and other neccessities. Anderson calls it "protoagriculture." Indigenous peoples all over the Western hemisphere used similar techniques.

These ideas would have struck a chord with Mother, but Anderson's story of how the First People took care of this land was not available in her lifetime. All the same, she echoed their ways in her seed gathering, layering, and transplanting, and in her campaigns against plants that were unbalancing the ecosystem she loved. She would have seen herself as "tending the wild," and I believe she began to grow into that role as she worked with the Napa land and mentored me in that work.

Mother would also have resonated with botanist-poet Robin Wall Kimmerer's *Braiding Sweetgrass: Indigenous Wisdom, Scientific Knowledge, and the Teachings of Plants*. Kimmerer loves languages and knows the Latin names of plants in European-based science. But she is also re-learning her ancestral Indigenous language—Potawatomi. Bridging scientific and Indigenous worlds, Kimmerer is relearning her people's ways of talking with plants, of being in reciprocity with them and with places like the Pansy Field. She calls it being "indigenous to place."

Kimmerer's inspiring stories feature modern people—Indigenous like herself but also settler people like Mother and me—restoring land and ecosystems from the degradation that came with European settlement, removing invasive plants and chemical toxicity. She says people who aren't Indigenous can become "naturalized" to place, like plants from outside an ecosystem that naturalize when they feel at home there, flourishing without taking over. For most Americans, becoming naturalized would mean a major paradigm shift. We'd have to stop trying to control what happens and work in "deep reciprocity" with the natural world, learning from plants and other beings and even taking direction from them. Andean healer Arkhan Lushwala calls it letting "things tell us what they are." Kimmerer calls it collaborating, not trying to impose our will. This was the role I think my mother was growing into, the one she was teaching me with the wild strawberry tendrils. If Kimmerer is right, closeness to the earth can transform the colonizing mind. An elder tells her of farmers who thought they were in charge, but "while they were working on the land, the land was working on them. Teaching them."

Those lessons can't have been easy for my mother. Although open to the land, she was highly educated, had a strong will and a developed sense of entitlement. She took great pride in what she'd learned from books and passing it on. Along with my father, she'd been an excellent student in the most elite honor societies. It was hard for her to be wrong about anything. And this was part of the complexity she transmitted to me. Like hers, my first reaction is to think I know already—that this weed should go and that plant should stay. By habit, I jump to conclusions and hold on, and I've had to retrain myself to listen more humbly for the truth, with plants as well as people and ideas. As a child, I didn't see that our habit of knowing what's best for others was the very mentality that took over the continent and dominated. The mind that thrived on slavery and turned fossil fuels into flooding and climate change. It's at the root of white supremacy and runs directly counter to Indigenous listening, respect, and collaboration. I am slowly working my way out of this contradiction, and I think my mother was also, in her way. With her native plant garden and the task of tending the ranch, she bequeathed something unfinished, a shifting paradigm, a mind-set moving from domination toward reciprocity.

Visiting Each Plant

How does a changing mind-set get passed on? Just as I was wondering who would care about the bunchgrasses and invasive broom in the next generation, I found a younger person as passionate as I am about listening to the natural world. Diana Benner, daughter of a friend and granddaughter of Mother's friends, is a plant ecologist who cofounded The Watershed Nursery in Richmond CA. She collects seeds and grows indigenous plants to restore creeks, shorelines, and even the land around highways, making sure the seed is local so gene pools don't get so mixed that they can't adapt to climate change. Like my mother, whom she barely knew, Diana knows the Latin names and travels with a hand lens. Plus, she carries tiny manila envelopes for seed collecting. We clamber around collecting late summer blue rye and bright red California fuchsia and sharing stories. At last there's someone eager to hear about Mother's efforts to restore balance and biodiversity.

Diana knows the science but also understands the reciprocity of working with plants. We respond when a thicket of broom calls us to stop and pull seedlings or when we find ourselves in some unique, beautiful microclimate. We gasp with pleasure at elegant red-brown manzanita trunks, self-mulched against too much underbrush. It's a joy to experience these things again with someone who shares the same feelings. Our time on the hill is more than seed gathering. We're visiting each plant, communicating, appreciating, stopping to remove the ones that don't belong, and reseeding species that evolved right here on this hillside. It feels like part of an ancient ceremony of renewal, making the earth whole again as the early people did. At first I thought we were simply continuing my mother's work. Now I see that all three of us continue a much older tradition of tending—learning to listen to what the land offers, needs, and wants.

Once Mother and Dad moved to Napa, I started reading everything I could find on Indigenous Californians. In the late 1980s, *News from Native California* began publishing Native-written stories of cultural resurgence. Before that, there were occasional booklets by white authors. I was drawn to stories of healers working with native plants, like respected leader Florence Jones of the Winnemem Wintu tribe north of us, near Mount Shasta. Born just a few years before my mother, and living well into her nineties, Florence Jones worked tirelessly to preserve the language and culture of her people in the face of development and loss of sacred sites flooded by the Shasta Dam. Dedicated to "waking up" sacred places, she had permission to do ceremony on lands controlled by the U.S. Forest Service. Drawn to the power of her work, a government researcher often accompanied her and felt she trusted him despite their differences.

In the 1970s, this man wrote a small book about the Wintu and Florence Jones, whom he called "Flora." One prophetic story touched me. In a grove of black oaks where there had been many Wintu healings, Florence told him of big challenges ahead. "This world is getting very near to the end," she said. "The white people are causing the world to end." She urged everyone with sacred spaces to "wake them up, the same as I am doing here." I don't think my mother knew about Florence Jones, but I wish I'd told her. In her own way, she was caring for the land in a manner that could help it wake up and heal.

Mother's Roots in White America

I've often wondered how my mother came to feel the deep connection with the California earth that she transmitted to me. After all, she was not from here. Her roots were in the gentle hills of middle Tennessee, a land of deciduous woodlands peppered with beautiful dark cedar trees. I think it was Cherokee land, but President Andrew Jackson's deadly Trail of Tears had cleared that region in 1837. On family visits, our grandmother told nothing of this in her stories about land that had been "ours" generations before the Civil War. Her stories were also silent about the Indian wars and the enslavement of Africans that had made our family's ownership and lifestyle possible. As children, we didn't know what was missing from our grandmother's stories, but we sensed the legacy of slavery on these visits and sometimes challenged our relatives about it. Our mother must have prepared us. She often said she was raising us "to be less prejudiced" than her generation. She had distanced herself from southern culture, and was the only California mom I knew in the 1950s who always spoke up when she heard the n-word.

The year after Mother died, I made a journey back to one of the home sites in my grandmother's stories. Cragfont was the first stone mansion in its region—built at the end of the eighteenth century, in disrepair for generations, and being restored as a historical site when I visited. I was uneasy. By this time, I knew many of the murderous details of conquest and enslavement that had benefited our family through my mother's line. But, left to myself on the grounds, I recalled the Buddhist practice of walking meditation—every step with full and loving attention to my own feelings and the messages of the land and its history. The March day was gray yet lovely with spring, the air alive with warmth after winter in New England. I felt a churning around my heart that I knew was outrage and deep grief, but the walking also brought a peaceful energy. The gentle sloping hills and open pastures felt like the Pansy Field or the first homeland of our species in East Africa and seemed to exert a healing force. I imagined this might be how my mother had felt about the Tennessee landscape, and maybe why she took so naturally to Unc's ranch. I'm guessing she had mixed feelings about her roots. She had moved away and sought to raise her children "less prejudiced." It was a first step.

Standing there on the Cragfont grounds, part of me wanted to shout in outrage mixed with shame, but another part wanted to humanize my ancestors so I could understand in a deeper way. With the basic goodness they must have had, what had led them to promote such great wrongs?

Outrage would not change things, but understanding could help end the grip of their mind-set on the world we still inhabit.

For the next fifteen years, as I flew back and forth to California for Mother's work of tending the Napa land, I turned to what I'd begun at Cragfont—moving from outrage to understanding. Many activist groups I joined in this period thought the best way to address racial injustice was to denounce or try to shame it. But would this work for my relatives? The Buddhist teachings I'd drawn close to after Mother's death encouraged the idea that all beings have innate goodness. Honoring ancestors meant healing the harm caused by their misperceptions, beginning with the attitudes we'd inherited from them. Genocide and enslavement lay invisibly at the foundation of my life. Learning more and seeking to heal could help me move beyond the shame I continued to feel, so I could take clearer action. To uncover my ancestors' true stories, I began following leads, sometimes on Google, and learning more about colonial and enslavement history in California and other places where our family had lived. I remember writing some angry poems about my ancestors but also starting to see some of them as human beings.

These efforts energized the resolve to stay active that I'd made after Wounded Knee. And somehow—perhaps because my mother had been on her own version of this path—I sensed that she and other ancestors were in this with me. In 1998, I took another Buddhist-sponsored journey into the past with African Americans seeking to heal themselves and our country from the wounds of slavery—the Interfaith Pilgrimage of the Middle Passage. There I heard indigenous West African teachings that said ancestors rely on living descendants to undo the harm they created on Earth and are available for support. I hoped my own would help as best they could. Their healing was also at stake.

Generational Differences

I wish I could have talked to my mother about some of this, but she was gone. We had never come close to discussing the downsides of our family history—the legacy of slavery and the massacres on land within view of Unc's deck. I doubt she even knew of them, because it wasn't easy to find out. Even in her last years, my own awareness was just beginning, so I hadn't been ready for this conversation, either. I'd loved my heart-to-heart talks with Mother—after breakfast, as morning sun lit up the oaks and stirred miraculous bird life. She listened to my stories of the students I was learning so much from and my experiences at Wounded Knee. But with all our common love of plants and the guidance we both seemed to feel from the earth, we were of two different generations when it came to the meaning of our own family's story.

In my younger days, there had been plenty of tension. In the 1960s, I'd been full of youthful outrage about war and racism and wasn't a very good listener. When I called myself a "peace activist," I think she heard criticism of her father's life of military service. And she was right—I was upset about people like us imposing our way of life over a whole continent and around the world. Now I know much more about colonialism and genocide, but even then I saw that we'd taken the California land and covered it with our plants, our pastures and orchards, our fences and malls—and hadn't honored what was there before. Slavery was a terrible face of it, but the mind-set of superiority behind this institution permeated the culture I was raised in. People like ourselves—European, Protestant, hardworking, and good at managing time and the labor of others—felt that God had set us up to prosper. We thought we were "better than," and that was the problem. I'm sure it would have been hard for my mother to hear this. By now it's easy to name it "white supremacy," but to us back then, being "better than" was just normal, "nice." Not visible and in-your-face like the Ku Klux Klan, which I'm sure Mother also found repugnant. Our culture was as successful as wild oats or French broom in the oak woodlands. And like them, we had destroyed some pretty amazing ecosystems.

Polemics like this didn't work with my mother. And even now my ideas about invasive plants standing in for the whole colonial enterprise would probably have gone too far for her. But somewhere there was common ground. We weren't that far apart. She had resisted the colonial legacy in her own way. Leaving the South and beginning to open her heart to the history of the Pansy Field. And she had, indeed, raised us to be less prejudiced than her generation. That meant we might change in ways that would be hard for her to accept. Even though we weren't in agreement, I honor her role in the long, slow transformation of our racial legacy. And I've always imagined that her strength for this came from her connection with the earth.

Now when I look back, I don't get stuck on our differences. For every mental picture of my mother riled by our generational tensions, there's another where she's beyond all that, filled with joy of the earth. Once when she was in her early seventies, I found her lying on her belly in a field of tiny lupine high up in the mountains. We were on one of her Sierra trips with grandchildren in a remote place called Pioneer Basin—accessible by Mono Pass, named for a local tribe. (I hadn't yet seen the ironies of these beloved place names.) Mother—by this time a lot rounder and more solid than she had been in the early Pansy Field days—was spread out in the semishade. Sun hat ajar, cheek against the earth, she seemed to be in a trance, embracing the ground of being in deep silence and concentration. Was she storing up energy, perhaps to address the cancer that had already begun to affect her lymph system? That was her kind of contact with the earth.

Our last time together in the Pansy Field, I made a photo of Mother about to climb the old stone wall at the far west border of Unc's former square mile. In her soft blue velour top, she looks over the wall at me, her eyes their own luminous blue, her face rugged and tanned from all her time outdoors. She seems aglow with health for a woman in her late seventies, her hair still naturally light brown, curling around her face with a barely perceptible touch of gray above her ears. Behind her are green spring grasses with dashes of wildflower color and a few live oaks. There is the blue lupine she called "my lupine." She gazes at the camera with such a deep, timeless look, conveying her love of this place, of the earth and her family. I don't think she liked the photo. Maybe it betrayed a vision of the future she didn't want us to see. But the rest of us loved it, especially a year later, when the lymphoma caught up with her and suddenly she was gone. In two more years, when Dad's time came, we hung this photo over his bed. He talked about it almost every day, how she was waiting there for him at the edge of the Pansy Field by the old stone wall.

Once I'm up in the field, my spirits soar. Just being here again—the open-ness, the gentle rolling slopes with their one or two huge drooping valley oaks. The grasses are about to turn summer-blond, a few pansies still blooming low to the ground. They're getting by with very little rain this year. Two months with less than an inch. But beautiful April storm fronts are rolling in day after day, new banks of clouds, rain always a possibil-ity—strange to be in a state of both rain and drought at the same time.

The sky moves with moisture. Mists covering—then revealing—the blue hills to the east rimming the field. To the south is the row of suburban-style homes that line up now behind the old stone wall. This big field, no longer a field among fields, no longer linked to open spaces that connect on and on into the distance. Just past the wall on a paved driveway, a delivery truck bounces along toward a new gray shingle house backed up against the stones, looking like a mini palace. Mother would have been aghast. I turn my gaze aside to feel the spirit of the field as it was when we were children. If I soft-focus, I can keep before me the shining spirit of the grassland, letting the new development go fuzzy behind the rock wall.

I find a spot where I can keep my soft focus, looking up a gentle slope past poppies and purple needlegrass. Up to an old valley oak, stark and ragged against the skyline. I plunk down and eat a quick lunch—avocado sandwich and carrot—remembering our childhood picnics. Just sitting on the ground to eat that food draws me deeper into the timeless heart of the Pansy Field. Close to the earth, I drift into near dream. Free of thought, I feel the cloud of presence that has always been this magical field. I am fully absorbed in it—until the moment my body tells me to look up again. The clouds have moved in. The moisture in the air is dense and my skin feels the sweet softness of light rain. The air is both bright and dark, the essence of a California spring storm. Clouds wash over the field, bathing me in their fine spray: the life of earth and of sky touching me all at once. I open my camera, ignoring the drops of mist on the lens, and make some photos of poppies and a few late pansies in the spring-storm light. The hills loom distant blue around my blurred field of vision.

Saying Good-bye

When Mother died, it was mid-May of a fairly dry year, the grasses already summer-brown, with only a few flowers still blooming along the creeks. All of us were together in the house—my sisters and their families, including Mother's three grandchildren; my father, still tall and thin, but bent over and short of breath, his once-strong heart swelling with sadness. He'd never expected to outlive my mother. After he'd written an obituary on one of his lined yellow legal pads, and we'd all discussed it, we took a walk together as a family. The place that called was the Pansy Field. We stood there at the far west boundary, where the old stone wall curved, as ever, with a few oaks shading it.

We stood there in the stickery summer grasses—shadows lengthening, the bright light highlighting tension lines in our faces. We stood there with our raw, numbing pain. It was the first death in this family, and she was the one who'd held us together. We stood there mostly in silence, some of it numbness and some of it deep connection. She had been the talker. My nieces stood close to Dad, holding his hands. We spoke just a few words about Mother and how she'd loved this place. The poetry was the field itself.

It was just a few years later that the couple who'd owned the Pansy Field since Unc's death and had so far protected its magic decided to plow it up for a vineyard. They'd given up their plan to learn the names of the wildflowers. As for all those others taking over the valley, a vineyard would make the land more valuable for their children, they told us sadly, and they'd leave a little strip unplowed along the edge so as to walk out and enjoy any flowers that remained. It was hard for any of us to return after that.

A warm April wind stirs the bunchgrasses and all seems shining, healthy, and in balance. But the old route to the Pansy Field is blocked by new, unclimbable fences. Finally it has happened. The Pansy Field we knew is gone, and I am taking my first walk to the new vineyard, grieving and raging, but trying to stay open to what I will see.

I take the neighbors' road up through new vines, walking slowly, imagining Mother with me. There's unplanted land on either side of the road, and we watch it carefully. It's filled with unfamiliar blooming clovers, perhaps seeded there to provide nitrogen to the soil—red, cerise, and yellow, all in bloom just where the hill steepens and we used to look for the first spikes of owl's clover. And there they are. Elegant little pink spikes right here in their home territory, poking up among the gaudy alien colors. I can almost hear Mother calling out, *"Orthocarpus!* The little Owl's Clover!" She's using that joyous voice we used to tease her about when she discovered some beautiful thing of earth. "They are still here!" I repeat out loud to myself, as if we are saying it together, "They are still here." At least this first spring of the new vineyard, they are still here.

A lump rises in my throat as the history of this place floods through me—the land as it was for the Wappo and the Patwin, for Juárez, in Unc's time, in ours as a young family. Destruction of a people and the world they tended. And now this new destruction of a small bit of that world that remained. The loss of my parents as living beings. Things arise and they pass away. That is the Buddhist view helping me through these times. But the changes have been violent, and now we're accelerating them, so that whole species pass away permanently. Can the owl's clover compete with the superstrength designer clovers and hold out in its favored habitat, or is it already a relic? Mother used to take seeds from this special patch to the field she was trying to restore—but it didn't work. They liked this spot. And for now, they have not given it up. They are still here.

Farther up, in what used to be the actual Pansy Field, more owl's clover is growing like a border guard along the edge of the new vineyard, where there's still a slice of the field's former glory. Brilliant colors of pink, free, for now, of invading industrial clovers and mingling joyously with blue-eyed grass, white and purple brodiaea, buttercups, *Lomatium*, and yarrow—with larkspur, lupine, and poppies. A huge thick colony of yellow Mariposa lilies in bud now, ready to bloom in a week or so.

And yes, amazingly, out there in the plowed earth there are still some pansies, a few wiry little clusters of *Viola pedunculata* surviving among the weeds at the base of the new vines. With all the disruption—plowing, chemicals, and irrigation—a few of them are toughing it out for now, blooming their golden resistance to it all.

CHAPTER 5

Dad and the Oaks

Slowly Letting Go of the Family Silence

The large live oak near our door, with field and hill beyond, March 2017.

*An oak tree is an oak tree. That is all it has to do. If an oak
tree is less than an oak tree, then we are all in trouble. . . .
Every time we look at the oak tree we have confidence. . . .
We know that if the oak tree is not there, and all the other
trees are not there, we will not have good air to breathe.*
   —THICH NHAT HANH, *BEING PEACE*

*Our people were given the responsibility to use fire to make
things beautiful and productive—it was our art and our science.*
   —ROBIN WALL KIMMERER, *BRAIDING SWEETGRASS*

Time with the Oaks

MOTHER AND DAD'S HOUSE stands in a dramatic grove of California coastal live oak, some with trunks four feet across. Branching from the base, they reach their long, thick limbs for sunlight, parallel to the earth. The land is open at their feet, but, far above, a weaving of great dark limbs supports a leafy canopy. Bird life thrives up there, and buoyant-tailed western gray squirrels dart up one sloping branch and down the next, rushing to earth with acorns to bury in the blanket of fallen leaves. Live oaks shed leaves every year, but they're the ones from two or three years back, not from the past spring. So there's an illusion they keep those leaves forever. Everyone who comes remarks on these huge trees—usually with awe. In the dry, hot summer, they cool the air and their shade is sanctuary. They host an endlessly fascinating ecosystem. For humans, it's peaceful and quiet under their great limbs, and the earth is alive.

How did these big trees come to be growing so harmoniously beside the small open field Mother had tried to restore? Some were over one hundred years old when the first Europeans came into the valley. I imagine them back then on cool, foggy mornings when the grass underfoot was dry but not too dry and the winds were quiet, plenty of humidity in the air. People from a village along the Napa River might be here for ceremony to renew the land. An elder offering prayer in the Wappo language as men and women light and tend small flames that burn quickly along the ground, consuming young oak, toyon, and other saplings that have grown up since the last burning. The people know how to manage fire. Flames wrap themselves around the massive trunks of larger trees, scorching dry mosses without harming the bark—which for live oaks is extremely fire-resistant. Tendrils of smoke curl up through the branches, mingling with the morning fog, soon pierced by rays of light as midmorning sun breaks through. Small flames lick their way through the bunchgrasses in the field, leaving ash to fertilize the soil. Imagine a smoky smell that feels like healing, not danger, a whole relationship with fire my culture has lost, known only from old stories and the tribes farther north who still practice this way of protecting the earth from imbalance, disease, and catastrophic wildfire.

My father, the one whose DNA linked me to the early settlement of Napa County, especially loved the oaks. He'd grown up on a family fruit ranch in the valley and, even though making his living as a city lawyer, had a deep affinity for hard work in the woods. The place he and Mother chose when Unc's land was divided was really his choice. Mother leaned toward the Pansy Field, but he loved this zone of oaks at the base of the steepening hills, where big trees were always coming down in winter storms and could be cut up for firewood. Mother tended native grasses and wildflowers. Dad was drawn to the big trees. And they were magnificent in this place.

Most of Unc's square mile has lost its rolling grasslands and oak-lined creeks to vineyards, upscale homes, and European plantings with a different rhythm. But Mother and Dad's place in the northeast corner is still classic oak woodland—not all that different from the way it was before settlement—mostly because of how they took care of it. Huge trees grow where valley land meets the steep summer-dry hills to the east, concentrating all their massive glory in this border zone. Wrapped in their arms is a small redwood house with wide windows and a deck that looks out through big tree trunks to the valley. Time here is time with the oaks. Light pours in between the networked limbs, filtered through a year-round canopy of the dark green leaves of live oak, crisp and prickly at the rims, like holly. Here and there, taller black oaks and valley oaks grow straight up toward bits of sky showing through the canopy and shed their leaves for winter.

The giant trees are vulnerable to strong winds, especially when heavy with spring sap or when rains loosen the soil around their massive roots and add the weight of wet leaves. Long before today's extreme weather, the big trees near us fell occasionally—a normal part of woodland self-maintenance. They could fall suddenly with a great crashing noise, blocking the road when Mother returned from the mailbox. These were the trees that called my father to get out his chain saw and pickup truck, cutting piles of prime firewood to split, stack, dry, and deliver to friends in the city at Christmas in the days before hearth fires were linked with smoky air and climate change. Everyone who knew Dad remarked on his great stamina for hard work—quiet, tall, and lean in old plaid wool shirts and worn out Levi's that hung precariously off his hips. As a child, I loved helping him and also loved the smell of those old shirts—a little smoky, with a mixture of tannin from the oaks and Dad's sweat.

Interbeing and Resiliency

Mother and Dad developed their place with a light touch—unpaved road, small lawn and pool. Landscaping was mostly this grove of oaks that had been here for centuries and the diverse ecosystem that had evolved with them. Insects in the high canopy feeding flocks of warblers, chickadees, titmice, and bushtits. Brown creepers and nuthatches moving down and up the trunks. Five kinds of woodpeckers plus two local jays careening from branch to branch and plying the blanket of leaf mold below for grubs and acorns.

Acorns are the big draw. Each year, one or several trees produce "mast" crops, carpeting the ground with shiny, pointy nuts. Mast years feed gray squirrels, wood rats, tree rats, ground squirrels, mice, and voles, as well as deer, raccoon, possum, and band-tailed pigeons. And others eat the eaters—hawk and bobcat, golden eagle and snake—occasionally a cougar, also known as a mountain lion. We've seen every one of them hunting among the oaks, sometimes making off with a mouse or squirrel.

Before colonization, humans were key to this system. For the First People, acorn was the revered staple, with cultural practices for harvesting, storage, and preparation that varied from community to community. (At least one Native author uses the singular, as in the word *corn*.) Though they told us in fourth grade that acorn was a poor food, we know now that it centered a diet high in protein from game, grasshoppers, seafood, and seeds. The acorn crop sustained California's unusually large Indigenous population, warding off malnutrition or starvation. In turn, the First People tended the complex ecosystem of the oaks with pruning, harvesting, brush clearance, and nourishing fire.

Oaks host countless other life-forms, such as microscopic wasps that create fanciful galls and the common parasite, mistletoe with its bundles of dark leathery leaves that draw nourishment from the oak's upper branches. Dad used to climb up and harvest an armful at Christmas if none fell to earth as gifts in a windstorm. Branches and trunks are thick with mini forests of moss and lichen. More kinds of insects than you can imagine live in the sphere of the oak. Underneath, in the fallen leaves, are countless bugs, microbes, and worms digesting those leaves into compost to nourish the tree. An oak's root network reaches out three times farther than its branches, with the remarkable ability for roots of different trees to bond to each other so the stronger ones can pass on nutrients. A second vast system of fungal strands supports the roots by picking up minerals from the soil and making them available. Mushrooms are the visible part of this network, and they carpet the earth here after every winter rain. Some are deadly, others delicious—such as golden chanterelles or fragrant oyster mushrooms. Nowadays, you find wild mushrooms from oak woodlands in gourmet groceries, and Indigenous gatherers complain that supplies are dwindling. In Mother and Dad's time, the craze was only beginning, and we feared most were poisonous. Dad loved mushrooms more than any other food but didn't realize the treasure under his favorite oaks.

An oak also embraces predators in its ecosystem—enough predatory plants, animals, insects, and microbes to kill itself many times over. But that's not what happens. Glenn Keator's *The Life of an Oak: An Intimate Portrait* describes the trees' miraculous defense system, making and releasing toxic chemicals, such as bitter tannins, to let other trees know when they sense attack. Overall there is balance: Some creatures prey on the oak, others on the predators. These organisms evolved together. The beings surrounding the oak keep the whole system afloat without killing their host—so far, that is.

The calendar says spring equinox. Even though it's been cold and raining heavily all week, every single live oak on the hill knows what day it is. They're all sending out new leaves, what's called a "flush." When you look up the steep incline, their graceful billowy shapes are aglow with rosy copper and amber and golden green—each one a subtly different hue. A few started weeks ago. Others are just beginning. Each tree has its own leafing-out schedule and its own color, because each tree is genetically different. No clones on this hill. This muted rainbow is biodiversity made visible. A week from now, they'll merge to a single glow of pale new green when the budding stage ends.

A few are already displaying tiny tassels along the new branches. These will grow to a couple of inches long, like the fringe on a silk scarf, tossing in the wind and releasing oak pollen to be carried by rain or wind to nearby trees. There microscopic male pollen grains will meet the tiny beginnings of female acorns. Each tree is designed so its pollen and acorn "flowers" mature at different times. This way, no tree can pollinate itself, but must "find a mate" with different DNA—keeping the gene pool vibrant, assuring a wide range of characteristics in any grove of the trees. Some individuals release their pollen early, some late. Some form small, tight clusters of new leaves, while others send out long shoots—each tree a different color in the oak rainbow. With so many variations, the species has a better chance of surviving and thriving in changeable weather—which was California's normal long before settlement or the present climate changes.

In Unc's day—half a century before we felt the climate crisis, though well into the period of industrial carbon release—California's seasons had already made it the poster child for extreme weather. Dramatic winter storms from the Pacific never seemed to unfold exactly the same way. Wind, temperature, precipitation, length of storm front were always changing. Dad started keeping figures on rainfall. They vary widely—some years over forty inches, others in the low teens. And whether it's a "wildflower year" or a "mast year" or a drought year depends on how the variables play out. With their diverse gene pool, one tree or another will thrive in a given year. So far, California coastal live oaks seem to be adapting to the dramas of climate.

I've watched the same trees year after year, like one raggedy one that Mother worried about and had sprayed for the oak moth caterpillar. For years, this tree managed to hang on—with lots of small dead branches that attracted bugs and birds. Then twenty years later, when I took a good look, it was as green and healthy as any other. You would hardly know it had caused so much anguish. I've seen a tree struggle with its own special form of blight, then regenerate—according to some cycle of health and sickness known only to that tree. This gives me confidence in the ecosystem and the complex relations that have sustained oak woodlands for millennia.

But there are imbalances. Without the First People's tending, live oaks reproduce with alarming vigor. Because of his love and loyalty to them, Dad never wanted to remove a young oak seedling. But without their evolutionary checks and balances, these trees have a tendency to take over, to become invasive right in their own territory. In a mast year, squirrels, jays, deer, and acorn wasps cannot keep pace, as a carpet of little two-inch seedlings springs up after the rains. Not all survive, but the next year sees thousands of taller seedlings under the same tree, and soon, a thicket of tough, competing little trees, waist- or chest-high, with inch-and-a-half trunks and tangled prickly branches, choking off one another's light and air. Wappo caretakers' light burning every few years once kept the thickets down, killing pathogens that might harm the acorns and fertilizing the soil. Lacking this care, the health of the indigenous oak woodland is compromised, losing the open look that is so appealing around our house. Host trees lose vitality as saplings underneath compete for moisture and nourishment. With all the new tinder, the threat of catastrophic fire grows.

My father didn't know about the Wappo or how they kept the woods healthy. But he understood very well what replaced their practice after settlement—cattle grazing. In his youth, the woods continued open and parklike because domestic cattle grazed there for a full 150 years. Even when I was a child, Unc's tenants still pastured dairy cows on the steep hillside. Heavy-bodied livestock damage bunchgrasses and spread alien seeds, but they also keep sapling thickets in check by eating the tender new growth, weakening those armies of seedlings. They were a kind of substitute for Indigenous care.

Through the 1950s and 1960s, the land was still shaped by grazing. But when Unc died and the land was sold, grazing ended and thickets began to form. It took a while to understand that this kind of growth wasn't natural, wasn't how the land had evolved. Even without knowing this, Dad had the sense to keep up the grazing effect by annual mowing in a zone consisting of several acres around the house. This was fire protection in his mind, but it also re-created the open look characteristic of Indigenous care that had charmed early settlers. But, deeper into the woods than Dad's mower could go, rampant growth began to assert itself. And as Dad slowed down, his mowing slackened, and tough, unrestrained little oak thickets laced with poison oak began to close in on the house.

What, besides fire, can restore balance? Ethnobotanist Kat Anderson calls for new technologies to take the place of what used to be, just as grazing took the place of Indigenous burning in reducing fire hazard. Dad would have loved the family's new giant orange Kubota mower. Its brush hog can chew through a chest-high thicket and level it to the ground with a roaring noise and no trouble at all. But there are downsides—as there were with grazing. We don't know the long-term effect of a big tractor in the woods. Will it compact the soil that sustains so much life? Will its disturbance encourage thistles and other invasives? And we can't mow the entire steep hillside where tinder builds up. Ecologists shake their heads and say the land needs a good burn. But the policies that have suppressed natural and Indigenous fires since California first became a state are only beginning to change.

It's a cold, raw day, the first of January, the kind of day that puts me in touch with Dad. Outside it's in the forties and windy. A storm moved in last night, dumping rain in intense ten-minute bursts. The road is full of big puddles—no trees down, but each slope is a torrent. Dad used to plunge out in his yellow slicker and rain pants, using his pickax to cut drainage trenches so the water would rush off down the slope instead of eating into the roadbed. I can see him out there—tough and hardy—energized by the sense of emergency. His effort would "save the day."

My father was the guy who grew up on a working ranch and rowed the tough fifth oar that helped pull his crew ahead in the 1932 Olympics. People considered him handsome, with his blue eyes and straight brown hair. I loved loading firewood with him or just walking down the street together—both of us tall, with a tendency to stooping shoulders, both of us a little daydreamy, a little shy. I knew people could tell I was his daughter, and I was proud and happy about that. Ever since he died, I've felt the pull on these raw days to go out myself with the pickax where the wind is whipping the branches and water is sheeting down, where the dry creeks are filling up and starting to roar.

I loved being in the woods with him. But I had big issues with my father during my early activist years, mostly unspoken. A property-rights lawyer, he didn't seem to question patriotism, war, and the whole unjust system that had evolved out of genocide and slavery. As I began to see differently, I had trouble standing up to his views. I wasn't confident about articulating my own and often just kept quiet around him—I, too, had inherited the family silence. It wasn't that Dad was overbearing or dominineering like some other fathers I knew. Rather, he was a modest, sweet-tempered man, humble about his standing in the world, never bragging about things like college honor societies, the oldest fraternity on campus, his pioneer ancestors, or his Olympic gold medal. These privileged identities were probably important to him, but he didn't speak of them. Despite his training as a lawyer, I think he didn't like facing controversies, especially those as threatening to our belief system as the ones I was interested in. My father prefered a quiet hike to discussions of politics or ethics, and I went along with this approach on most of my visits home in the 1970s and 1980s.

My mother, a big talker, called Dad "the strong, silent type." Later, I would see how this stereotype expressed the whole culture we'd come from—both sides of our settler colonial family. Silence about the harmful side of our history was our default mode. I struggled with it myself, learning only slowly how to face disagreement without either backing down or exploding in outrage. Doing the research for this book, I grew curious about the soup Dad had grown up in just three generations after genocide. He'd absorbed Unc's Bear Flagger stories and the idea of a better people taking over. When he was thirteen, the Napa Valley saw a large mobilization of the Ku Klux Klan, and a blackface troupe was normal in his all-white high school. How had my father understood this culturally sanctioned hate and diminishment? He'd played high school sports with fans loyal to the "Napa Indian" mascot—which was only changed a century later, as I completed this book. Did he realize the lack of respect in this? There was no counternarrative in his time. He and my mother had no friends of other ethnicities. How could Dad have known what we younger generations were learning when it was so hidden away? Yet changes were happening below the silence. There was an openness in my father that I would see only after he was gone.

Dad Learns about the Patwin

Not long after Mother died, in the early 1990s, I was visiting and just beginning to learn the valley's colonial history when I had a touching conversation with my father about some of it. This was the period when I was doing public presentations about the Wounded Knee Ride and the Columbus Quincentennial, so I had developed more of a voice for speaking about the truths that so many white Americans didn't know. Plus, Dad and I had grown very comfortable together. He was more chatty on these visits and didn't hesitate to bring up subjects other people never mentioned. "What do you make of these street names?" he asked me one day as we drove the more rural way to the ranch. "Trabajo Lane? Wintun Court? What do these words mean?" Mother had studied Spanish after moving to Napa, with its large Latino farmworking community. But Dad had grown up in the valley knowing English only.

"The first one's easy," I said. "*Trabajo* means 'work' in Spanish. And Wintun is the broad tribal name of Indian people who lived around here. Their specific name was Patwin." In fact, a sign told us we were at that moment passing the Wintun Elementary School. I was just learning what I'd missed in my own elementary school and knew enough to tell him something about the people who'd lived on his family's land.

I didn't know the Wappo role yet, but I knew the Patwin had had two villages along creeks near the lower Napa River. We had passed one of them, Suscol, back where we'd turned onto the main drag, which was now lined with gas stations and car dealerships. The other, Tulucay, must have been not far from where we were driving at that moment, and had given its name to the creek we would cross as we drew close to Coombsville Road—named for Dad's family. A branch of this creek had drained the southern parts of Unc's place. Tulucay was the name of the Mexican land grant that included what became Unc's ranch and also the cemetery where

Coombses and Dunlaps were buried. The Patwin branch of the Wintun had lived on the land Dad's family had taken over, and, despite all his education, he had not known their name until our conversation. Neither had I until I made the effort to seek it out.

I told him Patwin villages near the Napa River had been home base during the winter, but during spring, summer, and fall, families had spread out, establishing seasonal camps up the creeks, where hunting and gathering were good, and near the big oaks at the base of the steeper slopes, where the fall acorn harvest was rich. Right near the place we now called home. Families claimed gathering rights to especially productive oaks, and visited year-round to clear and improve the ground beneath them. I knew he would like hearing about the oak trees. Over centuries, over millennia, there must have been many family campsites where the First People had cared for oaks along the creeks we knew so well. It's a zone rich in acorn.

I told him another tribe, the Wappo, speaking a completely different language, had lived farther north, beyond the tidal reach where Napa is now. Their villages were also along the river, so they would have lived in the rich land near Yountville, where his family had started their fruit ranch. I hadn't yet found the information on massacres and enslavement that marked the takeover. And I didn't realize then that Wappo territory included the two creeks on the part of Unc's land where he and Mother had built—and the very oak trees he loved so much.

"I'll be darned!" said Dad, with genuine interest.

It was no surprise that my father didn't know any of this history. He was raised in times when those around him kept quiet about these things. White Californians didn't talk about Indigenous life, even if they knew. I once asked Dad if he had any childhood memories of Indian people. He thought about it and said he wasn't sure. There had been one old man sitting outside the Yountville Catholic Church every day who used say hello to him. Maybe he was Indian. In the early years of Dad's century, Native Americans in California still had to hide their identity to survive the dangers of being Indian. Many had to claim Mexican or Portuguese descent, which was probably why the 1910 census had showed so few in

Napa County. At the same time, white Americans romanticized what they thought was a vanished people or set them up as mascots for sports teams.

Dad—for whom the law was a source of justice—would have been shocked to learn how early California legislation had blocked paths to citizenship for the First People and systematically enabled their enslavement and even "extermination." If I'd understood this then and told him about it, I think he would have had trouble believing me. He'd come from so much entitlement and believed so firmly in the justice of our laws. Like so many well-meaning people, he couldn't see the injustices at the root of our system. Evidence of what happened in California is plainly available now in the scholarship on genocide. Documents and political speeches in his grandparents' day had used that vicious word *extermination*. And his own great-grandfather had helped to make the laws. Now that I understand all this better myself, including the unconscious supremacy of the culture he and I were raised in, I'd love another try at talking with my father.

There was something Dad didn't tell me in these conversations, something I learned long after his death from my Uncle John, a major player in the story of our family's inherited silence. This uncle, younger than Dad by twelve years, was only fifteen when I was born, a wonderful bridge between the generations. Uncle John was the youngest son in a family that was present throughout the genocide and proud of its history—a Republican family with many ties to the pioneer narrative. But somehow as a child, he took a different path. I've begged him to describe how his consciousness changed. He says only that he thought his family's "better than" attitude was wrong. He wanted to be more egalitarian.

When I was growing up, Uncle John became the family rebel, declaring himself a Democrat and running for state office as a liberal during the 1960s. In an era of restrictive covenants, he and his wife signed an ad saying they would rent to people of other ethnicities. My cousin tells me this resulted in white crosses, like those of the Klan, placed on another uncle's lawn. These days, Uncle John is a legendary elder, venerated in Napa for clear thinking, tact, and humor. Whatever their politics, people go silent with respect when he speaks, and it's been supportive to talk with him while working on this book.

Once, without my even asking, Uncle John recalled a story about my father and the First People that amazed me. Dad was in law school then, already a young man. Uncle John, still just a kid at the time, remembers Dad taking him aside one day to tell him something important. "Johnny, I've been thinking. We gave the Indians a very bad deal. We virtually destroyed them." I picture little John nodding, feeling the seriousness of this time with his big brother. "It wasn't right. I've been thinking what I could do to make it right." Uncle John says Dad had decided the only way he could do anything to help would be to "marry an Indian girl." But he fell in love with my mother first.

I have no idea how serious this was for my father. But his little brother took the conversation to heart and has remembered it for ninety years. Dad's idea of a solution made me uncomfortable. He probably didn't realize how common "marrying an Indian girl" had been for Anglo settlers—for sexual satisfaction and the labor of running their homes and also as a tool of assimilation and control. Even in Dad's time, such a marriage would probably have reinforced the power and privilege of the dominant culture. This wasn't the kind of solution that came from learning the needs and wishes of Indigenous people. But, all the same, I was touched to learn that Dad had seen the injustices of our history. Like my mother, he'd begun to step away from the consciousness that held the false history in place. I guess that's the way transformation happens—small changes in one generation enlarging the field for the rest of us to move further.

When he inherited a share of Unc's land, my father returned to his roots as a Napa farm boy. In the late 1970s, when he was well over sixty, he planted a small orchard, laid out a quarter mile of gravel road winding through the trees to the new house, and carried down load after load of flat rocks from the hill for paths, a barbecue, and a beautiful indoor fireplace. His pride and joy was the wood-burning furnace in the basement, a marvel he and Mother found at the seventies-era Whole Earth Access store—a back-to-the-land version of the one in Unc's house.

Besides being the guru of well-split dry oak, Dad was a master builder of hearth fires. Back then, these fires were a luxury in privileged Bay Area homes, before we realized how they added to smog and the CO_2 releases causing climate change. Left outside or composted, those oak logs would have sequestered carbon for a long time. I never saw my father struggling with a smoking mess, not even on rainy mountain trips. In his homemade barbecue pit, he used only thick dark slabs of oak bark, which burned slowly and held the heat. Indoors, his secret was space for air and a careful choice of wood. Black oak was better than live oak because the trunks grew so straight. Valley oak—known to our relatives as "mush oak"—had softer wood that didn't produce a hot fire. Dad spread his ashes out under the oaks to return minerals to the soil—another practice that mimicked the effects of Indigenous burning. He coached me on fire building, and for some years I spent long evenings with "his" fires, staring into their scarlet caves and shimmering heat waves and admiring the impermanence, the shape-shifting, the new flames darting up from places that looked dead.

We all had lots to learn about fire. Once—I must have been about ten—Uncle John called for help with a grass fire along the county road. Somehow, I was allowed to go with the men to fight it. When we arrived, things crackled and smelled of danger as small flames whipped up the pasture toward the Pansy Field. My uncles worked with shovels and wet burlap sacks. I carried buckets of water from the creek so they could douse their sacks and lift them, dripping wet, into the air to slap down onto the flames. Dad, shirtless and wearing work boots and blue jeans, was in his element. Uncle John remembers they had to call the Napa Fire Department to stop the blaze before it reached the Pansy Field. The fear was that half of Unc's land would have been lost if the fire had not been contained.

Now we know differently. That fire looked scary, but its light, quick blaze was just the kind our ecosystem had evolved with, what the First People called a "creeping fire." Grazing might have been interrupted until the grasses grew back after fall rains, but those grasses would have grown back much healthier. The Pansy Field itself would have loved a good quick burn to return nutrients to the soil and restore the benefits of Wappo and Patwin burning. The next year, that field would likely have produced the most prolific wildflowers we had ever seen. Today, I can hardly recognize the place where we fought that fire. The slopes are all vineyards now, and the little creek where I ran to fill buckets is buried in invasive brush—Himalayan blackberry and French broom. People sometimes stop their cars and throw trash into the tangle. The overgrowth there now could fuel a major firestorm, putting today's expensive homes at risk.

Two years after Mother died, Dad got the word that his heart was failing fast, maybe only a couple months to go. With hospice, he stayed in a nursing center ten minutes from the ranch, where I could be with him almost every day. He told my sisters and me three things he wanted to do in the time he had left. It was fall and the rains had already brought out some green under the oaks. Dad wanted one more trip to the ranch to see the new grasses. He wanted to tape-record the story of climbs he'd made in the mountains with his family. And—a lifelong agnostic—he wanted to learn to pray. Things were not easy, but accompanying him those final months drew me very close to him.

Dad accomplished all three of his wishes. Every day, we cued up a tape recorder and reminded him where he'd left off on the long list of climbs set down in angular handwriting on one of his yellow legal pads. The east face of Mount Whitney with Susie and me, North Palisade with Sarah, and smaller peaks with his grandchildren. Our nature-loving family had taken to the mountains like many other Americans of European origin seeking deeper connection with the land but unaware that the very places we admired as "wilderness" were known and sacred space for Indigenous peoples. Even so, a little of that sacredness touched us. For me, the awe of approaching a peak helped me to appreciate Black Elk's stories and rejoice when Indigenous ceremonies took place in national parks.

I like to think Dad also found something spiritual in the mountains. But his stories explored a different dimension—route finding among boulders, rotten rocks falling in chutes. My sister Sarah, who has an impeccable memory, said lots of his detail was off. But I was impressed. He filled three cassettes with these memories. If you listen now, you can hear his oxygen machine beeping. Dad kept going until the whole thing was done—just like on the climbs themselves.

About two weeks before Christmas in 1995, he finished recording his mountain stories. By then, we'd been able to visit the ranch and see the green seasonal grasses spread out like a delicate lawn under the oaks. Dad had meditated with me and talked to Mother's pastor about prayer. On what turned out to be his last night, I was with him as he began writing his Christmas cards, starting with one of his old crew buddies, a good friend to whom he'd delivered holiday firewood for many years. I'd studied all the great poets, but Dad's greeting was about as eloquent as you can get. "We send you warmth this year," he wrote, in letters that wobbled only slightly more than usual, "without the fire."

Oaks Weathering Climate Change

Years later, in January 2007, I drove my car west from Boston for a longer visit to the Napa house. After ten days on the road, I pulled up in shock under a live oak that looked dead—the huge, beautiful old friend with eleven big lateral branches. It was winter, but there should have been two years' worth of older leaves giving the tree its "live" look. Instead, the vast branching system was gaunt and bare, the canopy simply gone, the high branches leafless and open to the sky. A ghost of the tree I knew. When I'd left after summer, nothing had seemed amiss. The devastation was sudden. Could it be the new disease that was decimating oak trees closer to the coast—sudden oak death (SOD)? Called a pandemic, it had wiped out whole sections of oak forest and threatened the timber industry in the state. Had it reached us? Had we lost this wonderful friend? Did that mean we would lose more, might lose the grove of oaks that were the heart and soul of this place? I staggered inside wondering if there was anything we could do.

I remembered scary headlines in the local paper. After two to three years, when the disease is hidden below the bark, the whole system fails and the entire leafy structure dies suddenly in a matter of weeks. I recalled a heartbreaking walk in the redwoods, west of us. Laced among tall evergreens, along a creek where salmon still spawned, were sheets of dead oak leaves—gray-beige ghosts among the living trees. SOD had also reached Napa County, where we saw sheets of dead leaves in the public park on the wetter western edge of the valley. And four miles south of us, where odd bits of fog linger in unique air currents, I'd seen telltale gray-beige patches where entire oak trees had died. Research is exploring whether live oaks are more at risk when bay trees interweave in the oak canopy—as they often do here.

Two or three years later, in the heat of summer, infected trees are so deeply compromised that they cannot survive normal dry spells. All is invisible except for occasional oozing sores on the bark, but suddenly the stressed-out tree succumbs—all its leaves turning brown at once. Scientists estimate a million California trees have died and that another million are slowly dying. Even commercially logged redwood and Douglas fir are affected. For Indigenous peoples like the Karuk and Miwok, a traditional and sacred food, the tanbark oak acorn, is at serious risk. Because this acorn is so much a part of their tribal identity, one Karuk woman sees SOD as "the next wave of cultural genocide." For the Karuk, oak trees are relatives within the forest ecosystem they are all part of.

The big oak outside our door felt like a beloved relative to us, too, and we took steps to help it. A county expert came as soon as I called, concerned about this disease spreading. So did a master arborist who wrote for the local paper. Both checked for oozing sores on the trunk, the only way SOD shows itself before the final onslaught. While bay trees nearby had yellow leaf tips, indicating possible infection, there were no sores on the oak. The bare twigs were still alive inside, like those of a deciduous tree. They said our dry side of the valley was not so vulnerable to SOD, though they were keeping close watch. The leaf die-off was a fungal disease called "twig blight." Late rainfall in May and June that year had combined with unusually hot weather. Warmth and moisture together were perfect for the fungus. "New leaves will come in the spring," the arborist assured me. "These trees have amazing resilience." We could help the big oak by spreading a thick layer of wood chips under the entire canopy and pruning out all dead wood, even the smallest twigs. Sadly, we'd also have to spray the tree with a fungicide to address the warm, wet conditions next time around. It could affect the oak's complex ecosystem, but the arborist recommended a spray with few side effects.

Months later, in full spring, I paused under the big tree as I returned from the hill. Up there, dark blue-purple iris had started to bloom along the trail to the dam. Here in the garden, Ceanothus was brilliantly blue, alive with fuzzy native bees and black pipevine swallowtail butterflies. Looking up, I could see the hill shimmering with translucent green and gold as I stood under the tender new leaves of the oak we'd worried about, now a leafy, healthy tree again.

All the years I've known these woods, I've seen big oaks look sickly, then revive. I've seen how individual trees in the spring rainbow of color have their own cycles and distinctive DNA, so the population can rebalance when things go wrong. But can we trust this process now? So much has changed in the environment these trees evolved with. Their friends, the Patwin and Wappo, are no longer here to offer ceremony, prune the outer limbs, harvest the mast crops, or burn away the rotting duff that fosters disease. Oak trees need that help from humans. At least one scientist says minerals in the ash of regular fires would protect today's trees from SOD. Fire is appealing, but hard to use, given the county's regulations and with so much tinder built up in the woods.

Most of all, I wonder about the climate. The twig blight that stripped the big oak got its start when hot weather began before the rains had quit—when the tree had to deal with warmth and moisture at the same time, a rarity in the California climate until now. But summers are coming sooner and rain falls at unusual times. Biologists have found that increased CO_2 levels cause some insect populations to thrive. They also limit how plants produce deterrent toxins. I haven't seen oak studies yet, but so many factors' being out of balance gives the edge to opportunistic infections. The oak's long-standing immunity—its ability to host the diverse set of predatory beings around it—is at risk. The "ghost oak" near our doorway may be the canary in the gold mine. These shifts may push the oaks beyond what they've tolerated all these eons of their development. Even so, they do their best to slow climate change with dense wood that stores more carbon than most others. I wonder how Dad, who was always interested in evolution, would have seen these massive changes in just the couple of decades since his death.

It's hard to know how the ecological miracle of the oak will react to climate change even in our lifetimes. Scientists keep learning more. One found that particulates in the air—including smog and smoke from forest fires—can weaken a tree's response to drought. Another showed that, with higher levels of CO_2 in the atmosphere, trees in arid climates are producing more green leaves. Even without more water, the greater supply of nutrient allows them to work more efficiently. And maybe they're storing away more CO_2 in the process. We just don't know yet. At the same time, many trees are visibly dying in the drought. When I talked to her about oaks and the climate, my friend Johnella LaRose from the Sogorea Te' Land Trust spoke about gratitude. The one thing she was sure of was how hard these trees are working to keep the Earth in balance.

There must be ways we can learn from the original caregivers to tend the oaks more effectively. There are still people who know how to listen to this land in the old ways, even to new messages it is sending. Their intentional fires, once forbidden and criminalized, are accepted in some parts of the state now. The Forest Service now works with tribes who are again practicing their ancient ceremony of burning. Maybe with their help, all of us can find a less fearful, more reciprocal relationship with fire. I like to think my father—with his fire skills, his woods savvy, and a respect for Indigenous peoples that was unusual for his generation—would have been on board with this.

One climb I remember with Dad didn't make it onto his list. I was already living back east and he was a youthful sixty. On a winter visit around the time Unc died, the two of us had hiked up to the "old stone house," a favorite destination up an old carriage road that traversed the steep hill above Unc's property line to a settler house from the nineteenth century destroyed by fire long before any of us could remember. On the way down, where the road curves back on itself, we'd stopped to look at the view and I'd taken a picture.

My mother loved the photo, which I found in her special drawer after she died. Dad sits on a stone wall, looking out toward the hills we admired from Unc's deck. His left arm is raised to shield his face from the winter sun. Spread out before him, as it was in my childhood, is the rolling land of Unc's square mile, the grove of oaks where Uncle John's house is now, and the Pansy Field—still pastureland—rimmed by the delicate dark line of the old stone wall. Beyond that, fields upon fields that had been in his family since Mexican days, the ancestral land of the Wappo and Patwin.

Even now looking at this very faded photo, I can feel how it was to be out on the hill with my father. Both of us liked to space out and not look at our watches—enjoying the moment like we did that day, maybe even in a sacred way. We didn't know then that those green fields below us would soon disappear into vineyards—even the Pansy Field itself. We didn't know the oak woodlands would choke up with underbrush after grazing ended, or that fancy homes would crop up on every rise, with dust and tractor noise in the vineyards. We had no inkling of global climate change, no idea we were looking at something fragile and impermanent. And we knew almost nothing of what this land had been before our family's arrival, about the Patwin and their acorn camps along the creeks, or how from here you could have seen the smoke of their winter cooking fires down in the village along Tulucay Creek or out along the Napa River at Suscol. We didn't know there had been mass killings out there in the panorama we admired. We had never heard a single word about the Patwin or the Wappo. We rested all too easily in that unknowing.

Looking at this photo now, I can feel all the uneasiness of our history along with all the peacefulness of the land itself. Past, present, and future merge into misty greenness with my lanky, plaid-shirted father, arm raised, beckoning me to look beyond the view to a legacy he would leave me a quarter century later. By then, we'd both know the names of the First People who'd lived here. And later I would learn of his concern for them as a younger man. Such a slow process. Like Mother, he had inched his way toward a change of consciousness. Like her, he's left me holding the contradictions he embodied. On the one hand, a sense of entitlement our relatives are hardly aware of and a habit of silence I am working to undo. On the other, strength, concern for the oaks, and a sense of justice. And—something I can feel when I sit quietly—his support for the work of healing.

CHAPTER 6

My Generation Takes Care of the Ranch

Leopard lily and Dairy Creek in late spring.

We must, all of us together, each with our own lives and
history, re-story the landscape so that together we are home.
> —GREG SARRIS (COAST MIWOK, SOUTHERN POMO)
> RESPONDING TO PUBLIC APOLOGY FOR THE MISSION
> SYSTEM, IN *NEWS FROM NATIVE CALIFORNIA*

We are related to the springs, to the water. . . .
If we don't take care of them, they won't take care of us.
> —PAULINE ESTEVES (TIMBISHA SHOSHONE ELDER),
> QUOTED IN LAURA CUNNINGHAM, *STATE OF CHANGE*

This land needs to be healed in a bunch of different ways.
We cannot just plant trees and think it's going to be okay . . .
underneath . . . is pain that we also need to set right.
> —CORRINA GOULD (LISJAN OHLONE),
> TALK IN OAKLAND, APRIL 2019

Water Is Life

A classic Northern California August is piercingly dry. Summer wildflowers sere and brown on the hill; maidenhair fern crisp at my feet like burned toast. Already the fallen leaves of poison oak lie in rosy curls near bare stalks. Summers have been like this my whole life, yet I find it challenging up here in the dry heat. Until I hear water ahead.

The air changes as I reach the green zone near Dairy Creek. Water rushes like a miracle over big rocks shaded by bay, oak, and madrone, which grow huge and lush in this steep, narrow corridor. Ferns, mosses, azaleas, spicebush, and brilliant, late-blooming scarlet monkeyflower, friend of the hummingbird—all surround me now in this riparian world. I stand quietly, taking in the coolness, feeling the contrast as my eyes adjust to the shade and the green. Even at midday, these creekside refuges are cool with abundant, moist life. Each breath affirms it.

Upstream, Lily Falls drops thirty feet among lacy five-finger ferns and trailing branches of ninebark. Mist from the falls darkens the rocks as I splash through the shallow pool at the base. Sitting on banks of moss, I look out on a giant clump of leopard lilies that have already shed their spotted gold-and-scarlet petals. Their stems, ten feet tall, are laced together with white umbels of the medicine plant angelica. Once we found a message from the past here, an obsidian arrowhead. Were the falls sacred to the First People? Did they come here to pray, to gather angelica?

I can't speak for my two sisters, but, already in the mid-1990s, when my father died, my attitude about inheriting land was different from most. What had been Unc's ranch touched me in a way that went beyond the usual idea of ownership. My parents' love for the place they had tended in the most natural way they knew—restoring bunchgrasses, native plant gardening, keeping oaks healthy, and especially the help my mother had asked from me near the end—all of this seemed like a sacred trust. I was grateful that my sisters seemed to feel their own versions of this. After Dad died, I don't remember a single difference of opinion about whether to keep the ranch. The three of us acted as a family, signing legal agreements to assure that Susie and I, who didn't have children, would pass our share to Sarah's children—our nieces and nephew. Somehow, though we all lived on the East Coast, we took care of things with visits from afar. Sarah handled finances and legalities, Susie and her partner, Don, the machines and water systems. I looked after the plants and the ecosystem. Our parents had built a small house for a caretaker. Dave, who'd lived there for some years, knew how everything worked and was a big help.

Just figuring out how to keep things going was hard enough, but, as development pressures grew in the Napa Valley, there were other challenges. As we dealt with them together, I would also begin my own learning curve. My share of upkeep meant long visits to be with the land—listening to when to mow the field without jeopardizing the native grasses or when to "be the fire" by clearing under the big oaks. I moved deeper into the mode of reciprocity that Robin Wall Kimmerer would decribe in *Braiding Sweetgrass,* the relationship I thought my mother had begun to understand. As I continued my research into colonization, I began to think less about how my parents would have handled things and more about the Wappo, the people who'd had such profound connection with this land before our family got here. All this and my time with the Shellmound Walkers would show me how owning land came with responsibilities for healing its history.

To begin with, we had to tangle with a Napa Valley now world-famous for vineyards, tourist development, and expensive retirement enclaves. Our first challenge was the competition for water. The Wappo had lived in harmony with a naturally fluctuating water supply for millennia, but Europeans began to extract and fight over it early on. Water was more than life in the world of modernity: It was what made the land profitable. Our era was the current chapter in a long and bitter postcolonial struggle for water rights in this dry state.

Around the time Dad died and the ranch came to us, the groundwater in our part of the valley began to fail. It was scary to see well levels plunge in such a dry place. Some lost water completely. Uncle John's well dropped below three hundred feet and tasted of strong minerals. Mother and Dad had relied on water from the two remarkable year-round creeks on the hill. Both had old-fashioned fieldstone dams, one from Unc's grandfather's time, and rustic piping systems. Dairy Creek had supplied their household needs—treated with chlorine like city water because of cattle grazing higher up. The smaller Picnic Creek helped with irrigation. But even though both had run steadily through the toughest droughts as far back as anyone in the family could remember, Dad was uneasy and had a well drilled in case they ever failed. Our house was now dependent on that well.

Dad hadn't realized that underground water would be more at risk than the creeks. Old-timers thought groundwater was forever. That was the mind of the settler colonizer, and underground water was plentiful for a while. Malcolm Margolin, who studied early Bay Area ecosystems for his book *The Ohlone Way,* says settlers "regularly struck clear, fresh water within a few feet." As late as my own childhood, Unc had drilled a well they called "an artesian"—water pulsed out of it without the need for a pump. But in the 1970s and 1980s, a second golf course squeezed in, and vacation homes with tropical plantings. All took water from the aquifer. At the same time—without Indigenous burning or the grazing that came with settlement—vegetation grew thick along creeks and zapped up some of what would have percolated down to become groundwater. Now everyone's wells were at risk.

In early 1999, I attended the county's public meeting about the crisis. Coombsville residents packed an auditorium, anxious about their wells "in overdraft." We learned that our aquifer was called the MST because it flowed under Milliken, Sarco, and Tulucay Creeks. The two creeks we knew so well fed into Sarco. An impermeable layer below the surface in this part of the valley diverts winter rainwater directly out to the bay, so it can't replenish the aquifer. With all the new wells, the MST had lost its ability to restore itself. California law has long regulated surface water—extraction from streams—but at this time and until 2014 no laws protected underground water. Landowners could drill a well and use as much as they wanted, even though it would deplete our common resource. We were stuck in the pioneer mind-set—the dream of unquenchable aquifers and the freedom to extract. But this aquifer, like others around the state, was drying up, and people in the meeting were angry about the "big guys" taking it all—the vineyards and the golf courses.

The county's solutions at that time left the basic thinking in place. A new ordinance would require drilling permits, but in the meantime, those who could afford to would drill as many wells as they could on their properties, "just in case." Later, a pipeline would bring reclaimed wastewater to irrigate local vineyards for a steep fee. A study would investigate eight year-round creeks thought to be where water entered the aquifer. A map circulated in the meeting highlighting those creeks. All of them dropped into the valley along the eastern hills—just the zone I knew so well. When the map came to me, I was awestruck. Each creek was shown in bristling lines like halos. Two of the eight were the very creeks I had known from childhood. "Our" creeks might help solve a big problem for the valley. I was eager to consult with my sisters and sign us up for the study.

The county kept saying there was no need for lifestyle changes. But to me, this crisis called for completely rethinking our way of life. Here we were in dry California in the late 1990s, with a shrinking pool of water beneath us and climate change upon us—though people in Napa said little about climate in those days. What if we could see the underground water as ours collectively, not individually? I pictured door-to-door conversations leading to a new mind-set about water as something to share, not own. It was really the very old Indigenous thinking that the land had evolved with. The change would mean more than shorter showers and greywater systems. Could we shift our very relationship with water? Use our common resource in a way that was safe for the next generations and kept the land healthy? Fifteen years later, these ideas would have resonated with a new national consciousness about pipelines and water protectors, and might have had a chance.

Our family joined the monitoring program in the early 2000s, and someone came spring and fall to measure our well. Fall readings dropped, year after year, but rose partway back in spring, depending on winter rainfall. It was scary to see net levels going down. A lump would form in my throat when I spotted the well reader's blue card in our mailbox. We matched the readings with Mother and Dad's storm-by-storm rainfall records. Except for a few years after an earthquake jarred the underground layers, our well continued to drop—at times steeply, maybe from new wells dug in the grace period before the drilling ordinance took effect.

It was late August of a dry, dry year and the water tank on Dairy Creek rang hollow and empty. The creek was running, as always, but water in the dam had dropped below the outflow pipe. Susie and Don, who took care of the dam, were in Maine, but this was an emergency. Our old-fashioned system, cobbled together over generations, was the lifeline for Dad's fruit trees and the lawn, which could die in a matter of days in the ninety-plus-degree heat. We were making do with well water, but that would strain the aquifer. Even though we used far less water than most modern Americans, we still lived in the colonizers' bubble and we were vulnerable. A failing aquifer and a makeshift creek diversion were all that stood between us and the extremes of California's climate.

We headed up to the dam with tarps, shovels, and wrenches—myself, my friend Skip, and Dave, the caretaker since my parents' time. Water poured out around an old trapdoor at the base of the dam. Someone had to get bodily into the water to plug the leaks until Don and Susie could get here for a full fix. I was in my sixties then, but I climbed up on the dam and lowered myself into the creek water, thinking of all the times Mother and Dad had plunged in to get the rustic system working.

The water came up to my floating ribs, startling me with its sudden coolness. Clouds of mud blocked visibility, but I'd memorized where the trapdoor would be and used my feet to spread an old tarp over it. No effect until I began shoveling mucky gravel from the bottom up around the tarp—all underwater and invisible through the mud. At last a shout from below. "Whatever you're doing, it's working!" Within moments we could see the water rising and moving through the pipe toward the tank. Soon the dam was full and the whole little makeshift system was working again.

Climbing out, I looked around me at the miracle of dark, cool water on this parched hillside; tangled pink honeysuckle and a giant fern arched overhead. A bevy of skater bugs stood on stiltlike legs above the trembling water—habitat restored. Shivering in wet jeans even in the summer heat, I reveled in the strange energy that had come to me in the water. Was it my parents supporting me from the ancestor world, helping to keep this shaky system—and the whole ranch—on course? Was it something older?

The hydrologist for the new study said our dams gave water a chance to soak into the earth—as an Indigenous ecologist would later confirm. In the end, measuring minerals in the water showed little sinking in along the two creeks. So probably they were not the key to aquifer recharge after all—not now, with so many water-hungry plants along their banks that hadn't been there in the times of fire or grazing. Where was the aquifer recharging? A working hypothesis pointed to the zone where hillside steepness leveled out enough for rainwater to soak in. But this raised another concern. Our second big development challenge was taking shape just at this altitude across our northern fence.

Neighbors Clear-cut for a New Winery

The story of the aquifer was weighing on me in the spring of 2000 when I took my first walk on the ranch after months in the East. I crossed Dairy Creek, heading for the northern boundary, where thick woods just over the fence line always hosted big colonies of robins and acorn woodpeckers in their nesting season. Delighting in the green underfoot and the big oaks along the creek, I didn't notice a strangeness up ahead, the feeling of something missing. There was more light than I remembered—and smoke and a roaring sound. As I approached the fence line, my heart sank. The dense forest of oaks and madrones on the other side was absolutely gone—clear-cut. Chain saws were still chunking up the trees, some piled into smoldering burn piles, fouling the air and adding their load of sequestered carbon to the atmosphere. Woodpeckers and robins wheeled high above it all, calling out for their lost nests. The property line separated two pieces of hillside that were really one—same slopes, same rock formations, same oaks and wildflowers. Their wild remoteness was something I'd imagined would last forever. I felt the devastation now in every cell.

New neighbors from Texas were clearing the magnificent oak woodlands for a vineyard—right in the transition zone between the valley and the steep hillside, the very zone so important to the aquifer. In the next months, they'd be excavating a cave on that hillside and making plans for a state-of-the-art winery inside that cave. The winery would require a county permit, which legally called for community input. In shock, my sisters and I reached out to Uncle John and other neighbors. Everyone was appalled. One had awakened to the roar of huge machines attacking burly live oaks and crunching them down before his eyes. We formed a neighborhood group to contest the winery.

Clear-cutting acres of living forest is shocking enough, but these big oaks were part of the system that turned rainwater into groundwater, our lifeline. This zone between the valley and the steep upper slopes was where, so far as we knew, the delicate groundwater mechanism recharged. Would clear-cutting bring erosion and rob the hill of its power to retain groundwater? Would it strain the aquifer to irrigate many acres of new vineyard—not to mention running a high-end winery? The vineyard had already run afoul of county law by bulldozing the tributary of a blue-line creek. (In California, a creek that runs year-round and shows up on maps as a blue line has special legal protection.) This must have been one of those creeks with a halo on the county's aquifer map. And what would be the effect of excavating a large cave in the very zone of aquifer recharge?

Concerns about the aquifer and commercialization of a quiet part of the valley drew forty or fifty neighbors to hearings throughout the two-year winery-permitting process. My sisters and I researched the law, read draft reports by technical experts, and wrote to the planning commission. We made flyers, hosted neighborhood meetings, and spoke at hearings, bringing different strengths to the effort. Susan and Don understood water systems from their life in the Maine woods and could spot evasive language in consultants' reports. Sarah, trained as a lawyer and married to one, had a sharp mind for strategy and could be fiercely defensive when the land came under threat. And I knew the ways of planning commissions from years teaching in the planning and policy field.

We had some impact on the water issue. The county sent the winery's owners back to improve their proposal. At the next hearing, they offered a recycling plan that would purify all water from wine making to reuse in irrigating the vineyard. Wash water would be trucked in, so the winery's net use of water from the aquifer would be zero. Even though their vineyard would still use water, this was a real victory for us and could bring more sustainable wine production to the valley. Our group accepted this compromise rather than suing for an environmental review. Besides zero water use, there would be restrictions on winery size, parties, and signage. We hadn't stopped the project, but we'd pushed back enough to keep it within bounds we hoped we could live with.

Signing Away Development Rights to Keep the "Natural" Look

Dealing with the winery set us thinking how to protect our place from the excessive development that was changing so much of the Napa Valley. Our parents had valued what they saw as natural land—oak trees, wildflowers, animals, creeks—and the family stories about them that arose in their generation. That was what they had passed down to the three of us—not just a piece of real estate. Napa County had laws protecting farmland. But all through the valley, picture-book vineyards, tasting rooms, and McMansions were transforming the landscape. The simple woodlands and pastures we had roamed as a young family were disappearing behind electronic gates.

I think I was the one who proposed the local land trust as a way to hold on to what we loved about the ranch, a way to be sure the place we'd known since childhood would be protected from development. In my work with policy and planning, I'd learned about such organizations dedicated to protecting land. The one in Napa was a nonprofit that I'd spoken to Dad about in his last years. He and Mother had been interested but cautious about the effect on land value, thinking their heirs should make any decisions.

Now we looked into how a land trust agreement would work. The ranch would still belong to us, but we could do what is called "donating an easement," giving away some of our rights as owners in order to prevent future development and preserve what we valued in the land. We could give away to the land trust the right to cut down trees or install new fences. The choices would be completely up to us, but they would be permanent. We would still own the land, but the land trust would take over the rights we'd given up and would monitor to be sure no one ever used them—no tree cutting or fences. We could sell, or pass the place on to heirs, but our agreement with the land trust would last beyond us. No owners—ourselves or any in the future—could ever build or develop in any way prohibited by the easement. With these restrictions, the ranch would be less valuable as real estate and would be taxed at a lower rate, but it would be protected from the kind of development that was closing in around us. An easement would address the contradictions of owning property that was very valuable on the market—more so each year as the valley grew more affluent—but precious to us on a different scale of measurement, in family memories and a look we saw as "natural." This satisfied my concerns at the time, though I would come to wish for more. For different reasons perhaps, the land trust idea suited all three of us.

On a March morning, we met with land trust staff at the ranch to start defining what our easement would look like. Blue *Ceanothus* and purple sage were blooming in Mother's garden. Wondrous black butterflies with wings tipped in iridescent blue lifted from flower to flower—pipevine swallowtails, whose host plant grows throughout these woods, the only one their caterpillars can eat. Seeing just one of these butterflies can make your day. But that morning, dozens floated about—too many to count. This was why we needed the easement.

We worked for months on an agreement to fit our unique case, deciding what rights to keep and what to give to the land trust. Outdoor lights in the natural darkness? Fences that might restrict wildlife? Could future owners enlarge the house? When it was over, we'd done our best to preserve the natural look—no tree cutting, roads, lights, or fences. Perhaps most important, we'd given away the right for any owner to use the land for any commercial purpose. I think our parents would have been happy that what they had wanted to pass on to us would last into the future.

We celebrated with a spring wildflower hike to Lily Falls for friends, family, and neighbors, visiting special garden spots hidden away on the hill. Returning by way of the northern fence line showed the group how a conservation easement matters. There where the woods had been were row upon plowed row of vines. Beyond on the hillside was a network of pavement and tunnel openings where the nearly finished winery looked like gun bunkers I'd seen as a child on wartime hillsides. The worst was right in our face at the fence line—just at the elevation where aquifer recharge was most sensitive. Here, in full view (though unseen from the winery), was what in the plan had been called a "temporary trash storage area." Too late, we understood that phrasing. Only the trash would be temporary; the storage area was permanent. Waiting to be carted away were coils of plastic and rusty tins of agricultural chemicals. Nearby stood a giant burn pile with yard waste, including French broom gone to seed and ready to spread—the same invasive plant my parents had struggled remove on our side of the fence.

As we worked on the easement, my niece Jean, just finishing law school, was often at the ranch on weekends. She encouraged our project but warned of its limitations, reminding us how the environment extended beyond this eighty acres. The ranch might seem to be protected—there was sanctuary here for the plants her grandmother had loved and for butterflies, deer, and mountain lions. But our actions wouldn't stop what went on beyond the fence. On our own, we couldn't restore the aquifer or stop development by neighbors, even when it threatened the golden eagle that soared over a wider region. The ranch wouldn't be the same surrounded by parking lots and heliports.

There was another issue we never discussed—the whole European notion of ownership. Since reading Black Elk in the 1970s, I'd been drawn to Indigenous ways of relating to land. Ideas like "The land does not belong to us; we belong to the land" made sense to me, given my childhood experiences in the woods and the Christian teachings about sharing and Earth stewardship that I remembered from childhood. I could see why Native thinkers saw European ideas of land ownership as a form of violence and greed. Something like an easement that removed "our land"— even partially—from the profit system was deeply appealing to me.

I don't think my sisters shared this interest. "The land does not belong to us" ran directly counter to premises rooted deep in our family's belief system. Our father had defended property rights in his profession as a lawyer, and our mother, with all her leanings toward reciprocity, was seriously upset if anyone crossed a fence to hike on "our land" without permission. These beliefs went way back into our lineage. Unc and his father had also been lawyers defending private property, and the pioneer Nathan Coombs was admired for buying and selling Napa land. As I looked into the deeper past, I would see how owning land had been the engine of settlement on the entire continent, starting when the fifteenth-century Doctrine of Discovery empowered Christians to take lands already occupied. Coming from a Europe where once-communal property had come under control of elites, settlers here pursued land with a passion. Our Puritan ancestors in New England even saw property ownership as a sign of spiritual worth. With title to land came control and individual entitlement, the ability to decide what could be done in your own private domain. Those ideas were now deeply embedded in our culture and social structure. I was hoping a land trust easement could begin to extricate us.

Before Coombs family members—or any other Yankee—came onto this land, the grizzled pioneer George Yount obtained a Mexican land grant halfway up the valley in a beautiful spot along the Napa River, not far from where Dad's family would later have their prune ranch. On Yount's grant was a Wappo village whose people, the Caymus, he promptly put to work. Yount had trapped and traded all over the continent. His biographer says he worked "hard and unweariedly" to learn the ways of Indian people. With Caymus labor, he quickly established wheat fields on the floor of the valley and soon needed a dam for water to power a small mill.

Yount's memoir tells of leading a work party upstream, where he sets Native men to work prizing up boulders to block the flow of water— much the way we children did on a smaller scale one hundred years later at family picnics. When they realize what Yount wants them to do, the Caymus workers stop and say they cannot continue. Angry and scowling, they turn their backs, put down their tools, and walk off the job. As Yount tells it, their headman explains that this site is home to a local spirit, a sacred place that cannot be violated. Yount says he "choked as he spake and wept." Yount responds saying he respects the local spirit. He waits while the headman speaks to the spirit, who, according to Yount, obligingly moves upstream a few yards so the dam can continue as planned.

I picture Yount grinning as he tells this tale to an admiring writer. To him, the creek was not sacred, but his property by virtue of his land grant from the Mexican government. To be used as he wanted, to be developed. We don't hear the Caymus side of the story. Their land despoiled, their community weakened by European disease, they survive by working for

Yount, but they will not violate the spirit of the creek. A similar story tells of Native work crews sobbing when ordered to cut down trees for settler homes.

Ownership and Belonging

As I did my work in Mother's garden—encouraging wild strawberries, re-seeding native bunchgrasses, removing tiny oak seedlings that fire would have managed, and pulling up French broom—my feeling of belonging to the land grew stronger. It wasn't because my ancestors had owned the place. It was more that my hands loved being in the soil. I felt welcomed whenever I arrived—in fall from the hermit thrush, in spring from the western flycatcher on her nest above the sleeping porch. I called to owls and heard them answer, played a staring game with bobcat kittens, and persuaded a neighbor not to poison coyotes. Twice a year, I made a serious dent in the French broom population. As much as possible, I wanted to restore the balance in our ecosystem that had been destroyed with colonization. That meant tracking ongoing changes. When a new kind of squirrel moved in on the beloved western gray squirrel, I reached out to scholars studying how this was happening all over the West. Their studies reassured me that rural places with as many acorns as this one were at least managing to sustain both species.

Changes from beyond the fence line continued to distress me. A new plant we identified as *Rhagadolius stellatus* began to spread aggressively under the oaks, taking over from indigenous plants. I couldn't keep up with the weeding and learned it was also threatening other parts of the county. *Rhagadolius* had two kinds of spiny seeds ripening at different times in early summer and could outcompete just about everything. I was concerned for the entire hillside and suspected this plant was spread by an even more potent threat from outside our ecosystem.

Domestic pigs brought here by Spanish colonists had escaped to the woods and gone feral two hundred years ago. Later interbred with European boars imported by hunters, feral sows were now producing as many as twenty-four young each year, throwing ecosystems out of balance all over the state. Once grizzlies were exterminated in the 1920s, the pigs had no predators but humans. In our era, hunters and gourmets sought them avidly, but that was not enough to keep such prolific animals in check. Not long after the easement went into effect, feral pigs began showing up in herds around our house. One night, thirteen of them just outside my bedroom woke me, foraging in the rich leaf mold under the oaks with eerie huffing sounds. Surreal, powerful, shadowy presences. Some were huge—especially nursing sows—with dark, scraggly hair and snouts that ripped deep trenches into the soil. Weighing well over two hundred pounds, they could be ferocious. Up on the hill, I began to find wide pig trails, trampled grasses, and precious wildflower gardens churned into piles of sod. Were they spreading the spiny seeds of *Rhagadolius* in these vulnerable places? Down near the house, they turned the field of native bunchgrasses into a demolition site and sometimes hit the lawn or the orchard. Their numbers exploded, like the settler population that had set the natural world teetering out of balance two centuries ago. Was there any way to restore equilibrium?

So far, my generation had made decisions carefully about any form of killing. Concerned that Mother and Dad had used poison on the field mice that got into the house—which put predators at risk further up the food chain—we shifted to plugging holes and occasionally using lethal traps. The forest-based dusky-footed woodrats that loved sheltering in our basement were more challenging, but I located someone who brewed a potion from medieval Europe that kept them away. It also worked for the ground squirrels that bothered Dad's fruit trees. But there didn't seem to be a nonviolent solution to the pigs. To keep their population in check, we would have to shoot them for food, either on the run or after trapping them. With a county "depredation permit," ingenious trap designs could hold a dozen pigs until the shooter showed up. After wet winters, when the pig population swelled, the hunter who helped us would donate pork to families of unemployed friends. More recently, drought and fire have restored a kind of balance. Since the big fire of 2017, we've seen almost no pigs and the trap lies idle.

Learning about the dyamics of this land and their disruption by colonization, I was inspired by the ways Indigenous peoples all over the world saw owning and belonging. In the Peruvian Andes—before colonization and even now—Indigenous people recognize an "ownership" totally different from ours. For them, it is the deep understanding of a place—its plant and animal life, its creeks and rocks, its interbeing. An "owner" is one who is devoted to the land's health, to maintaining its balance of energy. A healer and teacher from that region, Arkan Lushwala, says such an owner "has an intimate relationship" with the land and is a "humble yet powerful guardian" who "both uses and cares for it." That was the kind of owner I wanted to be. And, like the many settler descendants in this country who loved *Braiding Sweetgrass,* I was drawn to Robin Wall Kimmerer's idea that settler people could be "naturalized to place" and help to reverse the ravages of colonialism. That kind of belonging was my aspiration.

The water from Dairy Creek is faintly milky with minerals from the rock. Sometimes you can see it in the pools of the creek itself, chalky, just a touch off clear, opalescent if you hold a glass of water to the light. When Buddhist teacher Thich Nhat Hanh speaks about water, he always stresses its entire cycle—what he calls its "interbeing." He uses a steep hillside stream like ours to teach the Buddhist idea of interconnection. He reminds us that the water rushing so actively down the rocky creek bed was not always creek water. It was once rain, once groundwater seeping toward a spring or pooling up to give itself to the creek. Before that, it was clouds and moisture forming out over the ocean, mist and fog—high fog and low fog. The water here will sink into the ground again or find its way to the Napa River, out into the bay, and once again to the ocean.

In Wappo and Patwin days, the People understood that oak trees helped nurture the flow of water. They carefully tended the land to support this relationship, practicing what is now called traditional ecological knowledge (TEK). For them, trees and vegetation were part of interbeing, and even fire could help the water flow by keeping the vegetation healthy.

Looking Back, Edging Forward

It's a quarter century since the three of us began to take care of the ranch. Susan is gone now. Sarah and I have returned to the West Coast. Her children are co-owners with us now but are mostly far away, deep into the busiest times of their lives. I still pursue my mother's dream of restoring native plants. As I learn more about Indigenous ways with the land and more about this land, Jean's reminder to see the big picture comes back to me often. Our easement was designed to protect what we remembered from the time we first knew Unc's ranch in the 1940s and 1950s. But the creeks we played in then, as well as the fields and oaks we knew, were not the pure and "untouched nature" we imagined. The idea of untouched nature ignored the caretaking practices of Indigenous people that had co-evolved with the land for thousands of years. Colonial settlement and the projects of our own family had interrupted this process and reshaped the land before our time. Even now—when we thought we were doing nothing, but withheld fire and other Indigenous tending—we were continuing the reshaping.

My research would confirm the many ways our relatives had disrupted the ecosystem. Their letters from the 1880s would show them plowing hundreds of acres of grassland in a failed effort to grow crops. Plowing destroys the deep-rooted native bunchgrasses and opens the way for the weedy invasive plants my mother and I had struggled with. Even the winery neighbors' clear-cutting was nothing new. Abrupt borders of wooded land at the base of the hills led me to suspect that Unc, too, had used forest clearance to open space for his cherry orchard and avocado trees. Were these long-ago acts less invasive than the ones we'd protested in the winery development?

Even though I would find he never lived on the land, the pioneer Nathan Coombs had exploited it. One of his businesses, with the Indian name Unoyome, had sold the waters of Tulucay Creek to city people. Selling these waters would have been unthinkable to the Patwin or Wappo, and even our modern laws do not permit it. Later family members started a dairy along what they named Dairy Creek and set up the water-diversion system we still use—including the dam we work so hard to maintain. California quickly became an agricultural state, where water extracted from its integral place in the ecosystem was a high-value commodity for irrigation. That was the colonial project and it remains in force.

Decades before my ancestors dammed and plowed in the Napa Valley, a European thinker—far ahead of his time—had shown how the same practices threaten water resources, land fertility, and climate itself. German scientist Alexander von Humboldt never came to western North America, but in other colonized locations he saw how—without its natural cover of trees—the land could no longer absorb water and channel it into groundwater. How heavy rains then washed soil off hillsides in flash floods that carried off topsoil and didn't allow percolation into the aquifer. The results: dessication of land, failing aquifers like ours, and—with trees gone—a loss of oxygen to the atmosphere. The very things climate scientists and Indigenous peoples point to today.

My ancestors' violence to the land was long past by the time of my childhood, and its physical scars had begun to heal. But the land I first knew and thought so pristine had already been altered tremendously from its balance under Indigenous care. The people who had been its companions and caretakers had been removed, and colonial practices had left their mark. Those practices had intensified around us in the development-crazed Napa Valley of the twenty-first century, even with global climate change very evident in the 2000s, when we made the land trust agreement. Even as the land was beset with wildfires, the ongoing colonial mind-set of Napa's policy makers now threatened more deforestation and further damage to the delicate living balance of water. Our family's dams created spaces for water to sink into the aquifer, but they also interrupted the flowing waters, just as George Yount's had done. Even my generation's minimal practices were part of the extractive mind-set that was causing aquifer loss and water shortages as California faced a drier climate than we had known in our lifetimes. The land trust agreement did not return the ranch to a mythical natural state, but simply stopped development at a moment in time—or tried to. Was this enough? Had we done what the land wanted? Come into reciprocity with it? We were trying to care for it and protect the life here but had only begun to grasp the depth of what was wrong.

Contradictions churned in me. We had dammed creeks, cut trees, poisoned plants we didn't like, and plowed the earth. In my generation, we had tried to stand up to harmful development practices—without understanding that the land had already lost the balance it had evolved with, without acknowledging that the majestic oaks and hidden waterfalls had once been home and sacred, cared-for space to a people our country had tried to destroy. The time I'd been able to spend caring for the land and looking into its history had opened my heart not just to the place itself but to the problematic concept of land ownership and the distant dream that this piece of land I loved could again return to Indigenous care.

Though I knew there was more to repair, I was grateful for the land trust agreement—where we kept the right to use and care for the land but gave away the right to profit from it. In my mind, this was a small step back toward the more reciprocal land relations of the Original People. That step made me happy, but I hadn't pushed this thinking on my family. I was sure their views about something so central to our history and culture would differ from mine, though I hoped that could change. The land trust idea might be the beginning of a paradigm shift, but it was only a beginning.

As I looked into my family's history on the land, I read a book by another woman descended from early Californians, another woman who'd looked high and low for information about her relatives and their land, information hidden by the story of colonization we'd learned in California schools. But her relatives went back much further than mine. They were Indigenous and their land three hours south of us was no longer available to her as the land in Napa was to us. Deborah Miranda was descended from Esselen, Ohlone, and Chumash survivors of brutality at Mission Carmel, whose founder, Junípero Serra, was recently canonized, despite protest from many California Natives.

Only 20 percent of Miranda's people survived the mission system, carrying the trauma of loss, separation from parents, whipping, rape, and near starvation, bearing this pain all the way down the generations into her father's and her own life. Miranda's book *Bad Indians: A Tribal Memoir* makes readers feel how her people continued to live out the trauma in violence, alcohol, and heart-wrenching tragedy. Alongside graphic detail of her ancestors' brutal beatings by supposedly loving priests, she shows her charismatic father driven to beat his own son with perverse brutality. There was no way to read Miranda's hard-searched-for stories of her lineage without feeling in your bones and flesh what genocide does to human beings, what intergenerational trauma really means. There was no way to ignore her family's deep belonging to ancestral land that others now "owned." It was hard to imagine the level of soul healing Miranda had been able to achieve in order to write a book so full of beauty, humor, and wisdom as this one.

She tells how a branch of her family that survived the missions was granted church lands that were secularized in the 1830s. Such grants were rare, but Miranda's distant grandparents Fructuoso and Yginia were able to return to live as farmers in beautiful hills and woods near their people's original village site on the Carmel River, in view of a sacred peak. Two or three generations lived on their ranch, El Potrero, until the 1850s, when a Yankee squatter drove them off to create a twenty-thousand-acre empire.

Awash in tears, I read in her final pages how Miranda was able to visit this land by the river once again—but only in a dream. In reality, she had learned it was now held by an exclusive land conservancy—an enclave with its own golf course—managing the rest of the land to look as it had before settlement. Set up differently from the one in Napa, this trust collects fees from wealthy home owners to restore native plants, grasses, and animals—everything that was part of the landscape except its human inhabitants. The land remains private, not accessible to descendants and never to be given back to them as Miranda had hoped when she first heard there was something called a "trust" there. Her people's land, cleansed of humans, is being preserved, kept parklike. But she cannot go near its oaks, its river, its view of the sacred mountain.

In her dream, Miranda goes to the land with her sister, walking the slopes that Yginia walked, seeing the view of mountains that their ancestors had looked at every day. Hugging each other and weeping, the two sisters explore the dream version of the land from which their people were removed, not just once but two times. They place their palms on the earth, then wade fully clothed into the warm waters of the Carmel River. They belong to this place in the most profound way but can be here only in dream time.

CHAPTER 7

Two Waves of Colonizers
on the Tulucay Grant

Cayetano Juárez and Nathan Coombs, the first and second colonial owners of the
Napa land. Images from Lyman L. Palmer, *History of Napa and Lake Counties*

The American landscape is palimpsest. Layers upon layers
of names and meanings lie beneath the official surface.

— LAURET SAVOY, *TRACE: MEMORY, HISTORY,*
RACE, AND THE AMERICAN LANDSCAPE

Long- long ago, mile after mile, in every direction, there
stretched endlessly, the "Rock Walls" or division fences
that were so laboriously constructed by the Indians on the
Rancho Tulucay. As time passed and the population grew,
land divided, sold and resold into smaller portions, the walls
have disappeared.

— VIVIENE JUÁREZ ROSE, *TULUCAY:*
THE PAST IS FATHER OF THE PRESENT

Old Rock Walls and Layers of Human History

HIGH UP ON THE HILL is a steep escarpment of rock that runs the whole north-south length of what used to be Unc's ranch. They say these hills are remnants of a collapsed volcano, so this rock layer is part of an ancient caldera. In places, the cliffs are dramatic, like where Lily Falls plunges thirty feet down their face. In other places, the rock has exfoliated in large squared-off chunks that lie in a jumble below. In other places, it has crumbled into the steep slope.

Exploring the north side of the land—near where the neighbors would clear-cut years later—Mother found what looked like the remains of a monumental stone wall completely hidden by trees more than a hundred years old and tangled in brush. It ran from our northern fence to the creek used for household water at the time. The other stone walls we knew were built on open ground to keep cows in a pasture or dispose of rocks turned up by the plow. Algonquian work crews built such walls in New England. In the South, Robin Kimmerer says, they're called "slave walls." In this region, the walls were built by Native people working on Mexican ranchos or by the Chinese laboring on Anglo ranches. They marked European uses of the land—colonial occupation. Like the wall around the Pansy Field, made of rounded rocks up to eighteen inches across, piled together waist-high.

But this was a different kind of wall Mother had found lurking at the foot of the steep slope. Its stones were three or four times larger, many of them squared off, as though quarried, but covered in moss. She talked excitedly about a California Stonehenge, a wall older than settlement. Overgrown now with huge oaks and madrones, buried in the spicebush and azalea along the creek, did it have some pre-European significance? Who had brought these giant rocks here and why? The old redwood water tank upstream was well over one hundred years old. Was this wall from then, or earlier? A Native ecologist told me his people here did not build walls. That meant these rocks raised questions about the colonizers. The answers came slowly, sometimes uncomfortably.

Our family name is well known in Napa. My pioneer ancestor, Nathan Coombs, founded the town in 1847 and played a role in the transition to statehood. Recently, Coombsville—the rural area named for him—became an official wine appellation, so he's touted on winery internet sites that sometimes get their facts wrong. I skimmed early histories to see how he fit in with the events of colonization. As I'd thought, he straddled the second and third waves. Reaching the valley in 1845, near the end of the rancho period, he bought up land from grants held by Mexican citizens. First, he traded his labor for land along the west side of the river, where he famously "laid out the town of Napa," selling lots as the town grew with the gold rush and Americanization. Ten years later, his home place was a 325-acre ranch northwest of town, where he raised racehorses, got elected twice to the new state legislature, and lived comfortably with servants. With his father-in-law, he bought an entire rancho in the hills from the original grantee. These acquisitions and more show up in all the books on settler days. Most of them say he ended up wealthy.

But none of this was the land I was interested in—Unc's ranch, the land that had stayed in the family. Just a little looking told me it had been part of the Tulucay Rancho, a grant of 8,866 acres made in 1841 as part of the second wave of colonization. A military man, Cayetano Juárez, had received this land from the Mexican government for service with General Vallejo four years before Coombs arrived in the valley. At some point after that—no one seemed to know just when or how—Coombs had acquired a chunk of the Tulucay grant from Juárez. The family then subdivided, sold lots, and likely named the area Coombsville. Of his four sons, Frank inherited this piece with an older brother, who died early. Frank was my great-grandfather, father to Unc, who took over after him. The parts of the Tulucay closest to the eastern hills, the Coombses kept for themselves, gradually selling off the rest.

That's what I knew to begin with, and I was eager to learn all I could about not just Coombs but also Juárez, who'd shaped this land I was so close to. The second wave of colonization had begun with Cayetano Juárez and his family. Two Patwin villages were sited on creeks within the borders of his grant—one old document called their people the Tulkays and the

Ulucas. What had happened to them? Wikipedia says Juárez had served under General Vallejo, "managing the land and native populations in Napa and Sonoma counties." I knew Vallejo had collaborated with the Patwin to form a force against other tribes. Was this how Juárez had won the Tulucay grant? What was his relationship with the Patwin and how had his family used the land?

Nathan Coombs's time frame—the third wave—matched the period now called the "California genocide." What was on his mind as he bought and sold land during the atrocities of those times? How did he relate to the first colonizers—Californios like Juárez? The original inhabitants? The land itself? Was he interested in it as a living reality or only in buying and selling? Both Nathan and his son Frank served in the state legislature— Nathan when it was less than a decade old and still setting policies that would define "the Golden State." So he was part of the institutional clout behind California's genocide and a founding father to what shapes the state's history to this day. I wanted to know not just what he did but who he was as a human being.

How did the Coombs family view Juárez? The Tulkays and the Ulucas? The Wappo upriver on land that became the Willows? Most histories don't consider the interface between the Indigenous and those who take over. But, if I could, I wanted to learn what contact was like on this land. Outsiders of European and Mexican descent had been in the valley just over ten years when Nathan Coombs arrived. Indigenous people still remained, though mostly as farm labor. But all over Northern California, the scalpings, village burnings, forced indentures, and attempts to clear the land for Anglo settlement would intensify for another twenty years with the gold rush and the arrival of Yankees.

Whoever built them into a wall, the big mossy rocks on the Tulucay land that was still in our family had witnessed events that hadn't made it into Unc's story or the articles about founding fathers in the local paper. How was I going to uncover the layers beneath what we'd been told? Many white people had written about Napa's history, but I was wary of their perspectives and uneasy about interpreting sources without the training of a historian. I hoped my long-ago experience reading between the lines of literary texts would help me find a truer history than the one I'd been given.

Digging into the Records

First I went to the Napa County Historical Society, a picturesque old stone building in downtown Napa, across from where I used to visit Unc's law office before it was torn down for urban renewal. Its reading room held memoirs of early days, including voices outside the dominant narrative—like that of Platon Vallejo, the general's youngest son, who'd been alive at the time of the ranchos. A Juárez descendant my parents' age had donated her papers and written a book about her family on the Tulucay Rancho. On its cover was her drawing of a spreading oak and curving stone wall like the one around the Pansy Field. Her writing showed intimacy with the land during childhood visits and a concern for Indigenous people that I appreciated. Viviene Juárez Rose, also from a colonizer family, felt like a soul mate in my quest to heal the wounds of our history .

But the society's files on the Coombs family were thin—news clippings with standard praise narratives and no personal documents to show feelings toward one another or the land. Nothing about the genocide that had opened the way for settlement. I wouldn't learn anything about my family's attitudes until much later, when a stash of old letters came my way—and even then I would mostly have to guess. As for the simple question of how and when the land passed from Juárez to Coombs, the archivist told me they couldn't help me at all on that. Records of deeds were down the street in the assessor's office. Later, I would spend days there, too, as my search dragged on month after month.

I looked at the Juárez family first—in the second wave of colonization after the missions. Unc had always spoken of those before us as "the natives," without distinguishing Mexican or Spanish colonizers from the Patwin and Wappo. I would learn this wasn't just his quaint way but part of Napa's pioneer Anglo culture and a strategy colonizers often used to erase the identities and history of those they'd taken over from. But a new generation of historians of color had been writing about the region, including two who'd grown up in Napa. From them and the two memoirs, I learned how Don Cayetano had been granted 8,666 acres of Patwin and Wappo land and I began to understand his family's feelings about that land and the people displaced.

Their lineage went back to the first wave of colonization. Both Juárez and his wife, María de Jesús Higuera, came from military settler families who'd come to California seventy-five years before the Napa land grant to protect the Franciscan missions that began to stretch up the coast from Mexico. Their ancestors had rounded up "converts" for the padres, marched them to the coastal areas, and intervened when Native people escaped back to their villages or resisted the brutal life of the missions. The military presence alongside the missions had accounted for much of their violence and brutality.

Vallejo, Cayetano Juárez, and the Tulucay Grant

Toward the end of this period, Juárez himself had a military appointment under Gen. Mariano Vallejo in the last-to-be-settled northern region. The two had gone to school together. Vallejo's base and his own large land grants were south and west of Napa, near the newest mission at Sonoma. At this northern frontier, a military presence was especially needed when the Mexican government secularized the missions in 1833, proposing to return land to the Indigenous people but instead strengthening their hold by granting more Native lands to former soldiers. While the missions had sought to break the culture and impose their own, this was outright take-over. The new landholders saw Native villages as part of the property they were granted; they expected the people of those villages to work the land as peasants had done in feudal Europe. Ranchos as large as thirty and forty thousand acres spread inland in the hands of *patróns* who ruled small fief-doms. Most were of Mexican descent and called themselves Californios.

One historian calls the most powerful landholders "*caudillos*"—char-ismatic strategizers like Sutter in the Sacramento Valley—out to create empires with the labor of Indian workers. Vallejo himself was a masterful *caudillo,* expanding his influence in the region through his link with the Patwin people and their leader, Sem Yeto, his staunch ally. Vallejo's strategy filled the North Bay valleys with settlers who could join campaigns against resistant tribes. These included his brother Salvador and early Anglo settler George Yount, who had his own feudal relationship with Wappo people on the rancho he'd settled in 1831. There are conflicting stories about how Juárez fit into this plan and received his grant.

Platon Vallejo, the general's son and a physician writing in the early twentieth century, saw Juárez as a problematic officer who lead a mutiny against Vallejo and escaped capture by swimming the Carquinez Strait— only to be court-martialed by the Monterey government. Platon's writing was a great source for the period, but I was not so sure about his story of Juárez. Platon was not born for at least five years after the supposed mutiny, so he is repeating family legend. He ends his story with Vallejo dramatically stopping Juárez's execution at the request of the women of the community. The general agrees to pardon Juárez if he will step down from the military and accept a land grant in Napa. If this is even partly true, it shows Vallejo's skillful manuevering to surround himself with people who would owe him loyalty. Juárez was useful as a colonizer in his plan to turn grasslands and oak savannas into a Europeanized landscape of pastured cattle tended by a resident Indian workforce.

The story Viviene Juárez Rose tells of her great-grandfather is very different. In her version, Juárez foils a mutiny and saves the day for Vallejo. As a civilian, he remains a key player in Vallejo's campaigns—often a skillful mediator, whether with "hostile" Indians, mutinous troops, or marauding Yankees. His ability to win standoffs without bloodshed and return runaway soldiers unharmed shows him a peacemaker, bringing parties to agreement in hot moments across the complex divisions of the times. In his kinswoman's version, Juárez leaves the military by choice, and receives the grant and another much larger one for loyal service.

It's hard to know which descendant spoke most truly. Both wrote with deep respect and admiration for their forbearers, whose times were complex in ways we'll never know. However it happened, in 1837 Juárez began to pasture cattle on the land southeast of what's now Napa—and likely started building stone walls. When the grant was final in 1841, he moved his young family to the gently hilly area east of the Napa River, just two years before Americans—including Nathan Coombs—began to pour into the valley. In six years, those Americans would control it, with statehood coming by 1850.

How did things look in the days of Californio settlement? I let the old face of the land talk to me each time I follow the highway north through suburbs and across the bridge over the Carquinez Straits that Juárez supposedly swam at such risk. Along this route, rising here and there above the crust of development, you see the rounded hilltops of the old landscape where Spanish cattle roamed. As you enter Napa County—where zoning favors vineyards—landforms are more visible, opening from flatter delta lands into softly rhythmic low hills that rise eastward into what the old-timers called "mountains." To the left along the river lie endless modern warehouses, a cemetery, a college, and malls. To the right along the road runs a picturesque old wall of rounded stones—one of the only old ones remaining in public view. In 1837, when Cayetano Juárez first drove his cattle onto this land, wide tule marshes rose up from the river into open grasslands studded with valley oaks and watered by a few year-round creeks—all embraced by steep hills to the east. This was the place Juárez chose for his rancho.

By the time they sold land to Coombs, Cayetano and María Juárez had lived and raised their children on Rancho Tulucay for seventeen years. Home was a small adobe, then a larger one, which still stands on the outskirts of town—preserved as a historical site and now a restaurant. How did they manage the land? Near where Tulucay Creek empties into the Napa River was a Patwin village where people spoke the Uluca language. The Juárez family learned to speak "Indian" as village people herded Juárez's cattle, built the stone walls, and constructed the family's two homes. Although María and her children also worked hard, the people they called the Ulucas made Rancho Tulucay possible.

Like other ranchos of the period, Tulucay's economy was based on selling hides and tallow from large herds of cattle, along with modest subsistence farming at the river margins, where irrigation was not needed. From this base, the Juárez family did well enough to afford a piano shipped round the Horn. They entertained *gente de razón* and others, throwing parties for everyone on the rancho and beyond. According to his great-granddaughter, Don Cayetano was iconic in his serape and dark wide-brimmed hat, riding his horse over the rolling land—in our day covered with the vineyards and exurban homes of Coombsville.

Viviene Juárez's Family Stories

Juárez Rose's book doesn't answer my questions about how her family controlled a colonized workforce, but it is filled with stories of the cross-cultural human contact I was hoping for. She writes of the Ulucas with great respect and is proud that village women came to play with her father as a baby and that he played with their children as he grew older. Her family treasured the Ulucas' handwoven baskets with quail feathers, given as gifts to Don Cayetano's wife, María, who started out with food and medicines whenever word came of someone on the rancho needing help. Family stories show that they deplored smallpox and cholera epidemics that hit the Indigenous population, where "servants would die before their very eyes and men in the fields dropped in their tracks." They treasured a story of two aged Native men traveling down from the north to thank Cayetano Juárez for having been good to them. Juárez Rose describes the kind of warm human contact with the Indigenous population I'd heard could happen among Californio colonizers. But, though esteemed in family stories, Ulucas on the Juárez rancho got paid almost nothing. One cow and one sack of beans per month—for the whole village—were supposed to supplement their gathering and hunting on the land.

Juárez Rose may not have realized how rancho grazing practices disrupted the Native people's subsistence, with cattle chomping down plants they relied on and trampling delicate water sources into mucky shit pools. While the Spanish and Mexican idea had been that Indians would keep their rights to use the land (usufruct rights), these rights meant little when the land's integrity was lost and creeks no longer ran clean. Stone walls and heavy grazing interfered with game, while weedy alien grasses and cattle-caused erosion disrupted the ecosystem that had grounded the Indigenous lifestyle.

A portrait of Cayetano Juárez shows a dignified face framed by wavy darkish hair—a well-trimmed mustache, muttonchop whiskers, perhaps beginning to gray, and a clean-shaven chin above a narrow bow tie. Light-eyed, he seems to look off into the future from a heavyset body clothed in a jacket with dark velvet lapels. Earlier, an itinerant Chinese artist had painted his family. Facing out from the canvas is Don Cayetano—dark-haired and slimmer than he would appear twenty years hence. Five sons stand on his right and María stands on his left with five daughters. The women wear white collars over dark gowns; the older males wear bow ties. All have dark hair and sparkly black eyes. An additional figure stands mysteriously between Cayetano and María with a hand over his heart—perhaps a son who had died two years before or perhaps Don Cayetano's brother Vicente, who had served with him in the military and lived with the family at Tulucay.

María de Jesús Higuera Juárez is striking in another portrait—high dark ruffles and a tiny gold cross at the neckline, wavy salt-and-pepper hair pulled back from her face, dark eyes and broad facial features that suggest Indigenous heritage. While Spanish colonists spoke of blood purity and claimed Castilian descent, their ethnicity was more complex. Historians say Californios mingled European, Native, and African roots. Pío Pico—the last governor before U. S. takeover—was partly of African descent. Historian Linda Heidenreich, herself Latina, describes the racial hierarchy of the Spanish empire as at once "stable" and "porous." Power rested firmly with those of European descent, but there were mechanisms for mixed-blood families to reclassify themselves by *limpieza de sangre,* "cleaning the blood." Colonial families like the Vallejos filed papers with the Inquisition, receiving certification of racial purity. Heidenreich says the Juárez family did not do this and that María's family had earlier been classified as mestizo, or mixed. Still, as landholders—at least one of them very European-looking—the Juárez family received preferential treatment in the next phase of colonization. Don Cayetano's portrait faces the title page in an early Anglo history of the county. María's appears on the cover of Heidenreich's book—hauntingly Indigenous.

It's likely my own blood family followed the same certifying process as the Vallejos in an older part of the Spanish empire—New Mexico. Proud of his European roots, Unc told us our Taos relatives were an "old Castilian family." I don't think he knew that Castile was a part of Spain, where African Moors, Jews, and Christians had blended for seven hundred years prior to colonization. In Taos, Juana Maria Lucero had married Yankee trapper Will Gordon and immigrated to California; their daughter Isabel had come to Napa as bride of the young Nathan Coombs. A professional genealogist has traced the Luceros—also a military settler family—back eight more generations to men and women born in Mexico as early as 1582. Ancestral names include Carvajal, de Herrera, Baca, de Montoya, Olguin, Lucero de Godoy, and many more. We can't tell just from names, but it's not likely the Luceros were purely of European descent. Heidenreich explains that soldiers of the Spanish colonizing force rarely brought European wives with them, but married Indigenous or mestizo women. Most followed the process to certify themselves as "Castilian," clearing any hint of mestizo—any hint of Indian—from their family names. When Nathan Coombs brought Isabel Gordon to Napa, he brought the Lucero lineage.

Given that her mother was a Mexican citizen and Isabel herself had lived in Mexican territory until the Treaty of Guadalupe Hidalgo, I'm assuming my great-great-grandmother spoke Spanish. The one portrait I have of her, date unknown, shows her in a rounded white collar like María's, and looking remarkably similar, if a little more European. I have only an internet version of this portrait, but it shows the likeness Uncle John remembers seeing as a boy on the wall of his grandparents' parlor. To him, this face looked darker than those of his other relatives; he was intrigued and wondered why. Isabel Coombs and María de Jesús Higuera Juárez—bicultural, if not bilingual, and both living in Napa before it was so named—could well have been friends. But there is no evidence, and I imagine there were tensions between the wives of Californios and those of new Yankee arrivals.

Juárez Rose's father recalled María as a lively woman five feet tall and a dancer who, even in her seventies, could perform intricate steps with a glass of water balanced on her head. Tradition says she was an expert rider, and courageous with weaponry. When gringos raided the Tulucay Rancho after the Bear Flag Revolt, María de Jesús Higuera Juárez met them at her doorway, defending her favorite saddle (and perhaps her person) with a long spear. In another story, she hides in the tules at dusk to escape the attack of a feral boar.

I wish I had known you, Viviene Juárez Rose, just my mother's age. We loved the same hills, the same plants, especially the indigenous ones. A generation apart, we roamed the lands of our great-grandfathers. I admired your drawing of the big oak and stone wall and the way you told the story of your ancestors so much more fully than others did. Your fourth-grade history course was probably not so different from mine, but you understood the mythmaking that whitens the stories in textbooks. Though not seeing the full harm of colonialism, you wrote about the Patwin people with respect and interest.

And you brought Don Vicente to life for me—Don Cayetano's brother —the one who carried on the Juárez tradition of herbalist and healer. Your family always had someone like that—male or female—in every generation, wherever they lived or traveled. Did you share Vicente's calling? I think I do, and my mother, too. I loved hearing how he headed off each summer into the hills with a big sack to gather medicinal herbs—and didn't return for weeks. The Juárez household shared remedies with the Ulucas, so Native herbalists must have helped Vicente learn which plants in these hills could heal. Nettles? Elderberry? Angelica root? All of them still grow here. I picture Vicente heading east from the adobe, across the low hills of Tulucay, and up along the big creek. Maybe he camped near Lily Falls among the azaleas and the leopard lilies. Things have changed, but not everything. Angelica still grows along that creek in the deep shade.

Juárez Rose embedded her family's story in that of the land. The Juárez clan had formed much deeper relationships with the valley and its First People than I would find in my own family. They were colonizers with entitlement, but they also gathered herbs and found ways to become naturalized to place, as my parents began to do generations later. But something was missing from their story, something Juárez Rose hadn't said much about and I almost missed myself. There was war in that period when the ranchos yielded to the third wave of colonizers. War between Cayetano Juárez's people and mine had disrupted the lives at Tulucay—and the Ulucas' lives, too. A war of conquest that my people had won. Except for the story of María saving her saddle from marauding gringos, the Juárez Rose papers were mostly silent on the Mexican American War and the Bear Flag incident. Although Don Cayetano had actively denounced Bear

Flagger atrocities and stood ready to attack Vallejo's captors, his family's stories did not take up this theme. Perhaps they felt a need to get along in the new regime. I could understand, but I noticed that I, too, had almost ignored a brutal war that was part of my own family's legacy. Silence kept asserting itself as I pursued this work.

Hunting for Maps and Deeds

I am in the county assessor's office to learn about land ownership. Nothing I've found so far agrees on when or how the Coombses acquired their piece of the Tulucay grant or how big a piece it was. Here, scrapbooks of yellowed surveys, patents, grants, and deeds go back to California statehood, in 1850—the start of a bureaucracy focused on property ownership. Paper submissions were required whenever land changed hands or was subdivided by an owner prior to sale. Every one of the documents from these early years, written or drawn by hand, is filed away here. On the walls hang old county maps showing property lines and acreage, with the owners' names at the time of mapping. I'm drawn to one dated 1895 and look there for landmarks I recognize in what is now Coombsville. The light is dim along this office wall and it's hard to decipher the writing.

What's now Coombsville Road has a different name, but it's on the map, heading toward the eastern hills, passing First, Second, and Third Avenues (our landmarks for visitors), not named on this map. Square plots of land line these roads, with unfamiliar owners' names. "The avenues," a loose suburban grid, must have been laid out to provide access and infrastructure for selling smaller plots. A bonanza at the turn of the century, when Napa was growing fast. Had this been Coombs land once? But further up the page, stretching to the eastern hills and north all the way to Hagen Road, are huge undivided spaces—owners N. and F. L. Coombs, Nathan's sons. This is it!

Now I look for the special place that's still in our family up against the hills, the square mile that belonged to Unc when I was a child. The Pansy Field. I have to squint to get a good look. My eyes are tired now, and I am distracted by copy machines and people applying for a marriage license. But up in the far northeast corner, I spot the delicate, wobbly lines of four creeks draining into Sarco Creek. Distinctive and valuable in a climate that can easily dry up, good reason for Coombses to hold on to this piece of land.

There's no road along the base of the hills, but another line catches my eye. Among the straight lot lines, this one curves gently along what might be the slopes that encircled the old Pansy Field. Could this soft, rounded line be the old stone wall that embraced the field in my childhood? I search the files for smaller maps that show this curve. Along with the creeks, it is my point of reference. Map by map, a richer story emerges. On one, the curving line is an "old wagon road"; on another, it is called a "stone fence." If I read these maps correctly, a stone fence alongside an old wagon road curved through the low hills.

The words *stone fence* confirm something. The wall of rounded rocks that encircled the Pansy Field of my childhood must have predated Coombs ownership. I could almost remember Unc calling it by its older name, "the stone fence," though we called it "the old stone wall." It must have been built by Juárez with Indian labor to keep cattle from roaming into the wild eastern hills, like the rancho wall in Juárez Rose's drawing. This guess gives me a sense of accomplishment, though it doesn't explain how the Coombses got this treasure of land and when.

It's late in the day and my eyes are weary, but one more big county map hangs on the wall—this one much older—from 1876. It's in a brighter place but behind a computer terminal where landowners research their parcel numbers. To look, I have to crawl onto a table and cram myself in behind the terminal. But here it is—a big open space on the old paper map, glowing ivory-colored under glass—the entire tract of what's now Coombsville, a squarish chunk of land still free of dividing lines, stretching between First Avenue and the hills. I don't have to squint to read what it says: "N. Coombs, 2,123.24 acres." The histories say Nathan purchased a small part of the Tulucay Rancho, but this is not small. This is nearly a quarter of Juárez's entire grant. I still don't know when or for how much Coombs bought this land—and whether he paid Juárez a fair price. For that, I'll need to find the actual deed. But now I know this big piece of land was his when he died the year after the map was made, 1877.

A Paper Signed in 1857

I continued to spend time in the deeds office, but Nathan Coombs conducted so many land transactions during the first two decades of statehood that the one I sought was a needle in the haystack. Then my cousin Helen—whose father once took care of the Coombs attic at Unc's Napa house—gave new life to my search. Coombses held on to paper. What had accumulated in their attic was now piled in a weatherproofed shed nearby. Helen pulled together a special stash for me—old deeds, elegant scrapbooks, and a huge plastic footlocker of frayed, yellowed letters from the 1880s and 1890s, unread in recent generations. Now I had another set of sources.

I bundled them up and took them to my small apartment in Oakland, waiting for the energy to begin. Then one night, I got home late and dipped in just for a preview. From the bundle of deeds, I pulled out some white folded sheets with red borders and struggled to make sense of them. Frank Coombs and the brother who died early, buying and selling more parcels of land—parties of the first part and parties of the second part, dating back to the 1880s. Knowing I should stop for the night but thinking I'd try just one more, I pulled out a folded sheet of blue-gray paper. This one was slightly larger and had an older feel than the others—crisper, more fragile—stained and cracked in places, a faintly scrawled math calculation on the outer page. Scotch tape had been added to reinforce the folds, but it was brown now and even more brittle than the paper. Sensing something important, I unfolded and spread the paper out in the light. This document was called an "indenture." As my eyes adjusted to the faded brown script, I made out the words, "Cayetano Juárez and Wife, Parties of the first part." With this very document, they were selling part of the Tulucay Rancho to Nathan Coombs. The date was in smaller script: "January 23, 1857." I had to remind myself to breathe. This was the document I had been looking for. The point of origin for our entitlement to that land.

I moved to better light, got out my magnifying glass, and began to decipher the fine print, a mixture of handwritten and preprinted language—

this sheet had once been a form with blanks to fill in. The details I sought were added in browner, more faded script, which didn't quite match the rest. Juárez and his wife had received "Four Thousand Three Hundred Dollars." The number was right there before me, but I had no idea what it had meant in the 1850s. In return, Juárez would "grant, bargain, sell, alien, remise, release, convey and confirm . . . to his heirs and assigns, forever." That was us. Specifics described the boundaries of the "Tulucay Ranch" in surveyors' language that read like a pirate novel: "Commencing at a sunken rock at the base of the mountains and on the bank of a small brook or branch" and "running with the meanders of said brook." The survey spelled things out in "chains," a sixty-six-foot measurement standardized in England in 1620 and required for official government surveys in the United States after 1785.

It described the boundary passing an occasional "pile of rocks" or stake. After following the creek (clearly Sarco Creek), that boundary turned south past more rock piles and stakes until it reached an oak "marked on the east side with the letters C & J cut in the bark therof." This was a "witness tree" in surveying lingo, where even trees were made into guardians of ownership. I could remember being shown that oak—long ago fallen or removed—at the corner of First and Coombsville. There the boundary turned southeast past another initialed oak to "a pile of rocks at the base of the mountains." Thence northwest to the "place of beginning." The acreage was handwritten in boldface: "TWO THOUSAND ONE HUNDRED AND SEVENTY ACRES OF LAND MORE OR LESS." At last I could trace the boundaries of Nathan Coombs's purchase.

Days later, I found another sheet of the old blue paper—this one smaller and less stained, perhaps less consulted, less touched by the hands of the old-timers. It held a hand-drawn survey map showing the mountains to the east as a bristling row of halos drawn in fine lines, naming the "sunken rock" in the upper left corner, tracing the delicate turns of the creek to the "pile of rocks," turning sharply south, then east at the first oak, and on up into the vaguer "mountains" and back again to the "sunken rock."

For weeks as I read through Helen's stash, I asked myself about this "sunken rock." Was it in a creek, maybe in Sarco Creek, some distance into what would become the parcel of the winery we had opposed? Had Coombs sold a sliver to some previous owner to even up a boundary? But most rocks in creeks appear sunken, so what made this one notable enough to legally mark a boundary? Then, looking up the hill one day, I realized that the "sunken rock" must have been the huge outcropping at our own northeast boundary. This massive rock, spread over an acre of steep slope, is visible from a great distance. Up close are crags and cliffs, but from afar it looks like one big rock mass sinking back into what in the nineteenth-century people called "the mountains." Terminology shifts with the centuries. I had always seen this rock as rising, not sinking.

West African teacher Malidoma Somé tells of rock outcroppings where his people believe we can contact the world of spirit. Andeans revere "standing rocks," formations where humans can feel the energies of Mother Earth. Andean teacher Arkan Lushwala says their shamans have continued—even after the devastation of conquest—to work with these rocks to balance the flow of energy between Earth and the stars. Through standing rocks, the universe transmits information about environmental change. They are centers for receiving what Native people here call Original Instructions.

Who Was Nathan Coombs?

After finding the deed, I knew for sure that my great-great-grandfather had bought over two thousand acres of Rancho Tulucay in 1857. He'd paid Cayetano Juárez $4,300 for it, but what did the transaction mean? In the money of his day, Coombs paid just under two dollars an acre for one quarter of the Tulucay grant! Two dollars back then was a ferry ride across the Napa River for a two-horse wagon. Ten years later, he would pay $3,500 for half interest in a racehorse. What did $4,300 mean in 1857? The internet said $116,216 today, around $90 an acre. But that didn't sound like anywhere near enough. Today, twenty-three acres in Coombsville sell for $5.5 million.

Early historian C. A. Menefee, who recorded how much things cost in Napa during that era, reports that five years earlier, in 1852, property tax assessments rose steeply, likely in the boom after the gold rush. Juárez's assessment, he specifically says, went from three dollars an acre to five dollars. So Juárez sold the land at less per acre than he owed in annual taxes for it—quite a bit less. The Californios had never been taxed under the Mexican system and struggled to hold on to land while adjusting to Yankee bureaucracy. There was a ten-year process to certify Mexican titles, where every document filed cost money, leaving Californios in an unstable limbo. Juárez survived better than most, but he must have been stretched thin. With all this and assessments rising so steeply, he would have been under pressure to sell just for cash to pay taxes. To put it mildly, the stained blue deed didn't show my ancestor paying a fair price.

Coombs drove hard bargains. I was hoping the stash of letters would show me his human side, but most were from well after his death. No affectionate words from the pioneer Nathan to his mother or his wife, no soul-searching about his children or the land he was purchasing, no exclamations about the green beauty of an early spring. Nathan Coombs probably had little opportunity for schooling and did not leave a paper trail. Mostly, I would have to infer his character from widely scattered information.

When he bought the Tulucay land, Nathan had just finished serving his first term in the new state legislature. I imagine he still had the scruffy pioneer beard and bad-boy frown that I had pondered so often in the only picture I had found of him. (It's all over the internet these days, advertising wineries in Coombsville, including a new one that is actually named for him.) When he bought this land, he was a thirty-one-year-old Yankee, in California for fourteen years. He had a very pretty younger wife, four children, and a fifth on the way, and was living comfortably on another ranch up the valley, with servants. How had Nathan Coombs accumulated the wealth to buy so much land—even if it was a bargain? He hadn't come west with money. It's said he got his first parcel in exchange for building a New England–style house for one of the Californios. On that piece of land, he laid out the streets of Napa and began selling lots as a wave of Yankees descended in the gold rush years. From the moment of statehood and before, this ancestor of mine was busy buying and selling land. One history credits Nathan and Isabel with the second land sale formally recorded in the new county.

My days in the assessor's office confirmed countless sales and acquisitions throughout the southern part of the county, many involving public lands known as school lands. These had been Indian, of course, but the federal government had claimed all land when annexing California, and had turned designated school lands over to the new state to support future public education. They were supposed to become a land bank, not fuel for speculation. Now and then, journalists dig into the story: In 1850, there were 500,000 acres of school lands, but now, despite school need, only 15,000 remain in public trust, thanks to the Coombs tradition of buying and selling.

To give a flavor of his success, in 1850, with the gold rush in full swing and Napa serving as a launchpad for newcomers heading for the mines, Nathan Coombs and two others opened Napa's first hotel—the American Hotel. Throwing a party, my great-great-grandfather spent four hundred dollars on celebratory eggnog, eggs costing twelve dollars a dozen (or perhaps six acres of land!). Throughout the 1850s and 1860s, he supported transportation and infrastructure projects boosting regional growth: two hundred dollars to make a private toll bridge free for public use; two thousand dollars to a citizen fund for a railroad. He bought into a water company, a stagecoach line to a hot springs, and a corporate dam-building effort in Lake County that proved so controversial, local citizens dismantled the dam after lengthy legal battles. As a civic benefactor, he donated land for Methodist and Presbyterian churches and served on many boards. All this showed that, as a contemporary put it, "[h]e believes in the manifest destiny of Napa."

His own prosperity rose with Napa's. The year of the Tulucay purchase, Nathan Coombs made the tough journey east via the Isthmus of Panama to buy two Kentucky racehorses. Shipped back to Napa by the same route, they anchored a strong obsession for the rest of his life—breeding, betting on, and racing horses on tracks around the state. Alexandria Brown says he employed two Black men recently from the South to help in this venture. The name Nathan Coombs became so famous in California racing that, in 1872, it was actually given to a horse. Racing historians on the internet say this horse outlived his namesake, continuing to wow the crowds. In those days, gambling and betting were thrilling to the popular mind, if not wholly honorable. The historian Menefee—always in awe of Nathan Coombs—told of the pioneer caught in a storm on a ferry to Benicia. Fearing for his life, Coombs reached into his pocket for his deck of cards to toss them overboard lest, found on his body if the storm proved fatal, they might tarnish his good name.

I found just two documents in Nathan's handwriting among the letters—one tracked efforts at horse breeding. The other, with cross-outs and odd spellings, expressed outrage about a toll road and rumors of missdoing. It dated from June 1856, the end of Nathan's first term in the State Assembly. "Now Sir," he says to an unnamed adversary, "it looks to me as though you was determined to just ride off that piece of territory and if possible to through the blame from your own sholders on to mine, these are my views and I have not formed them from idle rumor." I leave out the *sics* and wonder why this challenge was saved for so many generations. Did family members hold on to this scrap of paper because it showed a side of Nathan Coombs they'd had to tangle with themselves?

Guilt by Association and the "Other Slavery"

Nothing I could find endeared me to Nathan Coombs. Nothing stirred my heart or made me grateful to share his DNA. Just about everything showed this man embodying the stereotypes of Manifest Destiny, the very vision that troubled me. The beautiful land he'd bought from the Tulucay grant seemed just another piece of property to be subdivided and used for profit: Roads could be built through it and lots sold; the very waters of Tulucay Creek could be sold for profit in the name of development. I was relieved to find no direct connection to the hideous massacres of Indigenous Californians that marked his times. Though some of the men he knew from Bear Flag days had triggered the terrible killing at Bloody Island in Lake County and rampaged through the valley, killing Indians, it didn't seem that Nathan had been directly involved. Scruffy pioneer beard or no, troubled guilty frown or no, his way of pursuing Manifest Destiny was the one of land purchases and water companies, where deeds and regulations made the destruction of Indigenous life indirect and invisible. That was until I happened upon his census data from the year 1860—just three years after the Tulucay purchase and during his second term in the state legislature—when Nathan was thirty-four and my great-grandfather Frank was an impressionable seven-year-old.

Someone had posted it on a genealogy website—data from the 1860 census for Nathan's home ranch northwest of Napa. Besides family members, it shows ten people living that year at the Willows and working for the household. They were laborers, a carpenter, a stock raiser, and two others—a servant and a cook—whose names were given as Nancy Coombs (twenty-eight years old) and John Coombs (twenty-four). These two names on my laptop screen were a kick in the solar plexus. They bore the name Coombs in the census, but I was sure these two were not our relatives. No family stories ever mentioned a Nancy or a John. And Nancy was only one year younger than Nathan's wife. I knew that in the South enslaved people were given everyday names like Nancy and John, followed by the master's surname—the infamous slave names. Later, I would learn of a document showing thirty-five people of African descent sold as slaves in Napa County in 1846, before statehood. And I would learn how emigrants from pre–Civil War slave states brought their slaves with them. At least one, or maybe as many as seven, were part of the Bear Flag Revolt, so highly touted as the pinnacle of white patriotism.

But the Coombs family was strongly Republican and anti-slavery. Stories I haven't verified say Nathan went east to fight for the Union a few years later. All the same, the names on the screen had the ring of slave names. What if Nancy and John had been indentured California Native people, kidnapped as children and sold into servitude? This common practice was legally sanctioned by a law passed after statehood, the same one that had criminalized cultural burning—the 1850 Act for the Government and Protection of Indians. And the very year of the census—with Nathan voting in the legislature—that law was strengthened to allow outright kidnapping and longer indentures for children. The measure was repealed in 1865 with the passage of the Thirteenth Amendment, but Californians apparently found ways of continuing involuntary servitude for Native people until 1937, the year before I was born.

Slavery was on Americans' minds in 1860 as Congress tried to hold the Union together, but here was California strengthening its indenture laws in ways that would surely encourage enslavement. To get Native children, who were typically sold and "adopted" into indenture, kidnappers grew more and more murderous, often killing the parents in violent raids on their villages. Genocide scholar Benjamin Madley recounts probably a hundred such raids and says that in 1862, after the legislation passed during Nathan Coombs's term, the killing of adults to capture and sell children into slavery rose to new heights. Madley reminds us that the removal of children from parents or villages, making it hard for a people to reproduce itself, is a defining mark of genocide. This tactic meshed in California with what he calls the "killing machine"—the state-financed militias that sought to exterminate the entire Indigenous population.

I remembered that Nathan's fellow Bear Flagger, one of the Kelsey brothers, was known for rounding up Pomo from Lake County and selling them to other settlers. And what better customer than his old buddy from Bear Flag days? Had Nathan's family—my family—gone this route? Over the hills in Ukiah, one of Madley's sources claimed, most white homes held one to three Indian children in servitude. All the clues I could find put my family in this majority. I concluded that, at the height of his influence, Nathan's wealth relied on many people working for him, including at least two who had been forced to give up their true names and were likely in involuntary servitude.

What was it like for those laboring for the Coombs family? And, since I was trying to understand the mind of my ancestors, what was it like to live in a white household with indentured Indians doing the daily hard work of cleaning and cooking? What was it like for the children growing up in that household, and for Nathan's young wife, Isabel? I can only speculate. In 1860, Isabel Gordon was twenty—having married at fourteen, now with five children. She also had ten hired hands to feed. That would have been a lot of work.

As someone born in Mexican territory, in Taos, Isabel had likely benefited from indentured or outright enslaved Indian labor all her life. Her mother's family, the Luceros, were military people for generations in settlements rife with slavery and forced servitude. Andrés Reséndez, in *The Other Slavery*—about the enslavement of Indigenous peoples—calls New Mexico "a reservoir of coerced labor." Despite prohibitions of slavery starting with Queen Isabella, every white man, woman, and child in early Santa Fe had two to three Native servants in what Reséndez calls a "kaleidoscopic" system of "layered abuse." Pueblo author Leslie Marmon Silko tells how, after Indians expelled the Spanish in 1680, colonial forces returned with a policy of divide and conquer, inviting one tribe to raid another for captives to be sold as slaves. Slave markets flourished in the Rio Grande Valley near Santa Fe and Taos. I imagine the Lucero family and the Gordon family were sustained by victims of this trade. Legend says that when the Gordons arrived in Northern California, General Sutter pointed them to rich wheat-growing land near Cache Creek, in what's now Yolo County, and "gave them six Indian boys" to work the land. Isabel's branch of our family likely saw forced servitude as standard practice.

And perhaps New Englanders like Nathan did, too. I began to see that indenture and slavery had gone hand and hand with settlement in the eastern part of the continent, as well. The clearance and farmwork needed to make a Europeanized landscape from what was there—the act of colonizing the land—required more labor than a family could produce. A study by Margaret Newell suggests that New England colonies warred with Indians explicitly to acquire captives as slaves. After King Philip's War (1675–1678), during which settlers fought confederated tribes, the colonial government posted lists of families receiving Indian captives—including the children of "praying Indians" who had supported the colonists. Captured children were "put forth into service" to Eliots, Flints, Jacksons, Morses, and many more. Adults were shipped as slaves to other colonies, such as Barbados. Indentures were supposed to last until a child's twenty-first birthday but often dragged on. Unless contested (as they were), an enslavement could last for generations.

When I lived in the Boston area, I went as often as I could to Cape Cod—for the solace of the glacial drift and little pine trees that reminded me of the California mountains. Once, in the town of Mashpee, I stopped at a beautiful old New England cemetery with mossy rock walls and gray slate gravestones. Half-remembered family lore placed Coombs graves near here, so I decided to look. A plaque honored Wampanoag people who'd taken refuge here when pushed off lands closer to Boston. The oldest parts of the cemetery were theirs. To my surprise, a prominent name on early Wampanoag graves was Coombs. Later, I found that Wampanoag people named Coombs had been nineteenth-century leaders in their community, and remain so in the town of Middleborough to this day. One of them, Linda Coombs, a respected interpreter of Wampanoag culture, is often in the news as the region looks back at the history of settlement—four hundred years after the *Mayflower* landed.

Middleborough, near Plymouth, where the Pilgrims settled, was also the birthplace of our family's Nathan Coombs. Google helped me find early Anglo Coombses in Middleborough, but they had no sons. I had to speculate. Somewhere—long ago—there had been mixing. Had Wampanoag people been indentured and given the Coombs name? Had there been intermarriages? I didn't know this part of our history. When I shared my questions with a Wampanoag friend, he laughed and called me "cousin."

How Nathan Coombs Came to California

At last I filled in the blanks in the family story of Nathan's arrival in California. Yes, he had grown up in Middleborough and traveled with his parents to Iowa, where his father died. Then he'd crossed the plains on the Oregon Trail. I didn't realize from the family version that Nathan—still in his teens and on his own—had traveled to Oregon and entered California with the notorious Lansford W. Hastings party. Hastings was author of the popular guidebook that described an untried "shortcut," which a few years later would fatally delay the Donner party. His guidebook describes the very journey young Nathan shared.

I read Hastings's book, hoping for details about my ancestor and his experience. The party did cross the plains safely, then headed south from Willamette. Hastings focused on the need for armed vigilance to protect against hostile Indians. That was standard for trail guides says Brendan Lindsay, the author of *Murder State,* where an entire chapter on guidebooks reveals the deep fears settlers brought with them, despite almost no incidents of hostility during plains crossings and the fact that several of them were killed by their own loaded guns. Those fears would be the emotional matrix for genocide. Hastings didn't describe the people in his party, so I have to imagine. Nathan was just sixteen, a boy really, but he had joined a band of "armed men" traveling into little-known territory in a state of fear. It was the late spring of 1843, six years before the gold rush, and a serious drought year. "Hardly any rain fell that whole year," wrote John Bidwell, who'd reached California two years earlier and settled in Chico, along the route.

As I write in another extreme drought nearly two centuries later, I would give anything to know what it was like for Nathan on the long ride down from Oregon. Hastings said little about the land, but I can picture what lay before them as they rode— likely more or less the route of the present Amtrak line. I can imagine—it was May or June—riding south day after day through those long, open lands north of the visionary Mount Shasta, the lands of the Modoc and the Klamath peoples. Relatively peaceful lands then—to become killing fields just thirteen years later when gold-driven settlers waged wars of extermination. The lands of the Shasta people, whose name we now use for the county and the mountain.

I can imagine the awe of drawing closer and closer to Shasta's snowy summit, which must have shone golden in the special light each evening and each morning. Even in a drought year there would have been broad grassy meadows between sage and rock outcroppings, and wildflowers. Over a hundred years later, one of my uncles moved his family up into this beautiful land and began to learn some of its terrible history. Coombs descendants still live there. To a person on horseback, that high country would seem to go on forever during the long days of late spring, near the June solstice.

I imagine the group had passed out of the highlands and reached the downslope, where dense forests take over from the open sage. Perhaps they had passed the dramatic rocks of Castle Crags, which you see from today's highway. Hastings said they were within sight of the big valley when they met a band of four hundred Indians. I wonder if they were Wintu—relatives of the Winnemem Wintu today, who so firmly defend their sacred sites from the waters of Shasta dam. I once met their chief, Caleen Sisk—successor to the legendary Florence Jones—who is known worldwide for her defense of sacred ground.

What happened next? The Hastings party fought. Surely there could have been other ways—negotiation, trade? Historians say bands of Indians typically sought to trade with those passing through their land. But Hastings assumed hostility. He sent the party's women, children, and animals farther down into the grasslands and prepared to fight. "Hoping to deter them," he "discharged a gun into the open air" and instead precipitated an attack. Heavily armed, Hastings and those with him fought for two hours in rough, rocky country.

I don't know exactly what happened there in the lee of Mount Shasta, but some say the Hastings party killed eighty of the First People. Hastings himself said twenty. Was that sixteen-year-old boy counted as one of the "armed men"? It's hard to imagine he went with the women and children that day and did not use his gun. Did my blood ancestor kill one of Caleen Sisk's ancestors? No family stories tell of this episode. Perhaps our silence shows shame for the bloody encounter. But who actually pulled the trigger is not the point. The mind-set was shared no matter what role a person played in the takeover of California. That mind-set continued to reverberate throughout settlement—increasing to unbelievable depravity during and after the gold rush—and it continues, latent, sometimes surfacing, in our culture today. This was how my great-great-grandfather Nathan Coombs—with all the confusions of mind he embodied—entered California.

For years, my friend Donna, a trained psychic and member of The Minnesota Chippewa Tribe, whom I've known since the Wounded Knee ride, has gently suggested doing a reading on the Napa land. For years, I have said, "Maybe, sometime." But writing this chapter has been slow and emotionally difficult; there's a reason I felt aversion to these ancestors as a child. The times they lived in and the history they shaped are painful to look at and even more painful to know I'm part of. I need help from somewhere. So on a December morning, Donna and I sit face-to-face under the manzanita tree, blooming a month early this year. Donna is on the wooden bench where I often write, and I am near a stone wall my father built—facing into a white cloud of faintly fragrant bloom. Hummingbirds visit the flowers, whirring and chirping as we speak, and the tree hums with bees.

I'm to keep looking at her and not close my eyes, but she is in semi-trance, her face peaceful, framed in the leaves and reddish twigs of the manzanita. I'm not sure how psychic readings work. But she explains, calls in spirit guides, and begins to tell me what she sees. At first nothing but green. Then her voice rises. Many people are assembling, standing near and behind me. Twenty Native people, she tells me in astonishment, men and women. A young girl about seven, playful and upbeat, squats on the ground at her feet, playing joyful games with fallen leaves.

Through Donna, these people tell me that grim times have afflicted them here on this land, the pain unfolding, layer by layer. But they are still coming here. They still love these big trees. The land has suffered but is healing, they say. It is not now in pain. I am deeply touched to find that they comfort me, thank me. They want me to be strong, want me to heal—not take on their pain. They need my voice, not my suffering, they tell me. An elder at my left shoulder brushes the energy there, cleansing me of my sorrow. He says that over time they will unroll an entire story that will widen my perspective.

Given a chance, I ask about Nathan Coombs. Their reaction is strong —he was known among them, but not in a good way. If they saw him coming, they would disappear as best they could. He was one who used force, though not bloodshed. They warn he may be a man with secrets he doesn't want revealed.

They tell me of sacred sites on this land that they continue to visit and care for. I will find these sites, but only when open to the feelings of peace that come when near them. And I can help to protect them with offerings and prayers. They want me to complete my book, to make known who they are, what this place meant and still means to them—and to show my readers that they can find their own sacred places wherever they are. The wound here, their own wound, was large and deep, but it was not the whole experience. "We bring love here," they say. "We have our sorrow, but it is surrounded in love." Somehow, I feel their reality. I am moved by their kindness, their affirmation.

CHAPTER 8

Manifest Destiny

Letters from the Second Generation After Genocide

My great-grandparents Frank Leslie Coombs and Belle Roper Coombs, photographed in the early 1890s. Photo of Frank by R. Maruki, Tokyo, Japan; photo of Belle by Burrell E. Wilson, Napa, California. Images courtesy of the Dunlap family.

If I could build it in one of those lovely knolls whose curves were an endless delight to my eye, how I should revel! T'would be Eden land then beyond question to me.

—AUNT ELLA E. ROPER, LETTER FROM WORCESTER,
MASSACHUSETTS, TO NAPA, CALIFORNIA, 1886

Where shall we find, unless in the European, that nobly arched head containing such a quantity of brain . . . the perpendicular face, the prominent nose, and round projecting chin? Where that variety of features and fullness of expression?

—CHARLES WHITE, 1799 (QUOTED IN REGINALD HORSMAN,
RACE AND MANIFEST DESTINY)

As one participates consciously in a dialogue with the
ancestors, the capacity for love and support to flow between
and through the generations is gradually restored.
—SANDRA EASTER, *JUNG AND THE ANCESTORS*

New Englanders Move onto the Land

THE SUN IS JUST down and I'm walking through the neighbors' vineyard,
heading toward the earliest house on this land. Family members built
it in 1884 and called it "Mountain Side." I see why back then, with no
neighbors for over a mile, they thought themselves in the wild mountains
here. And I am awed by the beautiful siting of that house. From a rounded
knoll, it looks out over onetime pastures and down to the wooded area
where Picnic and Dairy Creeks join. Southward are gentle hills once part
of the Tulucay Rancho—in shadow now. Even with all the development
in the valley, you can still feel their rhythm rolling westward toward the
former Pansy Field and the old stone wall—all the way to what was once
the Coombs property line on First Avenue. It must have been even more
awesome before the vineyards and McMansions, before the suburban
lights at night out across the valley. Just rolling grassy hills, green in winter and spring, brown-gold in summer, fading to silver in fall.

And beyond the low hills, that circle of steeper ones, the long skyline
we used to see from Unc's deck, a reminder to me now of the killings that
opened the land for settlement. That skyline circles the whole valley to
Mount Saint Helena and back along the hills behind us here. As I watch,
the light shifts and all the hills behind me turn a rosy gold, reflecting the
sunset. And rising up from the nearest high place—shining more golden
than the rest—is the old boundary marker, "the sunken rock." I imagine
my great-great-grandparents enjoying an evening at Mountain Side. A
view like this gives a sense of vast entitlement, a sense that the world be-
longs to those enjoying it—is their destiny.

The first two generations called it "the Cayetan," a term for Unc's ranch that I hadn't known until it showed up in the stash of letters, perhaps an affectionate way of remembering Cayetano Juárez. With all his other holdings, Nathan Coombs never lived on this land, as far as I could find, and neither did the two sons who inherited it when he died, in 1877. They must have ridden out from town to survey the grasslands and oaks, to lay out First, Second, and Third Avenues and sell lots along them. I imagine they admired the land and felt some connection beyond its value as real estate. But so far as I can tell, they were day visitors only. They didn't see the stars from these hills or hear the owls. They didn't wake up among the oaks on a foggy morning or discover mosses turned green overnight from early rains. I don't think they spent time wondering what the land had been like when the Wappo lived here.

The first of our relatives to actually live on the land were the Ropers from Massachusetts, the parents of Frank Coombs's wife, Belle. Neither they nor Belle had ever met Frank's pioneer father, and they arrived in California after that violent third wave of colonization to a place where white people had already managed to forget. I found no evidence they thought about recent atrocities as they settled in and got to know the northeast part of the Tulucay grant.

I had a way into their thoughts and feelings that I didn't have for the pioneer Nathan. This generation wrote long letters to one another, and someone had saved them. To get their story, I would read everything in the big plastic bin of family papers that my cousin had found in her shed. I was lucky to have them, but it was a huge undertaking. Stamps removed from envelopes, letters—most from the 1880s and 1890s—unsorted. Many of the letters, which numbered close to a thousand, were from East Coast correspondents I didn't recognize—all with 140-year-old handwriting that was faded and hard to decipher. It took months to read through them all, one random handful at a time. What plants did my relatives find? Had the land begun to teach them as it had my mother? How aware were they of the violence that had happened around the valley? Did any of them question it? I wanted to know how this set of ancestors had responded to the land and the wounds of our history.

I wasn't expecting a lot. Frank and Belle's generation was the second since California's founding, coming of age at the end of the heightened period of genocide. They had died before I was born, a generation caught up in the mind of Manifest Destiny—the belief in white American exceptionalism and destiny to control and improve the continent and beyond. Even before studying this mind-set, I knew that my great-grandfather Frank Coombs—widely read and an accomplished speaker—had stood for these views in his publc life. Years ago, we'd found his efforts at a novel about his father as a Yankee pioneer. His writing expressed the deeply racist views of the era, repugnant to our generation. As I moved through the letters, I knew a lot would stir distress and outrage. But I also hoped that listening to the voices of my ancestors would somehow help me feel compassion for them, no matter how stuck they had been in the worldview of their times.

One of the first letters I pulled from the bin was from Belle Roper—Frank Coombs's bride from Boston. Belle's voice would become a familiar one. She wrote the classic, often daily, letters of the Victorian era, staying in touch with her parents across the wide continent. She was my great-grandmother, though I knew her only from the stiff, dark-eyed portrait I'd seen as a child in the Coombs house and an embroidered teal silk gown that still hangs in a closet at our Napa house. I had never warmed to her, but somehow there was something charming about this letter. Months after arriving in Napa, Belle wrote home to New England in the green spring of 1880, ecstatic about a horse and buggy drive into the beautiful Napa countryside. I recognized the tradition—the beloved Sunday drive of my own childhood. But this drive had a mission—collecting ferns. Frank wrote about the same excursion. After traveling east to marry Belle in December, he was now working as district attorney on a tough murder case. Frank's voice, too, would be a major one in the letters. He was eloquent, deeply involved in the issues and ideology of his times, and a very loving husband and father. His letter tells of taking a break to get some fresh air, driving out to see the ranches and gather ferns. "Belle found many that she had not seen before," he wrote, and said that she planned to get more.

On their porch already were "two hanging baskets . . . filled with ferns, maidenhair, lichens and moss." They hoped for a "wonderful collection of growing ferns."

Fern collecting came up often in the letters, particularly from a third relative, who turned out to be very important to my inquiry: Belle's single and adventurous aunt Ella Roper. A graduate of Mount Holyoke College, like Belle, Ella taught school in several eastern cities, traveled a lot, and wrote frequently to Frank, her niece, and Belle's parents, who would soon move west. Ella dreamed of fern hunting along the Napa creeks, asked for roots of specific ferns, and described gathering expeditions on the East Coast. Something rang a bell, so I checked the internet. Sure enough, the 1880s and 1890s were the height of a Victorian craze known as "fern fever," or pteridomania, a wildly popular way to connect with the natural environment, especially for middle-class white women who otherwise faced many restrictions.

Fern fever began in England but spread to New England, where Ella had first shared her passion for ferns with Belle. When Ella's letters described fern hunting in wild forested landscapes, I could now picture Victorian women in hats, bustles, and wide skirts scrambling up steep, brushy hillsides to dig up fern roots, identify them botanically, and grow them at home in specially constructed ferneries. In an era of scientific collecting expeditions, this must have been their way of participating. It was a pastime for the educated—people who could handle Latin names— and both Ella and Belle were graduates of one of the country's prestigious women's colleges.

I thought of the banks of maidenhair fern that still show green in the winter woods and the rare five-finger ferns at Lily Falls and knew my own mother would have enjoyed these details of Dad's relatives and California plant life. Would she have worried about the effect of fern fever on the ecosystem? Plant species were often collected to extinction, and maybe this had made our five-fingered fern so rare. For millennia, the Wappo had harvested them sustainably for basket making. But collecting was different.

From their point of view, Frank and Belle's country drives were idyllic on what was, after all, their honeymoon. More than one letter writer mentioned the couple's charmed life—so much went well for them in the Golden State. Frank's family status and his eloquence would lead to a long career in state politics, diplomacy in Japan, and a term in Congress. The couple had met when his parents sent him east to school in the 1870s. There's a photo of him setting off—handsome and a little diffident, standing beside a huge trunk. In Boston, he boarded with a local family and attended Dorchester High School, a public school that was coeducational ahead of its time. There he was drawn to classmate Belle Roper, who was from a local family. Afterward, the two pursued further education—she at Mount Holyoke, he at Columbian Law School in Washington, D.C.

This was a lot of privilege and education to have in one's family, especially back then. Belle went on to become a teacher in Boston, and Frank returned to Napa to practice law in 1875. It must have been a hard return: That year, his mother divorced his father, who died two years later. I found no letters at all between Belle and Frank until the very end of my search. But by December 1879, Frank was in Boston for their wedding, after which he took Belle west by train to a town just thirty years old, with unpaved streets, dusty in summer and muddy in the wet winters. Within a few years, Belle would persuade the Ropers to follow her and live on the Cayetan.

The next year, their family included little Nathan, the one who became our Unc, named for his pioneer grandfather and the subject of many letters in the stash. Frank fondly described the "noble shape" of his head, referencing the popular "science" of phrenology, which favored European features. Belle wrote about taking him to the spring countryside, where he was "just wild" about flowers. While she and Frank picnicked in the grass, Nathan would "travel off several yards . . . sit down back to us and pick the flowers pulling them to pieces in his lap—thinking we wouldn't see him, little mischief." She didn't allow him to touch flowers at home. I pictured this toddler, who would become our portly Unc, tearing away at poppies and lupine—not the first child, or the last, to do them this kind of harm. Belle and Frank were more amused than concerned.

They could hardly have known the future history of the landscape, and wildflowers probably seemed endless.

More children were on the way, and Frank would soon be serving in the state legislature. It must have been hard to find family support. Frank's mother lived hours away by carriage in Lake County. Plus, Belle missed her parents and younger siblings and was concerned about their health—a major theme in those letters as disease hit people hard in the years before antibiotics. A younger Roper sister had died in the short time Belle had been away from Boston, and two brothers had died earlier. Belle kept urging her family to move west for their health. In late 1882, Foster Roper made a trial visit, joined by his sister, Ella, to check out a climate that might be easier on his debilitating asthma. Belle had a plan: Eight hundred acres of the former Tulucay Rancho were ideal for dairying—rolling grasslands, dotted with shady oaks and watered by year-round creeks. If it were stocked with milk cattle, Foster and his teenage son Howard could develop the place and manage the land. No one believed Belle could persuade her father (who apparently had a mind of his own), but, a year after the trial visit, the Ropers—with their four sons, one still a small child—left their house in Boston to join their daughter in California.

Foster and his wife, Sophie, would take up residence on what had been Wappo and Patwin land, then the Tulucay grant. Their presence was central to the letters. Foster didn't write much—he may have been a man of few words. But I don't think there would have been a letter collection without Belle's mother, Sophonisba Peale Roper. Known to friends as Sopha or Sophie, this great-great-grandmother traced her lineage to the famous painter Charles Willson Peale, who'd made portraits of George Washington and started the country's first natural history museum. To judge by what others said, Sophie wrote a lot, and beautifully, but left so little of her writing in the bin of letters that I knew it was she who must have collected them. Her own were likely saved in attics on the East Coast. All the same, I felt Sophie's presence in what others said—she was mother to Belle, confidante to Ella, gardener extraordinaire, and beloved friend to all who wrote. Her correspondents often echoed what she'd said. I came to feel very close to Sophie.

The Ropers Build a House
and Call It "Mountain Side"

From their arrival in November 1883 well into the next year, Foster and his son, Belle's brother Howard (age seventeen), worked hard to build their new house, Mountain Side. That house still stands, though much changed, less than one hundred yards downslope from the one my parents built, now screened by a dense growth of live oaks. A letter from Ella, worrying about her brother's health, suggests there was no money to hire helpers, so Howard must have done most of the work. His two older brothers had found paying jobs in Sacramento. Foster had worked the business end of a New England furniture company, but Howard had bulding skills. He's said to have laid the hand-hewn oak floor—still admired after modern remakes of the former Mountain Side—and crafted a beautiful walnut table now in our house and a desk now at Uncle John's. I'm guessing he installed the water tank on Dairy Creek and built the stone dam to hold the pool of water where I'd plunged in to plug the leak. Maybe he'd built the stone wall that had intrigued my mother. As children, we had known him as "Uncle Howard," an elderly relative in loose denim coveralls with suspenders who helped us find eggs for breakfast right in his backyard in town.

By October 1884, the Ropers were living in their new house. Ella's letters were enthusiastic. She had been "mightily taken with that spot" when Belle drove her there by carriage on her earlier visit. She recalled visiting an outlook in the hills and "beholding the fair Cayetan lying under us spread out like a map." Was that where I'd photographed my father on our hike? Ella wondered if their "water comes from the spring or brook which we saw pouring over a precipice?" Had she made the climb to Lily Falls? Maybe, because she added, "It makes me so crazy to get there and have a scramble with you." "Mountain Side," she wrote, "is becoming a home to me rather than a myth now."

I was happy to find so much detail from long ago and to hear Ella's enthusiasm, but I wasn't hearing directly from Foster and Sophie and I sensed they were not fully at home here. According to Ella's letters in January 1885, they tried to plow; they plowed for weeks. But the crops they planted—alfalfa? wheat? I wish I knew—failed that year. One hundred head of dairy cattle rebelled, ran for the hills, and kicked Grandpa Foster during milking. A fire of some kind burned the calves. Relatives in Massachusetts wrote that it sounded very hard, that making all that butter was a lot of work for Sophie.

I wondered how they managed. Foster and Sophie were not young—he well into his fifties, she in her late forties—and they were not well. Foster, even in the warmer, drier California climate, was sometimes paralyzed with asthma—coughing and breathing with great difficulty. Sophie had problems with her eyes, severe headaches, arthritis in her hands that could flare up so badly, she had to stop writing the wonderful letters everyone loved. Hand-churning one hundred pounds of butter a week must have been agony.

And there was child care. Foster and Sophie had their own young child plus three grandchildren to care for when Belle and Frank were in Sacramento. Little Nate—Unc to us—was apparently quite a handful. More than once in the letters, he was said to have fallen into the creek and come home muddy. My grandmother Amy Louise (named for her Roper aunt, who'd died as a child in Massachusetts) was supposed to be a moderating influence. There was also baby Frankie, who would die of scarlet fever in 1891, and six-year-old Ralphie Roper—their uncle, actually, old enough to ride a horse and help with the cattle.

Sophie's life can't have been easy at Mountain Side. The many letters from friends who used to visit her home in Boston attest to her sociability. Yet here she lived in isolation—a four-mile wagon or carriage ride from town, over rough dirt roads like the one I'd seen mapped along the "old stone fence." No one to visit with. Ella commiserated with her about difficulties befriending their only neighbor, Hagen, a lone German who'd started a winery north of the dairy—where the winery we contested is now.

Sophie Tells of Her Garden

Socially isolated and working very hard, Sophie took time to enjoy a garden and the California spring. One of her her eastern relatives replied to a letter from Sophie, saying, "You wrote about your flowers. Here we are sitting around fires . . . and you with your windows open." And a child wrote, "I would like to see your nice garden and help you pick some of the roses . . . I should go wild with joy to ramble over the fields with you." What had Sophie written to draw such an ecstatic response from this child? I think my great-great-grandmother had a feeling for the land as well as a way with plants and gardens. While the men were building the house, she must have been planting those roses, because there wasn't all that much time for them to get established before things would change at Mountain Side.

I began to see answers for some of my ecological questions. Given the fascination in her era for exotic species from around the world, I'm guessing Sophie was the one who planted Himalayan blackberry behind the dairy barn—unaware that a century later it would fill acres of woods with impenetrable brambles, choking out the ferns her family prized and zapping water from the creek. These berries were the newest agricultural marvel in California at that time. Larger and juicier than the native blackberry, they'd been introduced from Asia by horticulturalist Luther Burbank, agricultural experimenter in nearby Santa Rosa. It took only a few farmers planting these energetic vines for them to spread like wildfire—through aggressive roots and seeds dropped by birds—into many pristine places around the state, choking out native blackberry, willow, and other plants Indigenous people treasured. Apparently, this species is invasive, from New Zealand to northern Europe. Himalayan blackberries are hard on indigenous ecosystems, but the fruit is delicious. If Sophie did plant them, she left us an ecological menace but also many family blackberrying trips—and delicious jams, jellies, and pies.

That same area along the creek has a stand of *Ailanthus altissima*, or Tree of Heaven, another overly energetic plant the Victorians found in India and introduced around the world. This feather-leafed, slightly strange-smelling tree is now a nuisance in many parts of the United States—a sapling so hardy in eastern cities that it twines itself into chain-link fences and forces its way through asphalt. It's on the "don't plant" list for nearby Lake County and is one of the few plants that compete in the Dairy Creek blackberry patch.

Even though I think Sophie introduced *Ailanthus,* it wasn't to spite the native plants of her new home. I'm pretty sure she loved what was growing in these hills, and at last I found something in her own voice that said so—a letter sent to an eastern magazine, introducing one of my favorite native plants: "The beautiful Manzanita is white with bloom and under its green branches the blossoms have drifted like a fall of pure white snow. It is our rainy season, but it does not rain all the time by any means. On the contrary, we have many more dry than wet days in the Winter, and they are simply beyond description. The sky is blue, the air balmy, and the hills and valleys green." Here was the natural world I knew and the Sophie I had wanted to hear. Her joyful words about the land could have come straight from one of my own journals. Finding this letter in one of her scrapbooks, I felt real kinship with Sophie.

But by December 1886, three years after beginning the Mountain Side project, Foster and Sophie were back in town—in a place on Second Street with a town-size barn, a cow, and some chickens. Ella wrote, "I should think you would miss the mountains, but it must be good to be near to Belle." Their sojourn on the Cayetan had been an ordeal. For the next half century and well into my own lifetime, the dairy and other parcels of that eight hundred acres would be rented for pastureland, with visiting rights for the Coombs family. Frank's family picnicked along the creeks, as did Unc in later years. Near Picnic Creek, I found what looked like one of the bottle dumps on old New England farmsteads— thick brown glass from the nineteenth century. I also discovered bits of crockery I associated with Belle's finery—blue and white willowware, a tiny demitasse handle. Eventually, Unc would build his house with the big deck a quarter of a mile south of Mountain Side, so that once again family members—including ourselves—would live on the land.

The road winds through a lush green New England June, flanked by the stone walls of early settlement, so much like those in Napa. But this is

Lancaster, Massachusetts, west of Boston, where Roper ancestors settled in the 1600s. A letter in the bin from Aunt Ella told her niece and nephews how their ancestors had suffered here. Decades later, Ella would write a book about these earlier Ropers. Before I found it, I learned the broad outlines. John Roper, who had recently emigrated from England, moved to this early farming settlement with wife, son, and grandchild—and soon had land to farm.

But this land along the beautiful Nashua River was already home to the Nipmuc people, a major force in the 1676 Metacom's Rebellion, which our histories call King Philip's War. The Lancaster settlers built garrison houses to shelter the farm families, but there was no real security. In one raid during the cold of February, the Nipmuc set fire to the garrisons, killing almost all the Ropers. John's son Ephraim lost his wife and child but survived to start a new family after the war.

On this land of the Nipmuc, my own family left their blood and tears. So often I've choked back sobs at sites where Indians were massacred during the taking of the continent—Wounded Knee; Big Hole, in Montana; the Modoc Stronghold, in California. But standing here, where my own kin met violent death, a whole new section of my heart opens up. I can feel the energy inside the garrison as forty-two human beings hear the men outside, hear that there are guns as well as arrows, tomahawks and war cries, hear the sound of fire ripping toward them. They look to their small children. Fear climbs the walls—perhaps they've feared this their whole time on the continent. Nipmuc war tactics are not so much to kill enemies as to destroy the built presence of the colonists and feed their fear. Descendants—if any survive—will bear this fear for generations, perhaps all the way down to my own, warping our ability to see our true history.

I imagine the Nipmucs—outside, carrying fire toward the garrison—hold a different fear. They have seen their own people betrayed and killed by the gun, their own children dying of starvation or taken into captivity and enslavement. The land they have loved and tended is defiled by cattle and fences. Their agreements with the English are not holding. This is a last-ditch effort to stop the loss, the genocide (if there had been a word for it then) that is taking place around them—to restore the balance.

What Was Said and What Was Not Said

I was disappointed to find the chatty Roper/Coombs letters all but silent about the First People of California. This was hard to understand when all around them pundits talked about "the Indian problem" and hideous anti-Indian cartoons filled the press. Months before Belle arrived, the Napa paper had fulminated against "redskins." There were more positive voices in the public eye: Acclaimed Paiute writer Sarah Winnemucca drew large San Francisco crowds to stirring lectures on her people's experience of colonization. Helen Hunt Jackson exposed injustices to Native people, and many read her romanticized but compassionate novel *Ramona*. Highly educated, Belle and Frank would have known of these views, but did they have contact with Native people in Napa?

In the 1870s, a local historian had estimated hardly one hundred were left in the county. But the fact was, there were still Patwin and Wappo people around the valley in the years of these letters. There were the mothers and children who had played with Viviene Juárez Rose's father in the late 1870s. And as late as 1927, a strong, beautiful-faced Patwin woman was photographed in Napa by an anthropologist—standing near trees in a head kerchief. In 1969, that photograph appeared in *Almost Ancestors*, a Sierra Club publication that began to break the white silence about California's Native population and touched me deeply at the time.

But Indian people weren't showing up in the family letters. Looking carefully through the whole batch turned up only three mentions—distant or romanticized, not people from the Napa Valley. Belle wrote home about her new mother-in-law, fascinated by Isabel's memory of Indians on the long ride from Taos to California and their stories of riches hidden in the hills. Later, she wrote of Frank's dislike for one of her prized Victorian hats, which he'd mocked, calling it a "Modoc war bonnet." I knew the reference—the Modoc War, which took place near the Oregon border, the last and a very lethal episode of the California genocide seven years before the letter. The orders of General Sherman, commanding general of the United States Army under President Ulysses S. Grant, were for "utter extermination." Negotiating for peace, the Modoc leader was forced into a months-long standoff in the rugged lava beds north of Mount Shasta, where the army destroyed most of his people. I remembered a detail from Dee Brown's *Bury My Heart at Wounded Knee;* Modoc warriors had worn huge headdresses of sagebrush as camouflage. Media from all over the world had covered this war, so I imagined the sagebrush had been played up in news reports, and that Frank had seen it as fuel for a lady's hat joke like those I'd often heard in my childhood. He was probably not the only Californian to make light of this devastating detail of the genocide.

Ella also mentioned Indians as she wrote her nephew about welcoming the Ropers to California, where she had already visited and been shown the sites. "Frank, you must show Sophie where those dead Indians were buried. It will be a delightfully tragic association for her." I knew enough Napa history to guess what she was referring to. At the time of the letters, a family named Thompson had developed beautiful orchards near the former Patwin village of Suscol, and they became the talk of the county . While plowing, Thompson had uncovered mass burials of two hundred Indians killed by Vallejo in 1835, and these also became the talk of the county. Years later, Platon Vallejo (who denied any such killing) said the burials dated from the smallpox epidemics of 1836–1838, when less than 10 percent of the Patwin survived. Either way, these bones would have been barely fifty years in the ground before being plowed up for the planting of peach trees and shown to tourists. Ella's phrase "delightfully tragic" made me want to weep. I wanted to tell her we now have a word for what she saw—"genocide," the attempt to kill off an entire people. I doubted she would understand, caught up in the national trend that saw the loss of the First People as sad and "tragic" but unavoidable. Even in my generation, white people couldn't see the truth until recently, and all too many still don't.

The letters showed white American consciousness before people like my mother began to chip away at the prejudice they were raised with, and it wasn't pretty. Coombses and Ropers had belittling things to say about everyone they considered outsiders, not upright Anglo-Americans. Their letters are a litany of "othering." Belle wanted a dairy because she was concerned about the "cleanliness" of Italians, who ran the other dairies in the valley. They "can't keep the milk sweet," she wrote her parents, and "are unacceptable to the community." Irish, Scots, and Swedes, who'd worked in Roper homes on the East Coast, were also disparaged. Post–gold rush California offered many more ethnicities for comment. Ella asked about farmworkers: "I wonder if you have those villainous looking Spaniards whom I used to see out driving. Do they speak Spanish? Do you ever go into the room where they are eating? I am curious to know what kind of manners they have. Mostly none I judge from their appearance." Did her stereotype of "villainous" Spaniards come from the centuries-old British rivalry with Spain? It's also likely the "Spaniards" Ella thought she'd seen were mestizo or even Indigenous people. Passing as their former coloniz-ers had become a survival option for the Patwin and Wappo.

Ella seemed especially drawn to observing and criticizing other cul-tures. Her views were most offensive when she moved to Georgia to head up a school for Black girls in the 1890s. A good antislavery Republican, like all those in her family, Ella worked diligently for what she saw as ra-cial improvement (which to us is paternalistic). Her letters tell mocking anecdotes about the Black cook and caretaker at the school. Her efforts to imitate their accents are unbearably patronizing to my ear. Perhaps she was trying to emulate Harriet Beecher Stowe, who had used this style to turn the tide of northern opinion on slavery thirty years earlier.

Ella had a strong sense of cultural supremacy. Generations later, my Boston students would help me see that I had some of it, too. Now I asked myself what kind of atmosphere Ella created for Black children in her southern school. Alongside the school stories, she told of admiring visits with renowned abolitionist Frederic Douglass, whose second wife had been Ella's Mount Holyoke classmate. Even here her letters voiced strong opinions: "[Y]ou know my feelings about mixed marriage." (Ella also disapproved of women's suffrage, which was Douglass's issue at the time.) This distant aunt was a fascinating study in contradictions.

On a related front, fear of "the Chinese menace" grew to brutal hyste-ria as Belle was adjusting to life in California. Labeled "Celestials," "Asiat-ics," or "Mongolians," Chinese immigrants had come during the gold rush, fleeing economic disaster in their home country. They stayed to build railroads, mine toxic mercury, do cooking and housework on ranches, and start small businesses. After providing labor to build the state's economy, the Chinese were targeted by vicious newspaper campaigns, white-only labor unions, arsonists, and lynch mobs. Linda Heidenreich says that in 1880 almost a hundred Chinese immigrants lived in the southern part of the Napa Valley, with two Chinatowns and several labor camps farther north. Animosity was intense: Gangs of white youth attacked the Chinese and threw rocks, while adults robbed and stabbed them on the streets. White newspapers of the time told a different story. Shortly after arriving, Belle wrote her parents, "You would just be frightened to death to live here—and read the papers—each day brings to light some new murder by chinamen—or some horror connected with them." Xenophobic fears mounted, and Frank's political career would rise alongside the movement to exclude Chinese immigrants from the United States.

At the same time, just two months after this letter and uneasy about managing a household, Belle wrote how happy she was to have "a China boy working for me." Chung was her first servant, "a Christianized Mongolian," who went to Sunday school every week at 6:00 A. M. He was about the size and age of her little brother and seemed to love working hard. "He scours everything," she said, and noted that he timed every meal to the minute. But Belle was concerned: "My bones fairly ache for this boy. He does not stop work for one minute, never sits down." (Decades later in the U.S. Congress, perhaps forgetting this, Frank would defend child labor policies with all his eloquence.) Belle wrote affectionately of a gift from Chung—a small box of China tea. I was glad for these details, glad to see my great-grandmother's kindly feelings for this young Chinese person with whom she had daily contact. I was glad to know that this bit of human caring could exist within the atmosphere of racial fear whipped up by the media of her time.

We don't hear how Chung fared during the shocking fires that ripped through Napa's crowded Chinatown in the last decades of the nineteenth century. There is nothing at all about these fires in the letters. Did Chung's people, like so many, have to flee hostility? From farther north, in the coastal town of Eureka, comes the terrible story of a young Chinese Christian snatched from his minister's house and taken to a makeshift gallows by a mob. Though saved by the bravery of another Anglo minister, he and all other Chinese residents, business owners, and even favored servants were loaded onto waiting ships and deported to San Francisco. That was in 1885. Throughout California, ethnic cleansing sought to ensure that this state would favor a white population.

Tonight on my walk, I looped over toward the old Mountain Side house because it's empty now, and on the market. Behind its modern facade and "French garden" plantings, I could feel the stark, old two-story farmhouse it had been in my childhood, when Unc rented it with pasture and dairy barn to a family named Vaz. Were they Portuguese? Many Azoreans came to California, and there are still Portuguese dairies in the area. At the time, I thought the Vaz family was Mexican, but what did I know? I remember they were lean and brown, with dark, straight hair. There was a son, Ray, in my third-grade class, who waited for the school bus with me every morning down at the county road, but there was always a kind of tension between us. Once, Ray and his brother yelled at us girls when our dog chased one of their cows into a barbed-wire fence. We weren't used to tensions like that and felt picked on, but Dad explained how dangerous dogs could be around cows and told us not to let it happen again.

I can remember standing in the doorway of the Vaz house sixty years after the Ropers left it—and peering in at a dark, cavernous space, like the inside of a barn. It looked strange to me, but fascinating. Afterward, the adults grumbled that the place wasn't being kept in good repair. Unc was the landlord, probably remembering the Mountain Side of his New England grandparents. This memory arose as I read Belle's and Ella's letters, feeling so critical of their views on Italians and "Spaniards." Half a century later, we hadn't changed all that much—the adults judging everyone by the standards of white New Englanders, and I, still a child, absorbing their ethnic stereotypes, distancing myself, and even fearing the people I saw as "brown."

Can I Love These Relatives?

The racial superiority in my ancestors' everyday thoughts was difficult and uncomfortable. I wanted to scream at them and sometimes did while sitting at my computer. But I also wanted to stay open to their full human-ity. Letter by letter, I began to feel some tenderness for these relatives as I got to know them. Ella's opinions were hard to take, but her boundless curiosity, affection, wide-ranging intellect, and feeling for family spoke to me. Like her, I am a teacher, an aunt without her own children, a stu-dent of family history, a lover of ferns and beautiful vistas. Sophie was less opinionated and felt more easily like a friend—the gardener and manzanita lover, whose letters everyone loved, whose voice I so seldom heard. I found myself talking out loud to Sophie while gardening just up the hill from her house, hoping she would understand why I removed Himalayan blackberry—the very thing she probably planted—now an invasive weed. "Sophie," I would say, "I don't think you understood how some things just take over."

It was harder for me to find common ground with Belle, the wife of a high-status political figure. Her letters home from Japan, where Frank was serving at the U.S. legation, share fascinating insights about living among strangers and the awesome beauty of gardens and ceremony in an imperial Japan just opening to Westerners. But letter after letter con-cerned shopping—prices for shirtwaists, embroidered handkerchiefs, bolts of rare silk, entire sets of fine china. They described plans to pur-chase sumptuously tailored gowns that Americans—getting a taste for imperialism themselves—were wild about. It felt like pure consumerism. But Belle also had a principled democratic streak that appealed to me. She complained of the Boston and New York elite turning up at the U.S. legation, expecting favors. I could appreciate the contradictions in her mind-set—critiquing elitism while at the same time passionate about the trappings of a privileged life. As a young person, I'd admired the very silks and china she brought back to California, treasures that showed up in the homes of every Coombs descendant. I knew I had some of that same mix in myself.

I knew Frank would be problematic. His political views and posi-tioning made him a prominent spokesperson for the attitudes of his time that most disturbed me. As a legislator, his signature issue was excluding Asians from California—helping to pass immigration restrictions and a

code prohibiting state spending for any "product of Mongolian labor."
All the same, he was honored in Japan, where his official letter of cre-
dence named him "Envoy Extraordinary and Minister Plenipotentiary."
Newspapers would later print his fulsome congressional speech defending child labor. These views shock my generation of Coombs descendants, but somehow I was able to stay curious while reading the letters
and ended up liking Frank as a human being. Though he could sound
pompous in his pubic persona, I had to admit that he wrote like an angel
when speaking to those he loved. And hundreds of clippings in Belle's
scrapbooks attest to his remarkable skill with people. Reporters said he
was "a leader and a mediator" and "had an old head on him." Both Republicans and Democrats seemed to appreciate how he balanced diverse
interests and brought out the best in others during seventeen years in the
California State Assembly, with two terms as its speaker. Although his
views and his rise to power as the privileged son of a pioneer made me
uneasy, he had some personal qualities I could respect.

Frank's letters to Belle and her family also touched me. He appreciated her and said so, not just as an ardent young husband but also twenty
years down the road, when he was writing to the family from Japan. And
she did the same. There was love between these people whose views I
questioned—love for each other, love for their children, and love for the
parents and in-laws in their lives. One of the last letters I read opened
my heart to them. It came from Frank in October 1879, less than three
months before their wedding. He wrote it at night, while waiting up with
a sick friend in Napa, listening to the first rains and thinking of a poem
they must have discussed together long before.

This was a love letter, the only one in the stash, but it was more. Frank
told Belle of his joy in receiving an unexpected letter from her, "the first
dawn of happiness for three dismal years . . . memories that seemed dead."
I caught my breath. This was a reconciliation. I kept on reading. "Belle,
the old love which we knew six years ago moves my heart with the same
pulsations that we felt then." Six years? It had seemed a very long engage-
ment, but now it was clear it had been broken by misunderstanding and
estrangement. Now I understood a coded reference to "the loss of F" in

one of Belle's letters. I understood why a friend had written her at such length, describing Frank's father's funeral procession.

The October letter was very long—Frank poured out what he had been feeling all this time, accepting responsibility for his part and expressing his happiness at again being able to love her. Without knowing the details, his words stirred me deeply, and I was thankful to Belle for having saved at least this one real love letter. It was important for me as a descendant to know this part of their story. Without reconciliation, there wouldn't have been a wedding, or a daughter Amy Louise, or a grandson David—who had made my own life possible. The letters in the plastic bin showed a chemistry between Belle and Frank that kept transforming as their lives unfolded—in Napa, in Japan, in Sacramento. Now I was moved by a profound moment at its root. Whatever our differences, I had begun to care about these people in the stiff Victorian collars.

When a friend who'd heard me grumble about racial attitudes in the letters asked what I was feeling from them, I was surprised by my answer. I was feeling love. Despite all our differences and all those years when I'd avoided thinking about them, I now felt a real affection for these people I had come from, something that went beyond their ideologies, worldly status, or beliefs and bound me to them as family. I welcomed this feeling alongside my disappointment in them. My relatives didn't seem to see that the land they enjoyed so much had been killed for; no one acknowledged or even mentioned the people who knew it as ancestral homeland. Instead, the Roper/Coombs letters expressed the mind of their era, filled with racist stereotypes, comfortable with the idea of a "white California" and a tragic willingness to ignore its moral price.

Frank's Novel and Manifest Destiny

They were the favored people—the ones whose bravery and intelligence, good governance and good values were going to make California and the world into a paradise, to bring all resources into their highest and best use. The letters confirmed what I'd sensed from the unspoken messages I'd been raised with. Then I read a scholar's study of race and manifest destiny—the idea that the so-called Anglo-Saxon race was destined to take over from all the "lesser" races of Earth (despite what is known now, that biologically we are all one race). After taking two centuries to mature, the idea reached its heyday nationally in the 1850s—with California statehood and genocide heating up. With little dissent, it had grown from the work of artists, writers, linguists, politicians, and so-called scientists who researched the shape of skulls to determine brain size. Many of them framed the idea in terms that evoke the Nazis of a century later. Most believed that—with or even without violence—the "Anglo-Saxon race" was so superior that its very presence would cause all others to wither away. The older local history books promoted the idea. California Indians were a tragically dying race, but the wonders of Anglo-Saxon culture and development were worth whatever might be lost.

As an educated political figure and leader in the world of ideas, Frank Coombs spoke for this ideology throughout his public life. During a period when he was not in office, he began weaving its themes into a novel about his father. It was the perfect project for someone of his literary and philosophical bent. The unfinished manuscript, a two-inch stack of yellowed paper, is stored in one of our Napa closets. My mother saw historical value in the typescript laced with Frank's handwritten edits—"gleaming" changed to "glistening." She hoped the Bancroft Library—repository of California history at the University of California, Berkeley—would be interested. They were not, but the faded pages are a window into the mind-set that shaped the history we're now facing up to.

Frank makes his father improbably handsome, a blue-eyed youth with a college education and a mission from the president to assess California for annexation—all fictional except the blue eyes. The hero converses at length with a Spanish "Signorita" in an atmospheric old mission. The sun always sets dramatically, the roof is mouldering, and rocks are mossy with age. An aged padre recounts an epic story of Spain bringing civilization to California. But Spanish institutions "have lingered past the grey dawn of their power." Frank's hero ponders "survival of the fittest." One culture after another is displaced by "the fittest" of its time, with our family's own white American culture—the fittest of all—winning out. "We took the west and made of it a glorious civilization. The world is better for it." That was the gist of the novel, and it pretty well sums up what my ancestors thought about the conquest that launched California and the lifestyle we know today.

The hero finds it sad that Indians are no longer working the mission farmlands (after secularization), which he thinks would have refined their natures. Without mission teachings, they are "turned away and wandering . . . a people lapsing into nothingness." Exactly the kind of spontaneous disappearance promised by the theory of Manifest Destiny. The worst is an episode as the hero rides east along what is now Coombsville Road. Near land that would become the Cayetan, he comes upon a scene that sickens me. I share it reluctantly.

The fictional Nathan Coombs rides toward a field enclosed by a stone wall where an ox pulls a rude homemade plow. "Hitched together" alongside the animal are two Indigenous men, described as foul and inhuman. "Goaded by the same master, they mingled their strength in the furrow." Their minds "dulled . . . with no desire but to sleep and drink and eat and grovel in the dirt, where the meaner senses make such toil contentment."

This is not the Frank Coombs I want for an ancestor. Instead of feeling anger or grief at the brutal treatment of other humans, his words demean them further. Frank's racial ideas had come down through the ages, all the way from European Popes declaring the rights of white Christians, superior beings, to take lands and resources from pagan, darker-skinned people. This is how our family—and other Anglo Californians—justified taking the land. It's what got transmitted to the child who became Unc, and what he passed on. In all its brutality, this thought still hovers, not so hidden, in American minds.

The words stare up at me from the page—my own great-grandfather, a respected leader in his time pouring his eloquence into demeaning a conquered people—a people who have actually survived conquest with inspiring resiliency. I'd worked to open my heart to Frank, to find what I could love about him. I'd worked toward understanding, not outrage. I needed a way to engage with him across the generations and all the dissonance.

One night, I lit a candle beside a photo of Frank Coombs from Wikipedia. He'd lived into the 1930s, dying just four years before I was born, so I'd seen many snapshots of him as a wrinkled elder with grandchildren and a grown-up Unc. In this portrait, he was young—perhaps in his early days as a legislator a few years after his marriage. I looked deeply into his face, turned slightly to the right, dark eyes sparkling with what I took to be intelligence, curiosity, maybe even a willingness to listen. In this face I could see his mother—her own dark eyes and the six generations of conquistadores in Taos, some with mestizo wives. It had not struck me until this moment, but Frank was one quarter Mexican. (Indeed, Wikipedia uses the same photo on its page on Latino members of Congress.) How had he been so comfortable with the Manifest Destiny doctrine? These ideas had led white Americans of his times to taunt Mexicans as "mongrel." I could see Frank's fine education—philosophers and poets along with history and law—his well-trained mind. I could see enslavers on both sides of his family. And I could also see human kindness. Something in this face reminded me of those dear letters Frank had written to his in-laws, to Aunt Ella, how deeply he seemed to care about Belle and his children, those turns of phrase in his letters to family that I had admired.

Seeing so many sides of this man made me hope he could understand my distress. Could I tell him how it hurt to hear his degrading words? Our zeitgeist had changed in three generations; many now repudiate the arrogance of Manifest Destiny, though it still shapes our laws and institutions, the systems we live by. My generation thinks we're free of the hatefulness, though many white Americans still hold the root idea—that we are "better than" and it's our destiny to save the world. I can see now that I inherited a subtle sense of specialness, reinforced by the idea of predestination in Presbyterian Sunday school—that certain people are God's elect, chosen for salvation. Even now I catch myself thinking this way, assuming I'm right without checking.

It's helped to have friends who are not part of white supremacy—a blessing I wish I could share with Frank. If only he could meet the wise and eloquent Corrina Gould from the Shellmound Walks—the one who urged us all to honor our ancestors. Some of Corrina's ancestors actually came from a Patwin village in Napa. One of those men pulling the plow could have been her great-grandfather. Frank's ideas had continued to create real harm for her people. I hope my great-grandfather would be able to understand this now.

Keeping the Heart Open

It wasn't easy to honor this generation of ancestors. I kept thinking of the iconic painting by John Gast in 1872—the year the Modoc War began and white Californians complained of the "Chinese menace." Frank and Belle were studying in Massachusetts, forming their ideas of the world and courting. The painting shows a tall, ivory-skinned woman with red-blond hair entwined in gauzy white garments that barely cover her. She is floating westward like a gigantic Greek goddess across open grassy plains above tiny covered wagons, stagecoaches, and trains trailing the smoke that would lead to climate change and wildfires. Sturdy "white" pioneers trudge underfoot like tiny toy soldiers. Fences and telegraph lines spring up behind. And far ahead, in the shadowy part of the painting, where her light has not yet reached, a small band of bent and tired-looking Indigenous refugees flee with goods and children bundled onto a travois. No acknowledgement of the village burnings and scalpings taking place in California at that time or the massacres that would continue for another twenty years. *American Progress* was the visual for Manifest Destiny and helped set the tone for settlement of the Cayetan. Its vision filled the mind of the Ropers, the Coombses, and their white contemporaries.

The silences of this generation went along with a mix of emotions. I had noticed a free-floating fearfulness in the Cayetan letters. Frequently uneasy about her brother's health, a general strike, or the wrong party winning the election, Ella wrote that fears often "get the better of my reason." Others worried about diseases like measles and typhoid—and there was cause, with little Frankie dying of scarlet fever and my grandmother Amy Louise hanging in the balance for weeks. Even after a century's medical advances, health threats still loom very real, as do our fears about climate and the other problems we face. But deep underneath is a propensity to fear, a habit of fear that was set long ago. Did this habit grow stronger for the Europeans who came here to colonize? Kathleen Donegan opens her book on early settlement with a scene of rampant fear getting the better of reason in the Jamestown Colony. Brendan Lindsay's *Murder State* shows the fear settlers brought with them across the plains—fear so powerful, they kept their weapons cocked for action and sometimes shot themselves or nearly killed their comrades, imagining them to be Indians creeping in on the night watch. There was trauma behind my ancestors' silences, and to learn about it I would have to look back into the deeper past. Both Ropers and Coombses had settled early in New England. Learning their stories might help me understand what they had brought with them to California.

I'd hoped that, once they were actually living on the Cayetan, my family would have begun to learn from the land itself. An elder had explained to Robin Wall Kimmerer that settlers came "thinking they'd get rich by working on the land. . . . But the land is the one with the power—while they were working on the land, the land was working on them. Teaching them." I didn't see much learning in this generation, but I knew the land had begun to teach me and my mother. It might have taught Sophie if she'd stayed longer. I couldn't honor these ancestors for their views or their actions, but I had touched feelings of love and compassion for them. I could hope that we were all part of an intergenerational learning curve, coming to understand the mind-set we had inherited so that we could transform it. I would look further back and try to keep my heart open.

Picnic Creek in October is overgrown with invasive blackberry now, but the place carries older memories. In my childhood, Unc held parties here at rough wood tables under tall black oaks. His friends drove big cars in through the pasture that's now a vineyard while we kids played in the creek. Probably Unc and Grandmother had played in this same creek while Frank and Belle entertained. This was where I'd found the bottle dump.

And before that? Upstream is a knoll, now overgrown with brush, that Dad called "Buckeye Flat." Stories said it had been a campsite for Coombs relatives who'd returned from prospecting in Alaska and had nowhere to live, but I wondered about an older human presence. When I first heard how Indigenous people came out from their villages for acorn camps in the fall, I knew one of those camps had to have been along this creek. All the big black and valley oaks and running water even in the dry season would have made it ideal. Some say buckeye trees are clues to Native campsites. Their big, round, bitter nuts were the backup if acorn crops failed, so new trees were planted or sprouted up around the camps. Had Buckeye Flat been a Wappo campsite before the Coombses came here?

This was the month when the Native people would have been here, and I was standing on ground spread with fat acorns from the black oaks—dark brown and about an inch long. I'd been wondering which species were the favored ones, and these seemed likely. So many huge black oaks grew here at the base of the steep hill. Then I walked down to a big valley oak in what was now the vineyard. I'd read that the Patwin people of the Central Valley had loved these acorns. This tree, too, was having a mast year—its acorns an appealing glossy bronze color, plump, and even longer than the others. To me, they said *food*.

As I crossed the great circle of fallen nuts, stooping over the shiny mass to gather a few, I thought of what I knew about valley oaks. My relatives had another name for them. Dad and Unc—and probably the whole Coombs clan—had called them "mush oaks." It sounded disparaging. Mush oak made poor firewood, did not burn with so hot a flame. I'd assumed the name was about mushy wood. But now I thought, Mush . . . Maybe the old-timers called them mush oaks because local Native people were still harvesting them for acorn mush. Whoever taught Unc that term probably knew Indians. And maybe everyone in the valley—when Unc was a boy—had observed an Indian preference for the nuts of the mush oak. Maybe. I didn't know for sure.

I stood there marveling at how insight can unfold when the thinking mind lets go. This new way of seeing the mush oak answered more than my question about preferences. Whatever the right answer, at last I'd reached into the minds of early settlers in Napa County—my own silent kin—and found a thought about the First People that they hadn't shaped into the official narrative or a racist meme. Maybe the Wappo and very likely the Patwin, who still lived in the southern part of the valley back then, came out in the fall to harvest these particular acorns. It would have been a normal thing to see them gathering under the "mush oaks." This was the kind of acknowledgment that was missing from Unc's stories, the kind I hadn't been able to find in the letters. The creek, the trees, the acorns themselves had given me a story about my own ancestors that I could trust.

CHAPTER 9

Healing the Deeper Past

This map of New England, published in 1676, reflects settler colonialism: English place names have been assigned to Indigenous land and few references are made to the people already living there. Map courtesy of the Mapping Boston Collection at the Boston Public Library.

When trauma is not dealt with in previous generations,
it has to be dealt with in subsequent generations.

  —EDUARDO DURAN, *HEALING THE SOUL WOUND*

It is a hidden and silent grief barely visible, pushed aside
and buried layer upon layer by the cultural and personal
justifications for survival.

  —FRED GUSTAFSON, *DANCING BETWEEN TWO WORLDS*

The silences in ourselves and our families are like scar
tissue over our wounds.

  —LARRY WARD, *AMERICA'S RACIAL KARMA*

Where the Silences Came From

AUGUST 2015. Today in the dry California heat I love so much, I'm out in the orchard doing summer pruning. I'm still upset with the generation of ancestors who wouldn't acknowledge the horror that made California a white person's state, but in the house I have a rare copy of Aunt Ella's book on Roper family history, which shows the story of our silence going much further back than California.

Maybe my mind isn't really on what I'm doing, because all of a sudden there's a crash and I'm on the ground, tangled up with a heavily loaded trash bin, barely conscious and spurting blood from my forehead. It's a concussion that will take me to the emergency room and put me out of commission for weeks with complex symptoms that will return years later as I am editing this chapter. My family's experience with the many-sided horror of genocide and our silence about it stretch back beyond California for another two hundred years on this continent. As I write about that story, I am breaking a pattern of silence that has held for twelve generations.

What I'd learned about the California Coombses and Ropers had not answered my questions. The answers lay further back in our story on this continent—both my family's and the nation's. This wasn't just about my own family and a special piece of land in the Napa Valley. I now saw a much larger set of issues than I'd set out to trace. What unfolded in California had begun long before on the other side of the country.. I had lived forty years in New England without realizing how deeply my own family history there connected me with the founding wounds of our country. My ancestors' silences didn't start in Napa; their mind-set had come west with them. Something much earlier had hardened their hearts to the genocide happening in California when they arrived and had woven silence into our identity.

A quick look showed that both Ropers and Coombses had been on this continent since the earliest colonial presence. Both branches of the family had come with seventeenth-century English religious dissenters—

Puritans and Pilgrims. Despite their distrust of Catholicism, the ideas of the Popes of previous centuries still held sway with them, elevating all Christians above the "savages" of Indigenous religions and entitling them to claim Indigenous land and labor as their own. The Ropers had come with the Puritans—arriving in 1637, seven years after the founding of the Massachusetts Bay Colony during its first war with the Native population. The Coombses had come on the *Mayflower* in 1620.

Some Americans would be proud of such a lineage, but I was deeply troubled. For years I'd felt anger at the arrogance of our country's founding on another people's land and a vague sense of shame that I might be directly connected with it. Now it was clear that my family had been part of settler colonialism from the very beginning. It was in our blood. No wonder my relatives ignored genocide in California. They had been present at its introduction to the continent. Generations earlier they had learned to remain silent.

Their story was our national story, the key to understanding the mindset that had accepted extermination of Indigenous peoples from the start and brought that idea across the country to California. I wanted to know the details, to find what had warped our sensibilities, our true humanity—so we could acknowledge, grieve, change, and make amends. And even though I couldn't be proud of our history, I hoped for a way to honor my ancestors as my friends on the Shellmound Peace Walks had urged. I would find that the colonizing process was hard on the soul, but I knew that somewhere very far back in time–before Christianity and empire in Europe—our own roots were indigenous. We, too, had likely believed, as does Malidoma Somé, that ancestors want us to undo the harm they caused and will even assist us. We had forgotten that teaching, but it was not too late to work toward healing. My family's history could illuminate the trouble and perhaps contribute to a change of consciousness. My first task was to uncover that history.

"Great Sufferers"

I started with the Coombses as the earliest arrivals. The same genealogist who had traced our Lucero ancestry placed Nathan Coombs's birth in

1826 in the town of Middleborough, Massachusetts, just inland from Plymouth, where the *Mayflower* had finally landed, locally considered part of Cape Cod. This matched family stories of early Coombses on the Cape. I tried the internet. Other amateurs were tracing the name in New England, finding information that might or might not be accurate. I screened out wild speculation, but I wasn't trying for accuracy. More than my precise bloodline, I was after the mind-set of the times, my heritage line, the cultural and psychic baggage our people had brought to California and passed on.

A Coombs family had moved to Middleborough not long after the *Mayflower* arrived. Franklin Coombs, son of a John Coombs, who'd married Sarah, daughter of *Mayflower* passenger Degory Priest. As Plymouth Colony grew and settlers claimed more land—logging forests and letting cattle trample Wampanoag cornfields—Franklin Coombs opened a hotel and drinking establishment (as Nathan did later in Napa). He was mustered to fight in King Philip's War in 1676 to wrest more land from the First People. Here was a possible lineage for Nathan, though sources said the Middleborough line had no sons to pass down the name. No one on the internet seemed to realize the Coombs name had reached the Indigenous population—where Native friends told me it was "a Wampanoag name." The Coombs/Middleborough scenario was inconclusive.

Then I found a more compelling version of our lineage in genealogical research done by distant relative Joanne Rigdon Williams in the 1970s. She traced us to a Frenchman who'd changed his name from Comeau to Coombs and settled in Maine, then was displaced to Cape Cod during King Philip's War. Through Nathan's mother, Abigail Hinckley, Williams documents our descent from three men who signed the Mayflower Compact—John Howland, John Tilley, and Thomas Rogers. Looking further into writings about the *Mayflower*, I found that Thomas Rogers—likely descended from "one of the first English martyrs" in 1555—had brought his teenage son, Joseph. John Tilley had brought his wife, Joan, and daughter Elizabeth. In this version of our history, six people on the *Mayflower* were my direct blood relations.

One way or the other, our family had shared the scarring experiences of the Plymouth settlement, one of the most heavily mythologized episodes in our national history. Most Americans know it as a story of heroic "suffering Pilgrims" but don't realize the traumatic backstory. That shipload of Europeans anchored in a land where 90 percent of the Indigenous people had been wiped out by a four-year pandemic of European disease. It was a terrible time of death all round. Half the Pilgrims' own number died of other illnesses during the long winter as the *Mayflower* lay anchored in Plymouth Harbor. Rogers was one who died, along with Tilley, his wife, and a brother and sister-in law—many deaths for our family. But a younger generation survived—Tilley's daughter Elizabeth, who later married John Howland, and Rogers's son Joseph.

Scholars now say the colony's leaders worked to turn the grim story into a narrative of triumph and resilience—what Abenaki writer Lisa Brooks calls a "replacement narrative," leaving out the messiness, psychological trauma, and brutality toward the First People. Notably, they proclaimed that the Christian God had favored their settlement by clearing the land for them. My parents' bedroom in Napa still holds my sister Susan's sweet childhood drawing of Pilgrims and Indians enjoying the first Thanksgiving meal together. Nowadays, Native oral tradition and new scholarship tell us that meal was fraught with guns and tensions as two cultures with different worldviews came together, one of which would soon subdue the other.

Literary scholar Kathleen Donegan looks at the "traumatic origins of colonial identity" in her stunning book *Seasons of Misery,* which is about Plymouth and other early British colonies. She shows these early settlements as "brutal places characterized by disease, death, factions, violence, starvation, ignorance, and serial abandonment," where settler suffering led to "mental ruptures" and unthinkably violent actions against both First People and fellow settlers. Infanticide and wife eating (neither in Plymouth) were the most shocking. Settlement, she says, was really "unsettlement," a breaking down of whatever social identity people had brought with them from Europe.

The story she tells of Plymouth starts with a fearful, sea-weary *Mayflower* party exploring pandemic-swept areas of what we now know was Wampanoag land. Their voyage had been delayed, it was nearly winter, and they were not prepared for the scenes of death onshore, where the bodies of an entire village might lie unburied, unsanctified. They found abandoned homes, buried caches of grain, and one fresh grave after another. At first, the Pilgrims respected the graves, but then they opened one and removed the ceremonial objects interred with the body. They stole Indian corn from caches. Gleaming ears of blue, rose, and gold—I have seen this corn myself, because it is still grown by a few people in New England. It was beautiful and they needed food. That was November 1620, so eating the stolen corn may have been their first Thanksgiving.

Arriving in Plymouth Harbor too late to build or plant, the Pilgrims spent a terrible winter of sickness and hunger on their ship. Not only were the living "scarce able to bury the dead," as William Bradford recounted, but their fear of attack was so great that they propped dying friends against logs with guns to simulate a guard. Donegan says Bradford left out details that didn't fit his nation-building message—including the impulsive killing of nearby Indians, followed by barbaric impaling of a Native head, which would greet visitors to Plymouth for years afterward.

How did those experiences shape the mentality of early settlers, including my relatives, who'd watched shipmates and beloved parents die that first winter? The family of John Coombs and Sarah Priest? Loved ones dead, the decayed head of an "enemy" above the town gates, stories of starvation, epidemics, corpses, and burials still alive in collective memory, though likely not talked about. John Coombs—whether my blood ancestor or not—was often on the records for drunkenness and not repaying his debts. Did his difficulties stem from the traumatized mind of the times? Does that mind somehow enter the bloodstream and get passed down to descendants? Geneticists now say it is likely.

Fast-forward two hundred years. Through brutal wars, this colony and others in New England expanded into Wampanoag lands, transformed the landscape, and prospered. But what about Nathan Coombs, who carried my lineage to California? Was he affected by the "unsettlement" of his people's early moments on the continent? Did he still carry some of their confusion and pain as a boy walking the streets of Middleborough? Apparently, his family still yearned for land, and their struggles moving west by prairie schooner in 1835 would add to his load. The Coombses settled in Blue Grass, Iowa, west of the Mississippi, on land taken from the Sauk and Meskwaki, the Oceti Sakowin, and the Kickapoo. There they faced a major drought as they tried to farm. Some say the big river itself dried up. A newspaper article in Williams's genealogy says they had to dig up their own seed potatoes and chew the inner bark of elm trees to stay alive. "The Coombs family were great sufferers." The malnutrition and disease that came with this drought echoed their *Mayflower* ancestors' experience. Twelve-year-old Nathan's father died in the winter of 1838, and "the mother rose from a sickbed to wash his shroud." Did losing his father to starvation activate ancestral trauma? Four years later, as his mother was about to remarry, Nathan would leave home on his own with the Lansford Hastings party, crossing the plains on the Oregon Trail, then heading south to California. What ancestral burdens did this young man carry west with him?

Though it didn't absolve him, I felt less critical when I saw the pattern of trauma Nathan had inherited from earlier times. I had no sympathy for the man who brought Manifest Destiny to California, gun-in-hand with the Hastings party—for the Bear Flagger, land speculator, water seller, and likely user of unfree Native labor. But in the larger arc of his ancestry—our unfolding collective narrative—I could see the Coombs "sufferer" among the forces that shaped him. His people were not the Pilgrims I had learned about in school—simple, good people who endured hardship and went on to create a beautiful, just country. That was the nation-building version. The true story was likely closer to Donegan's—a nightmarish, button-your-lips suffering that warped the mind, closing it to compassion for other humans and encouraging brutality against perceived enemies and the Earth itself. These ancestors struggled with a punishing legacy that still afflicts us. Maybe it showed in Nathan's face, in that one photograph I had seen of him. I was beginning to feel compassion and to wish for Nathan's healing if it were possible.

January 2014. All my years living in New England, I yearned for the green refuge of a California winter, for the ferns and mosses of Unc's hill. It was a joy to return, but there is deep reluctance climbing that hill now. It's more than my aging legs. The hillside is suffering, dry and gray in what should be a time of lush rains. This is drought—the third worst on record. And the first must have been that bad year of 1843, when Nathan Coombs arrived in California. No family stories say so, but 1843 was a drought year. A year of almost no rain, with Yankee settlers filtering in to claim the land.

The 2014 drought seemed to let up when early rain touched the hills with green, but that green faded quickly. Every plant and animal must be in stress now. It's hard to acknowledge what is happening as the climate wrenches into the new patterns my ancestors brought here. But extreme weather has been the norm in California—life-forms have genetic memory of surviving dry, difficult periods. Even the delicate white wildflowers we call milkmaids that fill the woods in early December. This year, they're only two inches tall. But they are here, setting seed for their species to continue.

I remind myself that I returned to California to be with the crisis, not to cower in the house or water the lawn. I'm here to witness all of it—not just pretty green things and rushing water and wildflowers, but sometimes a live oak with all its leaves suddenly brown, unable to cope. I want to embrace the earth and our history here in all its contradictions, to listen for wisdom and guidance. I will keep walking that hillside. I will keep listening and writing.

Six Generations of War

The Ropers' story, too, led back to traumatic times, and, again, an earlier relative had done the groundwork. Aunt Ella had a deep interest in her family's hardships. In 1904, she published a book about Roper history, with more detail on the Lancaster story than she'd mentioned in the letters. When I read it, I realized that the painful story I already knew was just one episode in a longer cascade of disaster. Ella's book was a family genealogy that included other details meticulously gathered from old New England records. With the help of modern scholarship, I could see that this branch of my family, too, had experienced radical "unsettling."

The Ropers did not have to face the raw shock of death and derangement that had met the *Mayflower* people. The Massachusetts Bay Colony, founded ten years after Plymouth's settlement, had been operating seven years when my family arrived. Food sources, a government, and social networks were in place. A whole family of Ropers—father and mother, sons and grandchildren—had sailed together for Boston. I wondered whether some suffering had brought them to this decision. Ella said their ship was one of the last before the British tightened restrictions on dissenters emigrating, so I thought maybe they'd fled trouble. Had they been taunted for religious views or experienced economic hardship, discrimination, a lack of safety? I had no way of knowing for sure.

During the 1630s, English dissenters were brutally punished during the repression under Charles I, who dissolved Parliament, imposed taxes, and restricted nonconformist religious practices. But Puritans were not a small minority in England and would soon control the government. Scholar Richard Slotkin says they were "tendentious and persecuted," part of "a rising, ambitious, new middle class." Many came to the colonies to find greater prosperity. Ella mentions that the Ropers shipped their own furniture from England, so I figured the seven of them were likely not fleeing poverty. Most Puritans who came to the colonies were people of means and education, sharing the Protestant belief in individualism and a religion that sought freedom from some restrictions while imposing others. For them, owning land was a sign of spiritual worth.

When the Ropers arrived in 1637, civil turmoil rocked the new colony. Boston citizens focused on the sensational trial of Anne Hutchinson. Her teachings—that human emotions could lead directly to spiritual insight—undermined the authorities, which some said threatened the very survival of the colony. I can only guess what my relatives thought. And English settlers couldn't keep up with the work needed to make the land productive in the ways they wanted. The very next year, the first vessel carrying enslaved Africans would land in Boston Harbor. Already, many New England households depended on Native labor that was not really free. None of this surfaced in Ella's account, but Margaret Newell's recent study, *Brethren by Nature,* says unfree labor was standard practice in this colony that saw itself holding the vision for a better world.

And the colony was already at war with the First People. The year before, it had begun hostilities against the Pequots of southern New England—in large part, some historians think, to acquire captive labor. I

didn't learn about the Pequot War until I was in my fifties and read about
its decisive event in *A People's History of the United States*. The Pequot
Massacre of 1637—the very year the Ropers arrived—has haunted me
ever since. In one terrible night, Puritans burned an entire sleeping village
on the Mystic River in what is now Connecticut—Pequot elders, women,
and children. It was hard to take in such brutality, but the worst was how
Puritan leaders gloated and praised God that terror could so afflict the
enemy, thanking Him for destroying five hundred souls at once. It was
a template for the extermination of villages in California two hundred
years later and a violent action I fear still lurks as a possibility in our
collective mind.

About the time of that massacre, the newly arrived Ropers were building a small home of sticks, clay, and rounded stones—crowded close to
others for protection in the new town of Dedham, near Boston. Though
distant from the action, they surely felt the war's influence. Colonial life
was discouraging, in any case; a historian says one out of six returned to
England. Later, the Ropers moved to Lancaster, a frontier settlement further inland on Nipmuc land. The colony had agreements with the Nipmuc
to let settlers farm, but it hadn't kept its side of the bargain, so tensions
were rising and fearful families mobilized against attack in communal
garrisons. The Pequot War had ended, but more wars with Indian combatants would follow for another hundred years. The next one, known as
King Philip's War, engaged a huge regional confederacy that fought the
colonizers with determination. "King Philip" was the settlers' name for
Wampanoag sachem, Metacom, whose kinship network reached from
Cape Cod to Boston and beyond.

It was in Lancaster in the cold of February 1676—the fatal attack Ella
mentioned in the letters, affecting four generations of Ropers. Ephraim
Roper—born in the early years in Dedham—lost his wife, Priscilla, and
their only child in a fiery assault on a communal garrison. Many were
killed or taken captive, but Ephraim escaped into the forest. Other survivors, fearful and destitute, called on the colonial government to evacuate
them in carts through winter woods that were nearly impassable. The day
it was to happen, Ephraim's father, John—who'd emigrated from England

as a younger man—was also killed by Indians. Only two elderly Roper widows were left to evacuate, a "grievous sight," Ella imagined. Two entire younger generations—except for Ephraim himself—had been totally wiped out. But this was only the beginning for the Ropers.

Fresh from his terrible loss, Ephraim fled through the woods to join troops searching for Metacom, moving through a landscape that the colonial mind did not understand. In a new study, Abenaki scholar Lisa Brooks, who has walked much of the land herself, shows how Indigenous peoples' understanding of hills, swamps, and vegetation gave comfort and refuge, where the English perceived only fearful wilderness. She also explains how in their version of warfare Indigenous "protectors" sought to rebalance what had gone wrong with their land, targeting barns and other built symbols of colonization, "actively invoking chaos" to terrify and confuse their adversaries, not wipe them out. On the other hand, as the war progressed, colonial forces developed a clear aim to exterminate—to empty the land for settlement, leading to horrendous massacres like one against Nipmuc elders and women at Turner's Falls, not far from Lancaster. From Ella's sparse detail it appears that Ephraim Roper joined Turner and became part of this terrible action. Historian Jill Lepore says this war fueled extraordinary settler brutality—English troops practiced such scalping, torture, murder, and dismemberment of their enemies, even of noncombatants, that colonists feared they would lose their identity as "civilized" people.

Ephraim Roper had fled from his own unthinkable loss into a world of extreme violence. Still immersed in its toxicity, he was in Concord later that year when off-duty troops committed what Ella called "an atrocious murder," killing "three squaws and three children" as they picked huckleberries. Today, we would call it a hate crime. Scholars tell us these were families of Nipmuc Christian converts who'd risked their lives scouting for the English. Ella said an "even-handed" court convicted and hanged two of the soldiers along with a Nipmuc combatant. Brooks says the gallows were set up on the Boston Common and included three Christian Indians falsely enticed into applying for amnesty. A year later, Ephraim married Hannah Goble, the widow of one of the two soldiers.

Amid so many atrocities, the trauma was clearly multiplying. The Roper family broken, young ones and elders lost to violence. The young father seeking retaliation in a toxic environment. I thought of the persistent trauma that follows today's troops in the Middle East, trauma that affects all who experience violence—victims and perpetrators—and can be passed to their children either genetically or through wounded behavior. I wondered whether my ancestors and those around them had taken the time to care for the trauma they experienced, to grieve, to release its hold on them and future generations. Had Hannah and Ephraim grieved their terrible losses? The two went on to have ten children of their own, nine girls and one boy to carry the Roper name—another Ephraim. All would figure in a second round of violence and loss.

After the war, Ephraim and his new family returned to Lancaster, still a border town with multifamily garrisons for protection. Over the next century, the colony would experience at least six more wars with European names, including King William's, Queen Anne's, King George's, as England, France, and Spain vied for power, each with Native "allies" to fight its rivals. Outlying Lancaster remained a target, and the colonial government prevented relocation. Ella says one Lancaster woman committed suicide in apparent despair. By the mid-1690s, settlers were again in a state of terror—torn between taking shelter in the garrisons and working in the fields to grow food for survival.

Then in 1697, on a fatal September 11, it happened again. The entire Roper clan—Ephraim's second family, with all their children—were in the fields, harvesting wheat and Indian corn, when a fierce attack came. This time, Ephraim, survivor of 1676, was killed, along with Hannah and at least one of their three daughters. Ephraim's only son—ten years old, also named Ephraim—saw it all but was captured and carried off to Canada. For the second time, nearly all the Ropers were wiped out. Native captives in this war were sold to settlers or in the Atlantic slave trade. But the boy Ephraim survived with tribes in Canada and two years later returned. All his relatives gone, he lived as an orphan before marrying in 1713.

Settling nearby, Ephraim worked as a sentinel, using skills, Ella speculated, that he had learned in captivity. But Ephraim died in an "accident" in the woods that Ella could not explain. One of his sons—a third Ephraim—returned from a colonial war in the West Indies to build his own house near Lancaster, again using the fortifying techniques of his grandfather and great-grandfather because hostilities continued—war after war with the European powers and tribal people allying to regain their land. At one point, the colonial government offered hundred-pound bounties for Indian scalps.

At last came the war we know as the War of Independence. The third Ephraim's family sent ten sons to that war, where they likely fought Indians said to be British allies. A modern scholar reading New England farm boys' letters home explains how George Washington's campaigns destroyed entire Iroquois towns, along with crops that were food for the next winter (an exceptionally brutal one). The ten Roper sons fought for independence, but the roots of that war were more complex. Like earlier wars, it aimed to clear the land for settlement. Consciously or not, the young patriots fought for extermination, genocide as we now know it. And that must have been hard on the soul. One of those ten Roper boys in the Revolutionary forces was father to a fourth Ephraim, who fathered the generation I knew from the letters—Ella and her brother Foster, the man with bad asthma who built the first house on Coombs land in California. He was the eighth generation of Ropers on the continent. Six had experienced wars of conquest.

I need the wisdom of the deep past, so one morning I call for ancestors—any who will speak to me. I'm amazed that someone comes, a woman bent over under blankets and cloths, an elder. I can feel her aches and pains, though I don't recognize her. Maybe she escaped the burning Pequot Village, but something tells me she is from Northern California, maybe a relative of the Coombs's "servant," Nancy. I'm awed and honored that she will speak to me.

Gasping, spitting out the words, she uses my language. "Do you realize what your people did in our village—shot the men they called 'bucks,' rounded up the others, pinching the younger women and laughing loudly." She speaks to the California history I'd read the night before. "You could smell the whiskey and the sweat on them. They took my daughter. Ripped her children away as they dragged her off—knife to throat—and threw her onto a horse. I could only crouch in the shadows, hidden among corpses and severed limbs. They cut the scalps from my son and my nephews, calling out to one another about how much bounty money they could collect for the body parts. When they were gone, I made my way to the creek, washed myself, and prayed for guidance.

"Here's what I say to you: Do not shy away from telling the story, but you must also do the grieving. Acknowledgment alone will not bring healing to your people or mine. You will need to give something up. You will need ceremony. In the woods that night, near the creek, I found a way to make an offering and grieve—you must do this, too."

Trauma and the Sin of Grief

As Jill Lepore explains in *The Name of War,* Americans in Ella's time had started to look back at colonial wars against the Indians as sad and tragic. White people had taken Native land for what was supposed to be a higher purpose and dealt with their feelings by romanticizing the victims. Ella was tuned to her times and also to our founding mythology and its theme of settler suffering. But I read a deeper kind of suffering into her story, an ongoing psychic suffering. Generations of Roper settlers had lived through extraordinary violence and fear that cut at their souls, not to mention the qualms they must have had about their own roles. Not just one traumatic Indian attack, not just a second. Two entire households wiped out and seven wars during our first six generations on the continent, with all the trauma wars carry at every level of involvement. What does it do to the soul to be a combatant in a war of extermination? For years, I'd thought about how devastating these wars of conquest had been for the Indigenous psyche. Now I could see they must have taken a deep toll on the colonizers, too.

These wars built on what Kathleen Donegan had pointed out in the initial colonial experience—chaos and catastrophe turning inward, weakening principles, inviting "mental ruptures" and transforming settler suffering to "settler violence." Somatic therapist Resmaa Menakem calls it "dirty pain," the unexpressed kind that goes underground, silent or denied, then gets blown on to others in anger or passed along as family amnesia. He says we can heal it, even now. Unresolved combatants' trauma was not unique to my family. It was the story of America's founders, the ones who inspired our nation's current path.

Looking back from the twenty-first century, where we now study war and trauma, I had questions that wouldn't have occurred to Ella. How did our relatives handle their pain? Were they able to grieve, for instance? The first Ephraim, who lost his wife and children, then fled to the woods and moved so quickly to retaliation? As a first-generation American, a Puritan and a male who likely believed strong emotions were weakness, what did he do with his feelings? Did they affect his second family of children? And the son who knew him only ten years—the second Ephraim—who saw parents and sister slaughtered in 1697 and had no one left to care for him when he returned from captivity? Ella called him the "slender thread" that ties us to this history. How did he carry the burden of catastrophe, the emotions of loss? Richard Slotkin says captive children often came home with minds "permanently impaired"—like Mercy Short, whose psychotic outbursts fed the panic of the Salem witch trials. With other child captives, my ancestor Ephraim may have lived in what Slotkin calls a "dense accretion of residual horror." Was there any healing in his lifetime, or had his mysterious death in the woods been his only release from it?

And Roper combatants—from the first Ephraim on down to the ten sons in the Revolutionary War—were any of them able to grieve or heal the deep wounds of those who kill other humans? Might any of them have questioned the policy to exterminate? Had they even been conscious of it amid the propaganda of war?

Was their religion any help? I suspected that Puritans—who distrusted emotions and rejoiced when five hundred Pequot souls burned to death in one night—would not have had practices to transform and heal the pain of grief, much less that of combatants. What I found was much more disturbing. The Puritan faith actually forbade grief. Church fathers considered it sinful and censured all grieving, including wailing and weeping—the honest expression of loss practiced in so many cultures. Literary scholar Mitchell Breitwieser studies mourning among them and says they saw grief as "poisonous," not among the "permissible feelings." Instead, he says, the faithful were to "sublimate mourning, to block and then redirect its vigor." A child's death was a teaching from God. The bereaved were to thank God for chastising them or to acknowledge that their own wickedness was to blame. To grieve or mourn in any way—even to feel the emotions—was to break covenant and endanger the entire colony.

Breitwieser analyzes the captivity narrative written by Mary Rowlandson, who was carried off with her infant daughter from the same burning garrison that destroyed the first Ephraim's family. When her daughter died on the ensuing journey, Mary wondered if God had taken her baby because she herself had enjoyed too much pleasure. She wrestled with impermissible feelings of sadness and worried they might be a sign of "Indianness" taking over her soul. A pastor's wife, a woman whose book was vetted by Puritan leaders, Mary may have been more devout than the Ropers. Ella gave no clue how long Puritanism remained a force in the family. But the Rowlandson book shows the cultural milieu all shared in this settler community. In prohibiting grief, their culture left them no way to heal from the trauma they experienced as colonizers—so the pain sat there accumulating.

In the early 1990s—long before I knew I had family in King Philip's War—I joined what is now an annual ceremony to remember the brutal treatment of an entire town of "praying Indians" in that war. Until then, I had never heard this piece of our history, though I'd lived for years along the Charles River, which had been their trail of tears.

A long day's paddle upstream from Boston, now a quick drive on the freeway, there had been a village especially for Indian people converted to Christianity. It was a project of John Eliot, who saw sharing the Gospel as central to Puritan settlement, though he was not in the majority. Others saw the praying towns as containment strategies. Historians say the Nipmucs in this village—including some from the Lancaster area—had chosen to assimilate and were loyal to the colonists. Some risked their lives taking sides against their own people as the war developed. Even so, the colonial government feared them and organized their removal downriver on barges to a desolate island in Boston Harbor. They could opt for being exported to slavery in the Caribbean. Arriving on Deer Island in shackles in October 1675, the people found no game or other food and no shelter from the intense winter. At least half froze or starved to death as the war raged on and were buried on the island in mass graves.

The worst suffering would have been at the icy peak of winter—the very time my own kin met their deaths by fire in Lancaster. I knew only half the story when I joined the ceremony—standing in prayer at South Natick, watching Penobscot, Passamoquoddy, Nipmuc, and Wampanoag paddlers come down the wooded parts of the river, and standing in circle on the island itself as the sun set beyond the Boston skyline. After the colonial period, Deer Island continued to be a place of suffering—an internment camp for starving Irish refugees from the potato famine, then a prison into the 1980s. The ceremony I'd joined was organized by descendants of tribes in the 1676 confederacy to contest a huge state-of-the-art sewage plant built on the very place of their peoples' mass graves.

I stood in those prayer circles with a heart full of sadness and shame for the harm at the very founding of my country, appalled at the mind-set that could allow such atrocity. If I could stand there again with what I know now about my own people, my grief would have more layers. Grief for the Nipmuc families—betrayed by my Puritan ancestors in the brutal winds of winter. Grief for my own kin—their psychic wounds as combatants and their own losses. Would I be able to feel just the grief—not the right or the wrong, the blame and the retaliation, not the shame—just the pure grief?

What struck me in those first generations of Ropers was a huge lump of what author and shaman Martín Prechtel calls "deferred" or "unmetabolized" grief. Some was for parents or children lost in the Indian wars. Some was that more complicated grief that piled up with every burned Pequot village, or murdered set of "squaws," or inkling of what it meant to be part of a war of extermination. Some was simply for the dailiness of hardship, when crops were destroyed or the New England winter was unkind, the colonial government unresponsive. Six generations of my family had lived intimately with the wars of colonization. From the seventh generation on (I am the twelfth), the direct violence of that past was behind us but still carried invisibly inside.

In the eighth generation, descendants of those Ephraims had come to California, arriving in 1883—just after the most flagrant period of the California genocide. I had found no mention in their letters of the violence that had made their new home possible. No sense of its horror. But the earlier history explained their silence. With their colonial identities and backlog of suppressed pain, it would have been difficult for the Ropers to open their hearts to a colonized people's suffering. The story of genocide I had wanted them to acknowledge would have touched a wound of their own that they had likely tried to bury or numb.

What was just ending in California when they arrived replayed their own history—but speeded up and twisted. Back east, there had been two hundred years of warfare, but here, Europeans like themselves had acted quickly, with the preemption that would mark many future American wars. Here in California, the fiery attacks on villages, the capturing and enslavement, all came from white Americans like themselves. In twenty short years, my family's fellow countrymen had quickly reenacted the long story of colonial violence their forbearers had lived out on the East Coast. With all the unhealed grief I could now see in my ancestors, silence—not looking at the truth—must have been all they could manage. I could see how it had become the emotional survival mode for white people all over the continent. I could see that the wound was raw—"dirty pain." It had been left to future generations to heal.

How to Honor These Ancestors?

Ella introduced her book with a kind of time travel, inviting all Roper descendants to join her in the small Dedham home of Grandfather and Grandmother Roper, newly arrived in 1637. She invited us to "come with loving reverence, for they are our very own . . . with tender sympathy, for they suffered sorely." Ella's words touched me despite our different perspectives on the story. Somehow, I was able to put aside my preconceptions and listen to this distant aunt closely enough to sense a suffering far more complex than the one she likely had in mind. I felt the reverence she urged because I was starting to understand how deeply my entire family had been unsettled by our history. Traumatic experiences as colonizers had separated them from their best selves as human beings. Instead of blaming them for their legacy of unhealed trauma, grief, and silence, I now saw their lives as part of a much larger drama. If they could be healed, it could help to transform what was stuck in our country. I remembered Malidoma Somé's teaching that, once they pass over, ancestors can see the harm they caused and are eager to help us right it. We were in this together. I began to see these ancestors with love.

It amazed me that Ella, back in 1904—by no means sharing my understanding of the story—had been the means of passing insight on to my generation. Ella remained the woman I had come to know in her letters—the one who disdained mixed marriage, made fun of Black servants, and appalled me with her venom about the table manners of farmworkers. Yet I was touched by her way of telling our story. She didn't demonize Indians—hadn't gone over to hate as other family historians might have done. She didn't pontificate. She had diligently sought the kind of information that, a century later, would help to clarify the spiritual burden our ancestors carried—and that she also must have carried. As Deborah Miranda had said about white people in her memoir of tribal survival from the California genocide, "the beginning of awareness is good to see." And I could see awareness beginning in Ella. She had passed information down the generations so that we would be able to build on that awareness. With all our differences, Ella now emerged as a kind of midwife to the work of intergenerational healing—helping with her own level of insight from more than a hundred years ago.

I wondered about all those others in the many generations of Ropers and Coombses on the continent—so many human beings whose stories were not told in the genealogies. Especially the women, whose lives left so little mark on those documents. What ancestors of mine had questioned the colonial mind-set in their own small ways or contributed to our evolving consciousness? How many, deep in their hearts, had objected to the wars? How many were shushed for speaking up for Indian people, or shunned for making friends with them? How many found ways to grieve despite the prohibition, or felt uncomfortable being considered part of a chosen race? I was sure the seeds of a more compassionate mind were there in our lineage, but those hadn't been talked about, either.

Because she had left so much writing behind, Ella was the only one whose thoughts I could see into. And as my own heart opened, I could appreciate her complexity. Ella was more than the privileged commentator on other cultures I'd found fault with, more than a booster of Manifest Destiny. She was also a dear elder, modeling "whole-souled" love of our ancestors and giving her descendants what we needed to help us look a full dozen generations back in time. Regardless of how she'd understood it in her conscious mind, the story Ella had transmitted made it possible to see all the way back to the foundational experience of settler colonialism, to understand the dynamics of our ancestors'—and our country's—silences. What I now felt for Ella must be what the Shellmound Walkers had called "honoring the ancestors." Aunt Ella Roper, with all her imperfections, was an ally in our mutual healing—something we still needed to work on. In the big picture, she had my respect.

I sat in my meditation space one morning, my distress levels rising—the beautiful hillside in climate crisis, the racial hatred, militarism, melting ice, disappearing species, and reversing rivers—a world that needed healing from the harm my people had set in motion. I held my pain where I could feel it hurting and just sat there without trying to get myself cheerful again. In the Buddhist way, I held it and just kept breathing.

After some time, I felt a kind of eruption inside; the stuck pain exploded and began to flow somewhere. I felt myself surrounded by weeping, screaming, howling ancestors. Those faces I had once seen on the dim parlor walls of the Coombs house now rose up around me. Frank and Belle and Ella were there and all the Ephraims and the Coombs sufferers. No longer posed portrait faces, real feelings bursting out, stored under the surface for generations. Misguided pride, anger, fear, and shame broke wildly through the silence. A howling mass of miserable spirit faces, grimacing, roaring with pain, baring their teeth, biting their own lips until the blood ran down their chins. Hair flying wildly out of pompadours, Pilgrim hats askew, tall collars awry, face powder running down cheeks.

These people were grieving—at last they were grieving—and I was howling and sobbing along with them because it was also my grief. This was what happened when you bottled it up for a lifetime, for many lifetimes. Did this pain come with us from Europe, from brutality there and loss of connection with those forests and open moors? We, too, had been colonized long ago by invading peoples, later punished for petty crimes on the rack, our women tortured and killed as witches. A likely ancestor of *Mayflower* pilgrim Thomas Rogers had died at the stake, "bathing his hands in the flames as if it had been 'cold water.'" Coming here, we surely brought the pain with us. Sherri Mitchell, Penobscot teacher from Maine, says we were drawn here because our deepest selves knew that people on this continent still had the earth-based understanding we'd lost. But we couldn't recognize it—things seemed miserable here. There was no food at first, our people died around us, and we lost our minds, attacked one another and those who lived here. We fed our fear, refused to grieve. Started wars for land and captives who could labor for us. We didn't call it slavery, but it was.

In those wars, we became as brutal as we imagined the enemy to be. We scalped and tortured, dismembered corpses, killed women picking huckleberries. And the enemy fought bravely. It was their land and their people were being massacred. They killed, too—burned some of us alive in garrisons, as we'd modeled combat in that first Pequot War the year my relatives immigrated.

There is no record of us grieving or mourning—either our own dead or our lost humanity as combatants. No mourning for whatever drove that journey across the wild, heaving ocean. Officially forbidden by our Puritan ancestors, grief was dangerous and to be sublimated into pious actions. Four centuries later at my little Buddhist altar, we are finally letting it out in a huge intergenerational wailing. The pain changes. It does not go away, but it changes. They don't look so tormented, and I no longer feel so powerless.

CHAPTER 10

Ceremonies for the Soul Wound

Napa oaks with "god rays" in morning fog, January 2008.

Sometimes it will take much longer than we want. . . .
Change happens over time . . . in a protracted way.
— ANGELA DAVIS, SPEAKING TO SURJ
(SHOWING UP FOR RACIAL JUSTICE), 2019

We are the continuation of our ancestors. We contain all the
beautiful qualities and actions of our ancestors and also all
their painful qualities. Knowing this, we can try our best to
continue what is good and beautiful in our ancestors, and we
will practice to transform the violence and pain passed down
to us from so many generations. We know that we practice
peace not only for ourselves but for the benefit of all our
ancestors and all our descendants.
— THICH NHAT HANH, *CREATING TRUE PEACE*

Longing for Ceremony

AS I PUSH MY WAY up the steep January hillside, the soil is barely moist. We're in a period of drought and my soul misses the mucky richness of a normal winter. Rock ferns and maidenhair leaf out feebly. I can't bear to see that the manzanitas are not blooming at all this season. Even on their favorite slope, where they are small trees—no sprays of white flowers, no circle of little white bells fallen to earth after bloom, no wintering hummingbirds, no subtle sweet fragrance, no magical touch of faint pink. A whole hillside that should be humming with bees is silent—as if the timing is off. As if this is not winter. Not manzanita-blooming time in the Napa hills.

These hills were Wappo and Patwin land, and still are in my mind. Would the First People have held a ceremony for a hillside in trouble? Manzanita was important for the hard wood of digging sticks and the rusty red fruits that dried on the bush and were soaked into cider or chewed as candy. Even more, this plant was a relative who took care of them as they took care of it. Ceremony renewed that relationship with healing all around. I long for this relationship. But the culture I was raised in lost its earth-based ceremonies long ago. Being out on the hill, in touch with the energy of this place, has been my way of ceremony. But as things grow difficult and the land shows its wounds, my doubts grow and the healing feels less potent. My friend Johnella LaRose from the Shellmound Walks has often told me, "You don't need us to offer prayers. Everyone can do it, and everyone has to. It's your responsibility, too. We're in this mess together." Indigenous ways can inspire, but it is time for the rest of us to reach deep into ourselves and our distant past for ceremony and healing. We need to transform the very mind my ancestors passed down. Those ancestors need healing. So do I. So does the land and all who've been harmed.

Things grew much worse in the world around me as I worked to understand our history. Not just the Napa land and other parts of California but also the great rain forests on southern continents burned. Even the peat bogs and tundra in the far north burned. Indigenous sacred sites were opened for mineral extraction, and destructive new technologies leached fossil fuels from dwindling reserves—though using them raised global temperatures to zones of extreme danger. Protections from lethal chemicals were dismantled. Wars brought on by extraction, drought, and abrupt climate change raged—with refugees treated as dangerous enemies by colonizer countries. Government money poured into nuclear weapons again as hostilities at home and abroad intensified and a pandemic threatened human health worldwide, especially for those disempowered by our history. All this was the legacy of colonialism that most Americans had not paid attention to. But now even privileged descendants of colonists faced the collapse that Black Elk had called "the black road."

I watched homeless encampments grow under city freeways, looked into the faces of men and women who had to live in them without protection from viruses or toxic ash. For years I had signed petitions against police killings of darker-skinned people. But of course it wasn't enough. Decade after decade, violence seemed to be rising all over the country. The media said one high-profile crime was the largest mass shooting in our history, but the numbers didn't compare to the Pequot Massacre or the attacks on villages and sweat lodges when California became a state. It seemed that Americans—far from healing the colonizer mind—were allowing it to grow strong again, caught up in a rising wave of racism and ecocide. White people marched openly with Nazi slogans and sometimes guns. The fascism Americans had fought abroad in my childhood was flourishing in our own country, all mirroring our unacknowledged history.

As the devastations of colonial mind worsened, I thought about the silences of my settler ancestors that had covered over the trauma they, too, carried. I remembered conversations with my friend Donna, whom I'd known since the Wounded Knee ride in 1990. In the early stages of researching my settler history, she'd invited me to join an Indigenous and settler group to discuss the "soul wound" on community radio. Later, I would read how Native psychotherapist Eduardo Duran had come upon this potent term while interviewing elders in communities with unhealed trauma from California's genocide. Both Duran and Donna's friends knew that all parties to our violent history were affected by this deep wounding—though differently. I was honored to be included in the discussion and to hear others' stories of psychic harm from colonization. I was just realizing my own then, but I knew that Indigenous people had worked for generations to heal. Descendants of perpetrators were only beginning to do our part. In those early stages, shame was the main feeling for me—a debilitating emotion to work with. It would shape-shift and deepen as I learned more of the story, but I began to find other ways of reacting—the universal paths of grief and forgiveness that my ancestors had blocked or forgotten.

During a February that was unseasonably hot, I headed up to the lupine slope on Gordon's Ridge, my heart filling with dismay at the special places on the hill that had been devastated by invasive feral pigs since my last trip. In beloved gardens of shooting star and buttercup, Mimulus and fern, I found the unique topsoil churned into deep ruts and mounds. Up on the ridge, there wasn't much damage. And even though it was blooming two weeks early, the lupine still smelled as heavenly as ever—its blue the most beautiful dark color you can imagine in a wildflower. I found one patch of Lewisia that my mother had transplanted from a rocky place the other side of the Pansy Field. It had hung on in this new home—for all these forty years of tending, hers, then mine.

On this piece of the hillside spared for now by the pigs, I knew it was time for the grief ceremony that Donna had offered me from a medicine person of her tribe. I found a place in the little bit of shade on the ridge—near the scent of the lupine and the memory field of the Lewisia, under fern, brodiaea, and wild cherry. As she had instructed, I found a rock, made an offering, and dug a hole for my grief. As I got down on the ground over this hole, my body surprised me and began to spasm, as if preparing to throw up. My eyes filled with sweaty tears from the untimely heat. Would all these lovely things blooming so early miss their pollinators? My tears poured into the little bowl of earth as grief came rolling out of me like globs of stuck energy—grief that also felt like disgust and shame. Grief for the Earth and the loss of our seasons, grief and shame for the taking of the land and the harm to its original tenders. Grief also for my ancestors' silent wounds.

And then I became aware of the sweetest, most wonderful smell—evocative, like the honey-smelling bee pheromones the time I helped move a swarm. But this was the moist earth itself, little grasses and mosses blending their scents into the mother odor of earth. I thought about the Patwin and the Wappo, about their losses. I thought about my own family history, the "unsettling" of my European ancestors and their prohibition of the grief that could have begun to change it all. Just as strong was a feeling for what the Earth is suffering now—the untimely heat, the explosion of feral pigs, the exploitation and homelessness in the city. I saw clearly that these many griefs are one. The losses of two and four centuries back—the blocked compassion and more—have morphed into deeper losses for Earth itself, losses now so huge that even protected people like myself, whose ancestors set them in motion, can feel them. Mixed in was a deep self-loathing for that part of us that let this happen. Crouching on the ridge, I let the stuck feelings go though me into the ground in a great shuddering of energy. When the fragrant earth had absorbed this purging, I scraped the soil back into the hole, replaced the plants and the digging rock—as Donna had instructed—gave thanks, and made my way down the hill with a lighter step.

New Voices

As we approached the year 2020 and the very worst of our nation's karma began to show itself, it was heartening to feel the strong leadership of Indigenous and African-descended people. Those who had born the brunt of colonial ecocide, genocide, and enslavement were healing from the trauma and some were sharing their medicine. New teachers and leaders arose and often worked in a way that took me aback with its peaceful, generous, and forgiving quality. Like Dr. King in the civil rights movement and the model I knew from Buddhism, they didn't demonize adversaries—even when demonized themselves. A local signer of the Indigenous Women's Climate Treaty reminded us at every action that we were not against particular people, only the mind behind them. Historic gatherings formed at threatened sites—the sacred mountain Mauna Kea in Hawaii, Standing Rock in North Dakota. Glued to my screen in the winter of

2015, I saw again the Lakota practices I'd experienced in 1990 at Wounded Knee. A younger generation had drawn together an even wider circle to protect water, burial sites, cultural integrity, and the Earth.

This energy had been building. A few years earlier, in 2011, I'd spent time at a 109-day encampment organized by my Shellmound friends to protect a sacred site not far from Napa. Their camp was a joyful place where children played, young people courted, and elders shared stories around a sacred fire—as they had in the original village there centuries ago. Ceremonial leaders joined us, and people once cut off from their culture began to heal. A young Ohlone musician told me of placing his sleeping bag where he could hear his ancestors speak lovingly to him out of the earth. Here, living on the land, people shared their lives and dreamed of how to restore true Indigenous stewardship.

When the action ended in a first-ever "cultural easement" intended to protect the site, my friends Johnella and Corrina expanded their vision. Knowing firsthand now that land was central to their healing, they created a completely new kind of land trust organization to care for donated land in small patches throughout the East Bay. Very different from the land trust that kept Deborah Miranda from her land or the one we'd worked with in Napa. For this one, a voluntary "Shuumi tax" paid by settler people like me who live on unceded Ohlone land supports their work. It was unique and visionary, completely outside the system of ownership that had grown from the colonial mind. Their first donated site is now a thriving garden of native plants, a place to hold ceremony, a place where Ohlone and other Indigenous peoples can once again truly belong. Alongside this project, they also pulled together a remarkable coalition, winning lawsuits on the long path to protecting the Bay Area's oldest shell mound from developers. The world now knew who they were. Corrina traveled to London, invited by a museum that held her ancestors' artwork. Signs and bumper stickers popped up locally proclaiming OHLONE LAND. One day as pandemic shut down the city and marchers mourned the murdered George Floyd, it lifted my heart to drive past one of the new Sogorea Te' sites, where a gentle circle of people sat, distanced, around a sacred fire, apparently in prayer.

Although her roots were in Minnesota, Donna now worked in the Sierra foothills with the Tsi-Akim Maidu people who were healing from the soul wound of California's murderous gold rush. She had taken me with her to meetings about a physical piece of the wounding—toxic mercury left in the rivers by century-old gold extraction that was still poisoning the people. In those times, they had lost a crucial ceremony, Calling Back the Salmon, an annual event to affirm the connection between the Maidu and the Salmon People of the Yuba River. The Maidu were to care for the spawning beds and the Salmon People would care for the Maidu. One hundred and fifty years after this relationship was disrupted by the genocide, the Maidu had been able to restore the ceremony. They did so in a way that included settler descendants in the healing. Because spirit runners had to travel miles along the river to spear the first returning salmon, they had to pass through many segments of land now privately owned. This meant Maidu leaders had to make plans with a diverse set of ranchers and owners. Despite tension and resistance, in careful person-to-person contacts a few settler descendants began to understand the racist history of their land and move toward new consciousness.

Two decades after its restoration, the Salmon Ceremony had become a five-day gathering of story sharing, music, and healing, attended by hundreds of locals, including schoolchildren and Indigenous visitors from several continents. When I joined them along the beautiful Yuba River, I knew a collective change of heart was slowly occurring.

Restoration was happening all over Northern California. The Winnemem Wintu from the Shasta area journeyed in ceremony up the great Sacramento River, praying for their salmon during the fall migration and reaching out along the way in their Run4Salmon. Near the Oregon border, three tribes along the Klamath River worked for removal of dams that had blocked their salmon and organized to restore ceremonial burning practices that had been criminalized in 1850 even though essential to the health of forests, river, and people. They worked with government and nonprofits to offer a training in the suppressed practice of beneficial fire and even invited artists to sketch it for the public. One tribe, the Karuk, developed a holistic Climate Adaptation Plan that would not only restore their culture but benefit us all in the heightened wildfire and climate chaos that were being called "the new normal." Wherever I looked, there were small and large stories of recovery.

Indigenous voices were strong in Napa, too. The Suscol Intertribal Council had established a beautiful land base for ceremony in the hills and begun an annual "healing walk." Years of educating current residents about the valley's genocidal history led to a series of workshops on the trauma of colonization as it still affects Native Americans in our region. This opportunity for health-care providers and other local residents to share tears and begin healing is in its seventh iteration as this book goes to press.

Shortly before the council began these workshops, I joined the final stage of another of their campaigns. Not living in the valley, I hadn't realized that the high school still retained its "Napa Indian" sports mascot—an emblem of colonizer mind dating from long before my father's football days. The mascot was not Wappo or Patwin, but a stereotyped Indian face from the days when white Americans romanticized a people they wanted to think had vanished. Despite a long educational process, the community was bitterly divided, with most people of Indigenous descent offended by the image and many white citizens clinging to "our Indian" and packing the auditorium to insist that the mascot was a sign of respect for Native people, respect they said came from Napa's founders. I was there with my cousin Helen to counter their claims with the truth of violence and enslavement I'd found in the Coombs family. So many vied to speak that I settled for writing my public comment as an article in the local paper. Star voices in the hearing were those of Indigenous students making clear how humiliating they found the mascot.

Afterward, we learned the transformative power of Indigenous voice as Native women filled the outer hallway, chanting the Women's Warrior Song while mascot supporters, shouting insults, defended an image of "the Indian" long ago worked into the flooring. The aggressive energy of the supporters would have alarmed me, but the chanting women evoked such peaceful and protective energy that I joined them with all my heart, marveling at the healing that must have taken place for these women to stand their ground in peace after the violence their ancestors had experienced so few generations back. The standoff ended with a beautiful nonviolent gesture. Lifting a wand of hawk feathers and calling out, "We are still here! We are resilient!" Indigenous activists filed out the door with dignity as mascot supporters gawked. Shortly after, the school committee—calling their process an "intense learning experience"—voted unanimously to replace the mascot.

On a clear January morning, I stand in a ring of people around a small fire, celebrating Ohlone land returned to Ohlone care. Traffic roars past on the freeway that cuts among small homes and remains of old glass greenhouses from the 1950s, which I remembered from the time when this part of Oakland was verdant with vegetable farms. A creek—mostly underground now—flows not far away. This grassy place is part of a small piece of land that's once again dedicated to growing plants and food. A nonprofit has donated a quarter acre to the Sogorea Te' Land Trust, the unique outcome of the Shellmound Peace Walks and the 109-day encampment. It's a placeholder for a larger plot that will go to Sogorea Te' when the mortgage is fully paid off. And it is the first of what will become many pieces of land under Sogorea Te' care as the Land Trust grows. For now, this spot of earth is once again a place Ohlone and other Indigenous peoples can belong, tend, and experience ceremony and renewal.

It's clear how deeply this belonging is felt around the circle. Those who once walked around the bay with us are older now, and the ones who were children are grown, with newer ones running happily in the grass nearby. As Corrina speaks, her voice breaks with emotion that all of us who know her can feel. It's been almost two hundred years since her people were herded off this land, cut off from the creeks and their ancient tending practices, sent to work in the missions and—after that era—punished or sold as vagrants for gathering in ceremony, for speaking their language. Now once again the land is welcoming them back.

Indigenous people were healing as they took brilliant actions restoring land, self-respect, and ceremony. But what about settler colonial descendants and the white America that had adopted their mind-set? We, too, suffered from the soul wound, but we had buried it under generations of silence along with the suffering we'd brought here from our own brutalization centuries earlier in Europe. Accepting the benefits, we had ignored the genocide, theft, and enslavement at the root of colonization—our ancestral karma. How could we do the work to heal it? Introducing the idea of "soul wound," Native psychotherapist Eduardo Duran had explained that "[t]he one perpetrating the wounding also wounds himself." He encouraged perpetrators to do our own healing work. While leaving us the responsibility to do this work ourselves, Indigenous people were offering encouragement. Edgar Villanueva, a Native American working in philanthropy, laid out steps for colonizer descendants to heal. Poet-artist Lyla June Johnston and ceremonial leader Sherri Mitchell were reaching out to settler descendants with warmth, teachings, and opportunities to engage. African American writers and teachers were also sharing their experience healing from the intergenerational trauma of enslavement—Resmaa Menakem, Larry Ward, Zenju Earthlyn Manuel, and others. Like Sherri Mitchell, many see our times as an age of prophecy, when major transformation can take place, and must.

"In Psyche, Nothing Is Forgotten"

Some healers of European descent have also devoted themselves to this work. Fred Gustafson, a Jungian who studied with Lakota teachers, sees "the American soil" soaked in "unrecognized and unresolved grief." He urges European Americans to acknowledge our history on this continent and reconnect with our own indigenous past—when we intimately belonged to the Earth, not it to us. Active grieving can heal the fear and paralysis that keep us from making repair and protecting the Earth.

Another Jungian, Sandra Easter, tells a moving story of her own ancestral healing in Jung and the Ancestors. Like mine, her lineage goes back to early New England—in her case, to Roger Williams, who founded Rhode Island after being expelled from the Massachusetts Bay Colony about when the Ropers arrived. Considered "dangerous," Williams had challenged the colony's right to grant land without having purchased it from the First People. Known for his Native alliances and his deep disappointment that the good relations he'd tried to build did not survive King Philip's War, even this presumed Native ally was not free of colonizer mind. Though he worked to build trust, sources say he also helped enslave

Pequot War captives. Easter believes her ancestor died wrestling with a spiritual dilemma. Unable to reconcile his respect for Indian people with the core of European entitlement, he passed this dilemma along so that, generations later, her own life could bring it closer to resolution. Easter has made acknowledgment, healing, and repair a life's work and helps others to do the same. The "long history of genocide, dislocation, and trauma," she says, "continues to haunt (our) bodies and psyches . . . until remembered, re-collected, witnessed and honored." Like Mitchell, she thinks the generations alive now are open to deep healing and transformation.

Easter's story of recovery from physical disease during her ancestor work reminds me that even though our settler minds may block the horror of what happened on this continent, our bodies remember. My own body seemed to remember—with digestive problems, falls, allergic reactions, heart attack, and a spine growing weak from old unhealed injuries as I researched and acknowledged the genocide. Perhaps I couldn't stomach the horror, couldn't stand the heartbreak. Recalling the stress-related asthma, arthritis, and heart disease of earlier family members, I wondered if they, too, had been reacting to our silenced history. My generation knows that our cells remember, that the shadow regions of our mind remember and can sicken us with unhealed history. Somatic therapist and best-selling author Resmaa Menakem argues convincingly that bodily trauma in his Black and white clients comes from old suffering that white colonists brought with them from brutality in Europe and passed on to the bodies of color (or culture) they found or brought here. He says this suffering, still stored in all of us, can be released only through the body. We can't think or talk our way out of it. Indigenous people have ceremonies for stored trauma—like those in Duran's work and the Wiping the Tears ceremony that centered the Wounded Knee ride in 1990. But white culture has no traditional practices to transform inherited suffering. Our religion and our history have taught us not to grieve or look back.

Our challenge is to find our way to the change in consciousness that Sherri Mitchell and the Jungians see as possible in this era, a change that's both personal and collective—a healing for what I've come to call the colonizer mind. I'd felt the change stirring in myself long ago—reading Black

Elk with my students and opening to the painful history I had not known. It quickened during the years I worked with Donna and our Indian activist friends in Boston, traveling to Wounded Knee and giving presentations about Columbus and colonization when I returned. More growth came with looking deeply into slavery, then the Shellmound Walk and the research for this book. At each stage, I learned more, made changes in how I used my resources, and also found ways to express the anger and grief that arose. And it wasn't easy. Every uncomfortable encounter along the way taught me more about my own entitlement. They say discomfort is part of any healing, even for a skinned knee or a head cold, so why not for white supremacy? Professor Vanessa Andreotti, a Brazilian-born scholar focused on decolonizing our thinking, speaks movingly of how messy and triggering it is to transform the toxins we've inherited. As the times cry out out for massive change, those most abused by colonization are taking brave and loving action to awaken concern for water, the Earth, and other humans—calling on the rest of us to do our own healing so we can join them without emotional obstructions.

Especially in 2020, the year I completed this book, white Americans' consciousness was changing dramatically, just as Sandra Easter had thought it might. More than a few white people from settler colonial backgrounds were looking at the full truth of our history and speaking and acting on it—like the veterans who had apologized earlier at Standing Rock for the military's role in subduing Indigenous people. White groups were learning to support leaders of color and Native groups without preempting their leadership. It became customary in many circles for people from settler backgrounds to acknowledge the tribal people whose land they lived on—unceded land, meaning stolen. Websites, books, new organizations, and study groups promoted the consciousness shift, seeing the connection with the wounding produced by enslavement of Africans and the hate focussed on Asians. Magazines and long-standing environmental organizations like the Sierra Club had been working to change their perspective. All this prepared white Americans to rise with passion in defense of Black Lives after the rash of lynching deaths in 2020. Sadly, the new consciousness also had its shadow—increasing racial hatred, bigotry, and violence in the divided public life of the country. Despite that enormous turmoil, the deepening awareness of settler colonial mentality was now collective, not something I struggled with alone. I took comfort in being part of a movement toward the dissolution of our inherited silence.

As I neared the end of this exploration, I had a chance to join a ceremony of apology for the violence of settler colonialism. At the invitation of a Lakota elder, over two hundred of us came together—descendants of commanders and foot soldiers, enslavers, and profiteers, along with later immigrants who'd accepted the privileges and comforts of the colonizer. In a way that touched me deeply, some also came forward from tribes to offer forgiveness for specific acts against their ancestors. People joined from Europe, Africa, the Middle East, and the southern part of my hemisphere. We didn't do a lot of talking. The ceremony focused on red cloth bundles tied with yellow string that held written apologies for our ancestors' actions.

Smudged wth sage and cedar, we carried the bundles into a ceremonial circle consecrated by a traditional sun dance, where we, too, moved to the heartbeat sound of a Lakota drum as the skies darkened, strong winds arose, and we began to hear the voice of the thunder beings. As they spoke, we filed out of the circle with our bundles to a large fire built to heat the stones of a sweat lodge. Its flames rose as we crowded in around it—young and old, descendants of the massacred and the perpetrators—all of us wounded by our history. Dramatic bolts of lightning lashed the surrounding sky as the ceremonial leader gave the word to release our bundles and their psychic burdens into the flames. Here was fire again, the element that caused so much fear in the world I was born into. But those who still knew their traditions were using it in a sacred manner, to restore an ancient balance that our ancestors had disrupted.

I was profoundly grateful—not just for the ceremony and the deep vision of those who offered it but also for the very idea of writing an apology. Distilling what I'd found in my research into one page of its most telling detail turned out to be a powerful act. I was able to go beyond the formulaic vagueness of apologies in white settler culture—say more than "I'm sorry" and reach deep for the language of my heart. My one page focused on the Coombs and Roper ancestry in California and looking back twelve generations. I apologized to the Wappo, Patwin, Wampanoag, and Nipmuc peoples—and to the manzanitas and the oaks. A voice that seemed to come from beyond myself spoke onto the page. As I expressed my sorrow, I sought to forgive my ancestors' actions and their silence and to enlist them in helping to change the mind they had planted in us. Over many years, I had been moving away from helpless shame and outrage. During this ceremony, I could feel my relatives as allies in the healing work. My father was wth me in his youthful form, giving me strength to stand long hours in the heat and cold. Ella, Frank, and Belle, the Ephraims and the Nathans were there in a cluster, holding my back when something was difficult. I felt their support and focused on their healing, too. The resonance of this experience still unfolds in my life, helping me see that I am on the right path and in the strong company of many others seeking to heal our past.

During early fall rains after the long drought, I held my own seed-planting ceremony for the Napa land. Between showers, I went out into Mother's field with seeds of the native bunchgrass I'd collected when it had grown so lush during the dry times. *Stipa pulchra.* The alternating showers and sunny periods would be a good time for germination.

Clouds clung to the hills above the open field, the air dense with potential rain, everything greener than I'd seen for all the years of the drought. I walked slowly around the perimeter—the walking meditation of my Buddhist community. Each step with full awareness of the earth underfoot, including its unhealed history. Each step, giving and receiving loving energy. Each step, gratitude. Then I went with my seeds to spots where gophers had prepared the soil—loose, airy mounds of tailings from their tunnels. I shook a half dozen seeds onto each mound—thin needle-like spines with a tiny grain at one end—and scraped the crumbly wet soil over them with my muddy clogs, wishing them well. I knew the next shower would settle them comfortably into position, ready to sprout. As I moved from mound to mound, the sun came out just a little. The damp earth began to release bits of steam, and everything sparkled—joyous, restorative.

Unfinished Work

Is the land of Unc's ranch healing from the affronts of colonialism even as it faces the hardships of a changing climate? Thanks to my parents and caretakers Robert, Clark, and Dave, we have tended the place with a growing sense of reciprocity for the forty years since Unc's death. I would like to think we're getting close to the beautiful vision of Indigenous botanist Robin Wall Kimmerer—becoming "naturalized to place." Sometimes we don't agree or the job is hard to handle, but a bond with the land is deepening. Especially during dry years, Stipa pulchra is growing back in the field, even though the little European plantain known as "white man's footstep" is taking over at one end. Yes, big trees keel over in drought, winds, and heat waves. Skies are often dim with smoke, and the hillside needs continuing care after the 2017 fire—all long-term outcomes of colonization.

Still, the land is beautiful—not as when the First People knew it, or even as it was in my childhood. But beautiful in its struggles—dwarfed milkmaids coming up to set seed in the drought, a rainbow of live oak foliage in spring, migrating birds finding refuge. Family and friends—including Indigenous friends—come here with awe and respect. Some of us are starting to understand what Corrina Gould said so eloquently— "underneath . . . is pain that we need to set right."

Repairing that pain is what's confusing and difficult. My relatives and I still "own" land the Wappo people never ceded to Cayetano Juárez, the Coombses, or any colonial entity. Our family's easement to a non-Native land trust protects the land from further development but doesn't begin to address the many-sided wound of colonization. I long for definitive closure—to join the growing number of settler families who give back land, fund Native projects, or organize to make amends. I appreciate the slow changes in consciousness I've seen in my family and felt in myself, but I am ready for healing that is more concrete. If an agreement we made years ago and the terms of our Land Trust easement did not prevent it, I would find a way to give back my part of this land. Is it the unhealed settler mind in me that wants to see things "fixed," my own accounts squared? That kind of thinking has been a hallmark of colonizer culture.

Can I accept a longer view, where small steps like this book can widen the circle of understanding and repair? Something we build over time with those wounded in different ways by the generations of violence. I'm grateful our bond with the land has become more wholesome, but I know how happy the oaks would be if the original tenders could help them again. I want that to be my legacy.

As she wraps up her book on King Philip's War, Abenaki writer and scholar Lisa Brooks resists the kind of conclusion expected in white majority culture. There is no "neat end" to a story like hers with so many layers, a story that is still ongoing. The healing we're looking for is much messier and takes more time than the colonizing mind can usually tolerate. Professor Andreotti, part of the collective Gesturing Toward Decolonial Futures, encourages us to look "deeper and wider" and commit to the discomfort of real change. Psychotherapist Eduardo Duran reminds us that healing is different from the colonizer model of "cure," where all is wrapped up and finished. It's a process of coming into relationship with the illness we carry. I'm grateful to have seen the beginnings of healing in my mother and father and to feel it continuing in my own life. Difficult and confusing as it is most of the time, holding these contradictions with awareness, speaking what has been unspoken, and acting from this truth in the world around me seems my best way out of the silence I inherited. Remembering to grieve and finding even small ways to repair the harm keep me from slipping back into that silence.

It's spring of 2019, a year and a half since the big fire that didn't touch the giant oaks or the house. A classic spring after a wet winter. No drought, no untimely heat waves here—though croplands in India are drying up, with floods in Bangladesh. What we're going through is uneven, but Napa is enjoying a beautiful spring—a respite from climate disaster. A chance to get up the hill to see how the ceremony of fire has played out.

Along Dairy Creek are massive spreads of invasive French broom. Two generations of weeding have not put a dent in their endless seed banks. But the fire helps us in a surprising way. Fire activates broom seeds so every one of them sprouts. Rigorous weeding this year may give us a chance to destroy the entire seed bank, and the land trust will help us with a work party. Parts of the hill have come back to life with unforgettable beauty after the fire. I find stands of the elegant *Fritillaria meleagris*, or checkered lily, I treasured as a child, and up where I once held the grieving ceremony, a slope cleared by fire is blue as the sky with lupine—like nothing I remember from before.

Above the broom patch is one of those pieces of the fire mosaic where the burn looked severe—a grove of manzanita up against a grove of madrone, the two hottest-burning trees on the hill. All of them incinerated to black charcoal stalks. But under the madrones, mounds of brilliant green leaves have grown back from the roots. Some say this vibrant regrowth pulls enough carbon from the atmosphere to offset releases from the fire itself. And new research shows that charcoal from these fires, if left in place, is one of the planet's best ways of sequestering carbon. This area had burned so hot, I'd feared the soil would not support new growth. I was just learning to trust the fire.

The first winter, things remained black underfoot, with eerie crusts of colored ash and strange tall mosses. Now two winters in, there's an elegant rock garden among the stark remains of the old manzanitas—soft mounds of familiar mosses, tiny blades of grass among delicate seedlings of sticky monkey and *Eriophyllum*, soon to bloom profusely golden. And glaucus gray–leafed manzanita seedlings—a sight I'd wanted to see for years. These manzanitas do not resprout when burned, but only after fire can their seeds germinate. Under the blackened scaffolding of the old are dozens of thriving new seedlings, enjoying the fertilized soil, reaching for the plentiful light. The manzanitas on this slope had looked unhealthy for years—dead branches, disease, a whole year when they didn't bloom. An aging population in decline, with no way to renew itself. Now the sick trees are gone and a healthy new grove is under way—regenerating with help from the fire they evolved with.

Touching the Earth

A deep appeal of Buddhism is its encouragement to hold painful contradictions, to move beyond the "right answers" and neat conclusions of colonial mind into the uncertainties of a world that seems to be falling apart. It's helped me hold my ancestors with love and honor even as I recoil from their sense of superiority and the devastation it brought on our world. Around the time the Shellmound Walkers addressed us all as "Earth People" and urged us to honor our ancestors, I found my way to a Buddhist ceremony that helped me do this. My Vietnamese teacher, Thich Nhat Hanh, had come to the West from a country devastated by modern colonial wars, bringing a ceremony he calls "Touching the Earth." This practice connects us with the earth's loving energy and that of our ancestors—both those who can help us heal and those who need healing. Vietnamese culture recognizes three kinds of ancestors. Along with our blood ancestors are "land ancestors," those who made the land what it is, and "spiritual ancestors," the teachers from any lineage who have shaped and guided us.

Hundreds of thousands of Europeans and Americans as well as Asians have studied with Thich Nhat Hanh and been touched by this ceremony. For each set of ancestors, we "touch the earth," placing our entire bodies facedown on the ground as a bell and guiding words resonate. (Or we can simply reach down and touch the earth with one hand.) Earth is our mother, our witness, absorbing and transforming our suffering and giving us strength and grounding—even now when her woundedness is so apparent. The teachings tell us the Buddha touched the earth at the moment of his enlightenment.

The first time I experienced this ceremony, though "the earth" was a carpet in an urban meditation hall, it felt like my belly was resting against the living earth, the way my mother had once showed me in the Pansy Field—grounded and communicating with deep insight and healing power. Many times I have found myself sobbing into the ground of being as I feel this contact and a deep connection with my family lineage and the words of the ceremony. Especially moving to me is always the part about healing the harmful energies in our ancestors that they were not able to address in their lifetimes. Thich Nhat Hanh encourages us to create our own versions of this ceremony, so I end this book with mine for the people I have written about and the Napa land:

First touching: *In gratitude, I bow to this land and to the Wappo ancestors who cared for it before Europeans came here.* (Sound of the bell—all touch the earth.) *I see them camping along the creek at the acorn harvest. Women tending the cooking fires, finding willow and fern for their baskets, searching the steep canyon for healing plants. I see the Patwin people, too, coming to nearby creeks from their villages, digging bulbs and harvesting seed. I see both peoples tending the fires that made this land healthy and free of underbrush—fires that kept the water flowing and the whole land in balance. I bow to the prayers they offered at sacred places on these slopes, greeting the land and the waters in the languages of this place. I pray for the healing of all harm that came (and still comes) to the Wappo, the Patwin, and their land, and for their well-being and spiritual strength. I ask that my words and actions may honor them.*

I feel the energy of the oaks and the creeks filling my body. I vow to cultivate and maintain this energy to transmit to future generations. I will work to transform the violence, hatred, and delusion that still lie deep in the collective consciousness of our society, so that future generations may live in peace and safety. I ask the land ancestors and the land itself for protection and support. (Bell to rise.)

Second touching: *In gratitude, I bow to all generations of ancestors in my spiritual family.* (Bell—all touch the earth.) *I thank those from the great wisdom traditions who have guided me—the Buddha and his lineage, the healers of Africa, and the medicine people of this hemisphere. I thank those teachers in the Judeo-Christian tradition who shine light on our true history and help to shift our consciousness beyond the mind of the colonizer. I bow to those friends and teachers who've helped me see the ways of Manifest Destiny in myself, the suffering hidden in the silence of my blood ancestors, and how to forgive. I am grateful for the teachings that show our deep connection with the Earth and free us to experience our essential goodness. I open my heart to receive the energy of understanding and love from my spiritual ancestors. I ask for guidance from the Awakened Ones that my words* *and actions may contribute to the end of suffering for all beings.* (Bell to rise.)

Third touching: *In gratitude, I bow to all generations in my blood family.* (Bell—all touch the earth.) *I see my mother, with her love and understanding of the land, and my father, with his strength and sense of justice—and I see all the contradictions they embodied. I see how they were beginning to break through their silence and entitlement. I also see my grandparents, my great-grandparents, and generation after generation of our relatives standing behind them. I see the Nathans and the Ephraims, the Isabels and Aunt Ella. I see my Spanish-speaking ancestors—colonizers in the Southwest. I see my mother's people caught in the mind of enslavement in the U.S. South. I see the line of my ancestors stretching back to the founding of this country—the painful acts and the suffering—and I see them long before then, living through trauma in the old country. I know their blood still flows in my veins, their infirmities in my body, their ideas in my mind, their suffering in my heart. I feel their love for me, their desire to give me the best they could imagine, and I also see the delusions they carried, their craving for land and comfort, their clinging to ideas of superiority to justify their actions. I see fear and suffering that could not be healed in their lifetimes. I hear their silences about the brutality of many generations. I see that some of them began to open their hearts, to question parts of their legacy.*

With the help of my teachers, I practice to acknowledge and transform my ancestors' silence and harmful views as they arise in myself and our society and also the fear, unspoken grief, and suffering that they carried and passed on. I ask these same blood ancestors for their strength, protection, and loving assistance in the work of our mutual transformation. May my words and actions lead to healing for them, myself, and all our descendants. (Bell to rise.)

It's mid-November 2020. I sit in early-afternoon sun near the quail bench, where I've come so often to listen to the land and write. In the fearful months sheltering in place in the city and the smoky, toxic air, my body has almost forgotten the peace of the big live oaks. But the air is clear now. Here near the manzanita, I can see what needs tending in the garden Mother worried about from her hospital bed thirty years ago. A gentle breeze loosens falling leaves and a few acorns—picking up as the afternoon lengthens, an early rainstorm blowing in for tomorrow.

Along with woodpeckers in the big oaks and a few distant robins, I can hear the drone of chain saws in nearby vineyard land where trees have fallen from drought and the harsher winds of recent years. More seem to be falling than in Dad's day, and within view of where I'm sitting are three smaller oaks with dead brown foliage. Sudden oak death has reached this sanctuary place at last. What is the land telling us? The summer's fires were more intense than those in any year so far. In other parts of the West, migrating birds dropped out of the sky, starving and with lung damage from the smoke.

But the young ruby-crowns are here again. Not so many as after the 2017 fire. But at least half a dozen—lifting off into arabesques from the lower branches of the live oaks like leaves in the wind. Eyeing me from little branches of the manzanita overhead. One of them—when I offered the bird-watcher's psssh, psssh sound—came closer, then fluttered up to my face for an intimate look. Affirming connection.

Last night, I lay on the lawn, looking up at the stars, like I used to do with my parents out in the field. We'd put our heads together so we could hear each other, but mostly we didn't talk, just looked up at the vastness, our bodies held by the earth. Last night, a glowing orange Mars and the Pleiades. I lay there for a long, long time as they moved slowly in their westward arc—trying to stay open to their messages. What do they know about the big changes unfolding? The worldwide pandemic, the fires and species loss, the social turmoil?

Next week, our country celebrates the arrival of those six ancestors of mine on the Mayflower. What do the stars know of the karma unraveling in our human world? Surely they saw the genocide and enslavement, the soul wounding. What do they know of the huge changes in rainfall, temperature, winds, and melting ice at the poles? How do they understand it? Can they advise us how to proceed? Can we heal this past and find a new way of being on the Earth that honors old ways? I don't expect a message, but they give me one, a meteor in the sign of Leo. A huge bright light, brighter than Mars, that falls away toward the southwestern horizon into the dark, lacy branches of the big oaks.

Closing Words
Action for Healing and Repair

It's in that convergence of spiritual people becoming active and active people becoming spiritual that the hope of humanity now rests.
—VAN JONES, IN PACHAMAMA ALLIANCE MAILING, 2020

TWENTY YEARS AGO, I joined women with ancestors from many continents for a day called Living on Purpose—to deepen insight into what each felt called to do in a troubled world. I came away with a scribbled green file card that still sits on my desk: "Fulfill my ancestors' mission to heal the mess they made." I was just starting to see the depth of that mess, but I was already dreaming of this book. I knew my ancestors wanted healing—to repair the numbing silence, the grief and shame, the entitled mind, our unhinged ecosystem, the harm we caused others and the Earth. Truth telling is a start but, as an activist and doer most of my life, I know how important action is—especially for people of European descent who've been sitting on this for so many centuries.

Over the years I have had lots of interest and encouragement from those who identify as Black, Indigenous and People of Color. But, near the end, as my project drew to a close, I found new support among likeminded people of European descent. Climate and racial violence were calling many of us back to our unhealed history, including younger people energetically taking up the work of decolonizing. Suddenly, my circle included people like Morgan Curtis (morganhcurtis.com)—ancestral storyteller and reparative-giving coach who knows her way through the complex financial world of giving back—and Hilary Giovale (goodrelative.com)—respectful, empathic cross-cultural organizer who's written

243

about "the unpayable debt." Both are wonderful writers with magnificent websites and resources for action well beyond what I offer here. Please go to their websites, explore, learn, heal, repair. It all begins with acknowledgment.

Here are the actions of my own journey, ranging from deeper looking to active repair. The psychic burden of facing our history can be enormous, so choose carefully what and how much to undertake, and do it with others if you can. As you take small steps, the burden will lighten and you'll be led to bigger ones.

Learn More

- Educate yourself about our silenced history but ask who is telling the story and seek out Indigenous authors. To balance mainstream news, try indianz.com and indiancountrytoday.com.

- Explore your own family's story. Ancestry.com is a popular tool, but match what you learn with social and environmental history. I was delighted to find writer/educator Christine Sleeter's approach— what she calls "Critical Family History"—at christinesleeter.org, including three novels drawn from her own family story.

- Go to native-land.ca to find the Indigenous people whose land you now live on or have lived on. Historically, maps were tools of colonization and many aren't reliable, so cross-check with local tribal websites.

- Explore *right relationship with native peoples*—a term borrowed from the Quaker project featured at friendspeaceteams.org. That project teaches hidden history, particularly about the church-run boarding schools that broke up Indigenous families and severed relationships with land, language, and culture. The Mennonite Church of Canada (mennonitechurch.ca) has an Indigenous–Settler Relations program, and other Christian groups are rethinking the mind-set that came here with the Doctrine of Discovery. *See Unsettling Truths* (Intravarsity Press) and *Unsettling the Word* (Orbis Books). On a more personal level, Myke Johnson's classic explanation of cultural appropriation, "Wanting to Be Indian" (on the mainewabanakireach.org blog), is a good starting place for right relationship.

- Keep learning. Don't be satisfied with what you learned ten years ago or even yesterday. There is much more to understand. Since finishing this book, my perspectives have widened reading a new history, *We Are the Land*, by Native Californian writers Akins and Bauer and the wonderful, *First Families* by L. Frank and Kim Hogeland.

Silence Is Violence: Speak Out

- Take inspiration from hip-hop artist Ariel Luckey, who created *Freeland*, about his family's history on stolen land, performed at campuses and communities all over the country. (DVD and curriculum guide available at speakoutnow.org.)

- Mention the silenced history in conversation or when speaking publicly. At a memorial for an unsheltered man murdered under our local freeway, I told what happened to the Ohlone here to explain the continuing violence. I spoke as directly as I could, acknowledged my position as beneficiary, and expressed my grief.

- Write op-ed columns on silenced local history. Local papers appreciate getting copy. I wrote one in May 2017, during the Napa school mascot debate (napavalleyregister.com). Holidays like Thanksgiving and Columbus Day, which obscure silenced history, are a good time for op-ed columns and conversations with family.

- Can you tell the story in schools, Sunday schools, libraries? There's a lot of interest in our hidden history right now and a need for voices to articulate it.

Support

- Learn how to best support Indigenous-led organizations in your area by donating, fund-raising, volunteer work, and spreading the word about their events. Listen for how Indigenous leadership would like you to be involved and how to help respectfully rather than jumping into the spotlight. Be a "humble ally," as Buddhist teacher Mushim Ikeda puts it. Places to look: Big cities often have intertribal organizations to serve the Native people from around the country who were persuaded to relocate in earlier stages of U.S. Indian policy. Idle No More, a Native woman-led group that takes strong action for the environment, has branches in U.S. and Canadian cities. In any work for climate justice, look for ways to follow Indigenous leadership.

- Support Native businesses. My favorite is tankabar.com from the Pine Ridge Reservation. Their buffalo bars offer traditional, healthy food, provide jobs where few exist, and restore the ecosystem.

- Center Indigenous voices. Even as awareness is growing, Native speakers at educational, political, or civic events—if invited at all— are given only a short moment to speak or asked to open with a prayer or song rather than share perspectives to be taken seriously. (Worst was when a Native friend was asked to submit her talk for vetting.) Build relationship with Indigenous communities by inviting their guidance in planning an event and shaping the content. To learn from their perspectives, one speaker is not enough. An entire forum with Indigenous environmentalists could provide the missing "medicine" to support life-saving changes in policy.

- Provide compensation for guest speakers. Activist groups, schools, and nonprofits don't customarily pay visiting speakers and may not have budgets for this. But because of systemic racism, Indigenous and other people of color often can't afford to share their time. When inviting a Native person to share time, wisdom, and effort, find a way to put him or her on a payroll, or fund-raise for a generous offering. The same goes when asking authors of color to write for unpaid publications. See the *Deep Times Journal* of August 29, 2017 (workthatreconnects.org) for a unique way to compensate such work.

- Centering Indigenous voices extends to all media, but whose voices are being heard? Groups like the OpEd Project (theoped project.org) help by supporting underrepresented writers, but readers can also pressure media sources to prioritize voices of color.

Repairing the Harm

Ta-Nehisi Coates reminds us that reparations will involve "a revolution in American consciousness." The Land Back movement—restoring land to Indigenous control and stewardship, with its clear benefits to climate—is a growing edge of this revolution. (See the inspiring talk by Dr. Cutcha Risling Baldy at youtube.com/watch?v=QQfrQyb4yw4&feature=youtu .be and the news for August 14, 2020, at lakotalaw.org.) There are many obstacles (baynature.org, January 23, 2021), but goodrelative.com has an excellent resource page on Reparations + Land Back.

For those not able or ready to return land or inherited wealth, there's a spectrum of ways to give back—from donating to Native-led land trusts to supporting with time and energy while working to shift the mind of colonial entitlement—including our own. Sometimes starting small opens the way for more as we find our way into this revolution.

- First on my list is the Native Land Conservancy on Cape Cod, dedicated to preserving what was once homeland for the people my Coombs and Roper ancestors displaced. Founded by Mashpee Wampanoag Ramona Peters in 2012, the group offers environmental education, often working with other local land trusts to provide an Indigenous perspective. It also provides a container for white landholders who want to give land back (nativeland conservancy.org).
- The Sogorea Te' Land Trust in Northern California—the Indigenous women-led nonprofit discussed in this book—created the voluntary Shuumi Land Tax for those now living on Ohlone land in the East Bay. Funds raised maintain land for food growing and ceremony, employing Indigenous people to tend their own

land. As I write, they've received several donations of land or ease-
ments, with more on the owners' decease. They have an inspiring
website (sogoreate-landtrust.com) and are making news. Other
settler-rent programs include those in San Francisco (ramaytush
.com) and Seattle (realrentduwamish.org), with more on the way
in New York and Boston.

- Other Native land trusts have formed around the country since
the 1990s. Learn more in a 2015 article in *Saving Land Magazine*
(landtrustalliance.org/news/source-all-sustains-us) or in Beth Rose
Middleton's book *Trust in the Land: New Directions in Tribal Conservation* (University of Arizona Press, 2011). A group of environmental organizations in Maine, with the motto Repair and Return
at the Speed of Trust, has more resources at firstlightlearning
journey.net.

- Individuals and groups have been returning land to First People on their own. In her autobiographical novel, *The Inheritance*,
Christine Sleeter tells of returning money from inherited land to
the Ute tribe. Other examples include Manhattan land returned
to the Lenape (nypost.com, December 18, 2016); a Jesuit mission
returning land (nonprofitquarterly.org, May, 24, 2017); a California farmer returning coastal land (nbcbayarea.com, October 20,
2015); a Massachusetts group returning Nipmuc land near where
my Roper relatives settled (telegram.com, October, 31, 2016); and
a small California farm partially donated for an Indigenous Bio-
cultural Heritage Oasis (nativeland.org/heron-shadow). The land
of the Ramaytush Ohlone (the San Francisco area) now hosts an
American Indian Cultural District (americanindianculturaldistrict
.org/) and a Native-guided farm focused on healing foods and
herbs (deepmedicinecircle.org). By the time this book reaches you,
there will be many more models for land return.

- A unique digital map shows ways to support Indigenous and African American land care projects, as mentioned in *YES! Magazine*
(yesmagazine.org), February 21, 2018. The websites of Curtis and
Giovale (above) suggest many other opportunities.

- Maybe you can't donate land or money but can share time and energy. Always ask what is needed and welcome. In Napa, the Suscol Intertribal Council offers volunteer and donation opportunities at suscolcouncil.org. The Tsi-Akim Maidu engage several hundred non-Native volunteers during their Indigenous Peoples' Days. I've held educational house parties/fund-raisers for our local Sogorea Te' Land Trust (sogoreate-landtrust.org), which has a website page on how to help and is developing guidelines for building respectful relationship despite the ongoing violence of colonial mind.

Restoring and Repairing the Land

If you are caring for land, even a small lot in a city, learn what you can of its history and how it was affected by settlement. Also listen to the bird, animal, and plant life that is there now. Take in the light, the wind patterns, the clouds. Think about what lies under the pavements. Where did creeks flow? Which animals and plants evolved here and which came with colonization? How did the First People use this land? How has their absence led to ecological imbalances—as in fire-prone California? To learn more, explore permaculture or consider an immersion course with Weaving Earth (weavingearth.org).

If you are able to undertake even small restoration projects, listen to what the land wants and be wary of imposing your own views. Learn about Indigenous practices from Native teachers in your region. The Spring 2018 issue of *News from Native California* features Indigenous land-care practices that increase biodiversity and water, making land less subject to catastrophic burns. Indigenous authors and their allies can help region by region: Robin Wall Kimmerer, *Braiding Sweetgrass* (several regions); M. Kat Anderson, *Tending the Wild* (California); Lisa Brooks, *Our Beloved Kin* (Indigenous land use in New England); Roxanne Dunbar-Ortiz, *Roots of Resistance* (northern New Mexico.)

The best sources I've found on fire are the profound video *Tending the Wild: Cultural Burning* (kcet.org); Professor Don Hankins's article in the Winter 2021 issue of *Bay Nature*, "Reading the Landscape for Fire" (baynature.org); and Redbird Willie's article "Fire and Water" (weavingearth.org). The Karuk tribe's work with fire and climate is inspiring (karuktribeclimatechangeprojects.com and as studied in Professor Kari Norgaard's *Salmon and Acorn Feed Our People*). Watch for new developments centering Native leadership in ecosystem management like the TREX program (wired.com, August 9, 2018).

Public lands need healing from the colonial onslaught. My region offers many volunteer opportunities to remove invasive plants and restore landscapes in parks and along creeks and shorelines. Check out your state's native plant society and look for opportunities as a citizen scientist (citizenscience.gov)—collecting data to avert invasions and extinctions. While volunteering, you can raise questions with other volunteers about the silenced history many may not know.

Self-healing and Ancestral Healing

- Hold the big picture in mind. As some of us work to heal the mind of the settler in ourselves, we must remember that the soul wound of colonization devastated others. Understand and find ways to support the monumental healing taking place in Indigenous communities, as in this program of the Suscol Intertribal Council in Napa County (youtube.com/watch?v=GQVno1coB20).

- Take care of yourself. All of us need self-support practices as we leave the comfort of cultural silence on racial history and the realities of fire and climate. Former Buddhist nun Kaira Jewel Lingo's "Befriending Eco-Anxiety" (ethical.net, December 13, 2019) beautifully shares ways to meet such challenges.

- Awaken to racial entitlement. There are more and more good tools for waking up and transforming the colonizer mind-set. In earlier years, I learned from Visions, Inc., Re-evaluation Counseling, The Peoples Institute for Survival and Beyond, Catalyst, and many unnamed projects that friends and colleagues developed. More recently, I've benefited from a new wave of spiritually oriented groups like White Awake (whiteawake.org), the East Bay Meditation Center (eastbaymeditation.org), ARISE Sangha (arisesangha .org), the Lotus Institute (thelotusinstitute.org), and many more.

My own small Buddhist practice group, the Deepening White Awareness Sangha, began after a study circle with Robin DiAngelo's *What it Means to Be White*.

- Get in touch with your grief. Joanna Macy's Work That Reconnects calls for expressing grief and other strong feelings if we are to heal and move forward. Along with the practices in her *Coming Back to Life* (2d edition), I've leaned on West African teachings on grief (malidoma.com and sobonfu.com) and other Indigenous approaches (martinprechtel.com). Francis Weller's work is helpful. More good resources from ancient sources are being shared in these times.

- Recognize and work to heal intergenerational trauma. Buddhist teacher Larry Ward's *America's Racial Karma* offers hope for transforming what our ancestors suffered and passed on. So does the work of Resmaa Menakem (*My Grandmother's Hands*), though he says it will take many generations. Both say it's our bodies that hold trauma, which cannot be addressed simply through the mind. Writers and healers close to their Indigenous roots emphasize ceremony. I've found guidance from Martín Prechtel, Malidoma Somé, Eduardo Duran (especially his talk at the Welbriety Journey of Forgiveness in 2016: youtube.com/watch?v=D4d2Y3PHJfo), Arkan Lushwala, and Sherri Mitchell, whose websites, videos, and teachings are easy to locate.

- Central for me is the Buddhist approach to ancestral healing—the idea that in healing ourselves, we are healing our ancestors. This teaching can be found throughout the work and body of ceremony as practiced by Thich Nhat Hanh's community at Plum Village, France—for instance, Sr. Dang Nghiem talk "Coming Home to Our Ancestors" (youtube.com/watch?v=mrThKTx-A9M&t=6s).

- Look for ways to unblock stuck ancestral patterns. There are many options and teachers now. I've found help from Family Constellations Work with Dan Cohen (seeingwithyourheart.com) and Alissa Fleet (everydaymystery.com). For a Jungian approach, try Sandra Easter's work (sandraeasterphd.com).

- Consider roots of trauma in remote family history when Indigenous European lifeways and connection to the land were destroyed. Poet/musician/thought leader Lyla June Johnston, with European and Diné roots, speaks eloquently to this (moon magazine.org/lyla-june-reclaiming-our-indigenous-european -roots-2018-12-02). David Dean writes and teaches on the subject (whiteawake.org). Sara Wolcott considers it in her work on colonialism and climate change (sarajwolcott.wixsite.com).

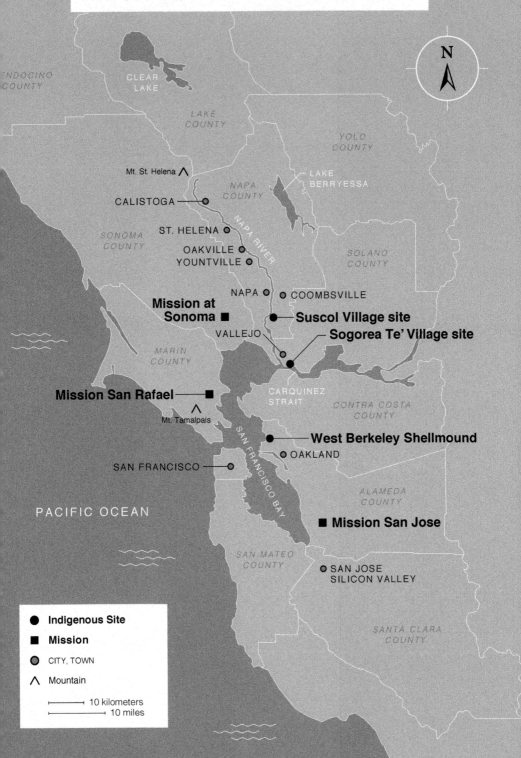

Some Indigenous, Colonial and Current Sites in Napa Valley and the San Francisco Bay Area

N

MENDOCINO COUNTY

CLEAR LAKE

LAKE COUNTY

YOLO COUNTY

Mt. St. Helena ∧

NAPA COUNTY

LAKE BERRYESSA

CALISTOGA

NAPA RIVER

ST. HELENA

OAKVILLE
YOUNTVILLE

SONOMA COUNTY

SOLANO COUNTY

NAPA   COOMBSVILLE

Mission at Sonoma ■

Suscol Village site

VALLEJO

Sogorea Te' Village site

MARIN COUNTY

CARQUINEZ STRAIT

CONTRA COSTA COUNTY

Mission San Rafael ■

∧
Mt. Tamalpais

SAN FRANCISCO BAY

West Berkeley Shellmound

OAKLAND

SAN FRANCISCO

PACIFIC OCEAN

ALAMEDA COUNTY

■ **Mission San Jose**

SAN MATEO COUNTY

SAN JOSE SILICON VALLEY

SANTA CLARA COUNTY

● **Indigenous Site**

■ **Mission**

◉ CITY, TOWN

∧ Mountain

├─────┤ 10 kilometers
├─────┤ 10 miles

Gratitude

MY FIRST THANKS go to the Earth and Indigenous friends who've encouraged this work, and especially to the Mishewal Wappo and Lisjan Ohlone peoples on whose unceded ancestral lands I wrote this book.

My own ancestral past was a source of shame and silence for me until I began doing peace walks with a small Japanese Buddhist order, Nipponzan Myohoji, that walked to heal hidden histories scripted into the land. From the icy hills of the Wounded Knee Massacre to the lush coastlines of the transatlantic slave trade, the monks and nuns had built close ties with Black and Indigenous people, who saw ancestors as diverse, active presences in our lives. Vietnamese teacher Thich Nhat Hanh deepened this understanding with his teachings on three kinds of ancestors—all of whom helped as I worked. Spiritual ancestors offered insight. Land ancestors, who had taken care of the Napa land way back into its history, inspired me. Even my blood ancestors, whose role had been so heartbreaking and problematic, seemed to lend me strength.

This work has been a family effort. My parents, Elizabeth Elliston Farrell Dunlap and David Coombs Dunlap, shared their love of the land, and when they were gone, I saw that they had begun to ask my questions in their own ways. They were not family historians, but I found others who were—Aunt Ella E. Roper, William Carey Coombs, Joanne Rigdon Williams, Frank Coombs, Gilbert Patchett, and even Unc, my father's uncle, whose tales filled my childhood. My cousins Helen Dunlap and Jill Dunlap Golis kept finding old letters, books, and genealogies. Peter Dunlap egged me on. My youngest sister, Susan—already an ancestor when I started writing—helped from the other side, and my sister Sarah Dunlap Galbraith wisely warned me not to sound like a preacher and was patient with my eccentricities. Her children, David and Jean Galbraith, and Jean's husband, Jeremy Tobacman, read draft chapters. And Kate Galbraith—author, skilled editor, and wonderful confidante—gave steady encouragement. My uncle John Dunlap, my father's youngest brother, and his wife, Mary Lu Kennelly, listened and shared. Uncle John's memory reaches further back than mine, and his own life is inspiring witness to the healing of colonizer mind.

In the 1990s in Boston, the Massachusetts Solidarity Committee taught me to follow Indigenous leadership; Women Transforming Communities (then the Women's Theological Center) introduced the "ancestor cards" along with Sonbonfu Somé and Malidoma Somé. Dr. Loretta Williams invited me to review books on racism. Community Change Inc. shared its antiracism library. My students at UMass, MIT, and Tufts showed me the deep harm of colonialism.

Returning to the West in 2010, I joined the Nafsi Ya Jamii book group focused on racism and started two writing groups for activists. These overlapping intimate groups became my book doulas, sharing their own powerful stories as I uncovered mine. Patricia St. Onge, Wilson Riles, Grace Morizawa, Laura Magnani, Lenore Goldman, Charity Whyte, Karita Zimmerman, Raphael Allen, Michael Yoshi, Diana Sands, Kazu Haga, Adrienne Bloch, Kris Yates, AJ Johnston, Phoenix Smith, Marti Pascal, Johnny Manzon-Santos, Zoe and Marcus Holder, Victoria Mausisa, Ty Blair, Donna Uran, Susan Shelton, Elaine Respass, Lakota Harden, Michelle Puckett, Linda Burnham, Margarita Loinaz, Arinna Weisman, and Kerry Nelson—our work together continues to be sacred work.

Other small groups added collective insight—Deena Metzger's Re-Visioning Medicine Council in 2016 and Joanna Macy's meetings on the Mother of All Buddhas. Buddhist sanghas kept my heart open, beginning with the Mindfulness Diversity and Social Change Sangha—Asa Brown, Ty Blair, Cecile Pineda, Refugio Arreguin, Tavi Baker, Steven Low. The Deepening White Awareness Sangha focused on healing from white supremacy—AJ Johnston, Max Heiliger, Cathy Cockrell, Joanne Connelly, Kathryn Werhane, Susan Schulman, Rain Sussman, Annie Gardiner, and Lyn Fine. The EarthHolders' Sangha and the Pleiades group listened and shared. Over the years, Buddhist teachers helped me understand our racial legacy—Hilda Gutiérrez Baldoquin, Larry Ward and Peggy Rowe, Margarita Loinaz, Lyn Fine, Arinna Weisman, Melina Bondy, Joanne Friday, and Kaira Jewel Lingo. A range of other teachers heard, understood, and encouraged me as I struggled for clarity of thought and word—Joanna Macy, Pat Schneider, Deena Metzger, Maxine Hong Kingston, and Wendy Johnson.

Dedicated friends read and commented on one or sometimes many chapters, often more than once: Skip Schiel, Stephanie Antalocy, Bill Shortell, Grace Morizawa, Helen Dunlap, Peter Wetherbee, Peter Dunlap, Ann Lacy, Courtney Martin, Kerry Nelson, Donna Uran, who is a guide as well as a reader, and Chairman Don Ryberg, who is writing about his Maidu ancestors. Special thanks to Linda Dittmar, who writes about her family's settler history in Israel. Bobby Marie and Shamim Meer shared remarkable stories of South African ancestors' lives also warped by colonialism.

Some read the entire manuscript at various stages: Arinna Weisman helped me find the "colonizer mind" in myself. Allison Cook enabled me to cut a very long manuscript in half. Climate activist and book coach Nadia Colburn provided expertise; longtime friend Ann Markusen read an entire final version. Clare Marcus, Elizabeth Turner, and Cathy Cockrell encouraged me to give talks and readings even before the book's completion. The friendship and common interests of many others helped me go further— especially Johnella LaRose and Corrina Gould from the Sogorea Te' Land Trust, David Schooley, Amy Hutto, Adelaja Simon, Edward Willie, Jenn Biehn, Joan Lohman, Sandy Boucher, Martha Boesing, Linda Seeley, Cassandra Ferrera, Nomi Green, Nirali Shah, Roberta Schnorr, Aravinda Ananda, Joseph Rotella, Cathy Hoffman, Betty Burkes, Cynthia Travis, Diana Benner, Chris Benner, Leny Strobel, Tek Tekh Gabaldon, L. Frank, and Ramona Peters.

Gratitude to Robert and Clark, two generations of the Lundeen family in Napa who, with Dave Hilaire, cared for the land over the years. Donald Cutler knew and tended its systems; Alan Galbraith offered generosity and know-how. Land trust monitors Chip Bouril and Penny Proteau climbed the hill with me often and helped pull out new generations of French broom. Charlie Toledo of the Suscol Intertribal Council showed me and many others how land can thrive with Indigenous care.

I'm grateful for help with ancestor photos from Kerry Nelson, map making from artists Ellen Toomey and Peter Soe, and brilliant coaching on ZIP files and Dropbox from Allison Cook. It's been an honor to work with Lynne Elizabeth's sensitive and skillful guidance at New Village Press, where I join a community of other authors supporting the Earth and a more just human community.

I thank my Oakland family at Temescal Commons Cohousing for loving support, especially Randy Yee's internet research and Courtney Martin's mentoring—the most savvy and encouraging any writer could want. I also thank the skillful hands, wisdom, and prayer of healers who've helped me stay healthy and clear—Giovanna Brennan, Thomas Mc-Combs, Christine Ciaverella, Phoenix Smith, and Arkan Lushwala.

Finally, I couldn't be more grateful for the fast-growing circle of other early-settler descendants bent on searching out their true histories, telling those stories, and righting their relationships with land and people harmed: Morgan Curtis, Hilary Giovale, Christine Sleeter, Sara Wolcott, Alissa Fleet, Cynthia Winton-Henry, AJ Johnston, Holly Fulton, Margaret Wrinkle, Paula Palmer, Michele Puckett, Emily Jacobi, Jeff Conant, and Brother Towbee. I am grateful to live in a time when so many are exploring the history that needs healing as we move toward a new way of living on the planet.

Selected Bibliographic Notes

While this is not a scholarly book, I've chosen sources carefully to get closest to the truth of our silenced history. At times, I had to use older mainstream authors with an obvious colonizer bias. But where possible I looked for Indigenous sources and others who treated their voices with understanding and respect. The first section provides key references that shaped my thinking throughout the book. After that, so readers can explore them, I list other references chapter by chapter. At the end are genealogies that family members commissioned privately or wrote themselves.

Key References

Anderson, M. Kat. *Tending the Wild: Native American Knowledge and the Management of California's Natural Resources.* Berkeley: University of California Press, 2005.

Brown, Alexandria. *Hidden History of Napa Valley.* Charleston: History Press, 2019.

Dunbar-Ortiz, Roxanne. *An Indigenous People's History of the United States.* Boston: Beacon Press, 2014.

Duran, Eduardo. *Healing the Soul Wound: Counseling with American Indians and Other Native Peoples.* New York: Teachers College Press, 2006.

Grossinger, Robin. *Napa Valley Historical Ecology Atlas: Exploring a Hidden Landscape of Transformation and Resilience.* Berkeley: University of California Press, 2012.

Heidenreich, Linda. *"This Land Was Mexican Once:" Histories of Resistance from Northern California.* Austin: University of Texas Press, 2007.

Johnston, Lyla June. "Reclaiming Our Indigenous European Roots." Moonmagazine.org, December 2, 2018.

KCET. *Tending the Wild: Cultural Burning.* kcet.org/shows/tending-the -wild/episodes/cultural-burning.

Kimmerer, Robin Wall. *Braiding Sweetgrass: Indigenous Wisdom, Scientific Knowledge, and the Teachings of Plants*. Minneapolis: Milkweed Editions, 2013.

Lightfoot, Kent G., and Otis Parrish. *California Indians and Their Environment: An Introduction*. Berkeley: University of California Press, 2009.

Lindsay, Brendan. *Murder State: California's Native American Genocide, 1846–1873*. Lincoln: University of Nebraska Press, 2015.

Lushwala, Arkan. *Deer and Thunder: Indigenous Ways of Restoring the World*. CreateSpace Independent Publishing Platform, 2018.

Madley, Benjamin. *An American Genocide: The United States and the California Indian Catastrophe, 1846–1873*. New Haven: Yale University Press, 2016.

Menakem, Resmaa. *My Grandmother's Hands: Racialized Trauma and the Pathway to Mending Our Hearts and Our Bodies*. Las Vegas: Central Recovery Press, 2017.

Nhat Hanh, Thich. *Being Peace*. Berkeley: Parallax Press, 1987.

Norgaard, Kari Marie. *Salmon and Acorns Feed Our People: Colonialism, Nature & Social Action*. New Brunswick,NJ: Rutgers University Press, 2019.

Savoy, Lauret. *Trace: Memory, History, Race, and the American Landscape*. Berkeley: Counterpoint Press, 2015.

Somé, Malidoma. *The Healing Wisdom of Africa: Finding Life Purpose Through Nature, Ritual, and Community*. New York: Jeremy P. Tarcher/Putnam, 1998.

Sue, Derald Wing. *Race Talk and the Conspiracy of Silence: Understanding and Facilitating Difficult Dialogues on Race*. Hoboken, NJ: John Wiley & Sons, 2015.

Ward, Larry. *America's Racial Karma: An Invitation to Heal*. Berkeley: Parallax Press, 2020.

Websites and periodicals: indiancanyontimes.wordpress.com; International Indian Treaty Council: iitc.org/gold-greed-genocide; karuktribeclimatechangeprojects.com; sogoreate-landtrust.com; suscolcouncil.org; and *News from Native California*.

Additional Chapter References

Chapter 1. Fires of Awakening

Courchene, Dave, Nii Gaani Aki Inini (Leading Earth Man). onjisay-aki
.org/turtle-lodge.

Cagle, Susie. "'Fire is Medicine': The Tribes Burning California Forests to
Save Them." *The Guardian*, November 21, 2019.

Guthrie, Woody. "Holy Ground." woodyguthrie.org/Lyrics/Holy_Ground
.htm. [Source TK]

Hankins, Don. "Reading the Landscape for Fire." *Bay Nature*, January 3,
2021.

Ward, Larry. "Larry Ward's Response to Insurrection and Guided Practice." Reproduced on Lotus Institute website. Lotusinstitute.org.
January 15, 2021.

Yamane, Linda. "How Hummingbird Got Fire." Read by Amah-Mutsun
tribal chairman,Valentin Lopez. KQED/QUEST. youtube.com
/watch?v=FolfLaVRy6g. July 18, 2011.

Chapter 2. The View from Unc's Deck

Neihardt, John. *Black Elk Speaks; Being the Life Story of a Holy Man of the
Oglala Sioux, as Told Through John G. Neihardt (Flaming Rainbow).*
Lincoln: University of Nebraska Press, 1961.

Chapter 3. Facing Our Silenced History

Who tells the story? Unsatisfied with articles in the local papers, I began
learning this history from Indigenous activists with the Shellmound Peace
Walk, the Sogorea Te' Land Trust, and the International Indian Treaty Coun-
cil's Gold, Greed and Genocide project. Only later did I find my way to books.
I'm especially grateful for the careful way Latina historian Linda Heiden-
reich tells our region's story and for the comprehensive research of Brendan
Lindsay and Benjamin Madley who make the story compelling for those of
us with colonizer roots who've begun to listen. I look forward to *We Are the
Land: A History of Native California*, by California Native scholars Damon B.
Akins and William J. Bauer (Berkeley: University of California Press, 2021).
The sources below were also helpful in this chapter.

Acosta, Estrella. "Blood, Gold & Medicine: Healing Maidu Country." Recorded for KMVR, Nevada City, CA, 2009. Available on Public Radio Exchange (PRX). beta.prx.org/stories/51025.

Alagona, Peter S. *After the Grizzly: Endangered Species and the Politics of Place in California.* Berkeley: University of California Press, 2013.

Beard, Yolande. *The Wappo: A Report.* Banning, CA: Malki Museum Press, 1979.

Chodrun, Pema. "Awakening in the Charnel Ground." *When Pain Is the Doorway: Awakening in the Most Difficult Circumstances,* disc 2. Boulder: Sounds True Productions, 2013.

Cook, Sherburne F. *The Conflict Between the California Indian and White Civilization. 1943.* Reprint, Berkeley: University of California Press, 1976.

Dillon, Richard H. *Napa Valley's Natives.* Fairfield, CA: James Stevenson Publisher, 2001.

Forbes, Jack. *Native Americans of California and Nevada. 1982.* Reprint, Happy Camp, CA: Naturegraph Publishers, 1991.

Gonzalez, Juan. *Harvest of Empire: A History of Latinos in America.* New York: Penguin Books, 2011.

Heizer, Robert F. *The Archaeology of the Napa Region.* Berkeley: University of California Press, 1953.

Klein, Naomi. *This Changes Everything: Capitalism and the Climate.* New York: Simon & Schuster, 2014.

Krause, Bernie. *The Great Animal Orchestra: Finding the Origins of Music in the World's Wild Places.* New York: Little, Brown, 2012.

Kroeber, Alfred L. *The Patwin and Their Neighbors.* Berkeley: University of California Press, 1932.

Lightfoot, Kent G. *Indians, Missionaries, and Merchants: The Legacy of Colonial Encounters on the California Frontiers.* Berkeley: University of California Press, 2005.

Lim, Jayden. "False Images and Young Minds: Sounding Off on History, Racism, and Education." *News from Native California* 28, no. 1, (Fall 2014): 10–12.

Mann, Charles C. *1491: New Revelations of the Americas Before Columbus.* New York: Vintage Books, 2005.

Medina, Vincent. "The Truth Shall Set Us Free." *News from Native California* 28, no. 2 (Winter 2014–2015): 48–58.

Menefee, C. A. *Historical and Descriptive Sketch Book of Napa, Sonoma, Lake, and Mendocino*. Napa City, CA: Reporter Publishing House, 1873.

Newell, Mary Ellen. *Brethren by Nature: New England Indians, Colonists, and the Origins of American Slavery*. Ithaca, NY: Cornell University Press, 2016.

Palmer, Lyman L. *History of Napa and Lake Counties*. San Francisco: Slocum, Bowen & Co., 1881.

Power, Samantha. *"A Problem from Hell": America and the Age of Genocide*. New York: Basic Books, 2002.

Preston, William. "Serpent in the Garden: Environmental Change in Colonial California." In *Contested Eden: California Before the Gold Rush*, edited by Ramon Gutiérrez and Richard J. Orsi, 260–298. Berkeley: University of California Press, 1998.

Raphael, Ray. *Little White Father: Redick McKee on the California Frontier*. Eureka, CA: Humboldt Country Historical Society, 1993.

Rosenus, Alan. *General Vallejo and the Advent of the Americans: A Biography*. Berkeley: Heyday Books, 1999.

Sandos, James A. "Between Crucifix and Lance: Indian-White Relations in California, 1769–1848." In *Contested Eden: California Before the Gold Rush*, edited by Ramon Gutiérrez and Richard J. Orsi, 196–229. Berkeley: University of California Press, 1998.

Street, Richard Steven. *Beasts of the Field; A Narrative History of California Farmworkers, 1769–1913*. Palo Alto: Stanford University Press, 2004.

Weber, Lin. *Old Napa Valley: The History to 1900*. St. Helena, CA: Wine Ventures Publishing, 1998.

Whistler, Kenneth Wayne. "Patwin Taxonomic Structures." Master's thesis, University of California, Berkeley, 1976.

Chapter 4. Mother's Legacy: Reciprocity and the Pansy Field

Cunningham, Laura. *State of Change: Forgotten Landscapes of California*. Berkeley: Heyday Books, 2010.

Knudtson, Peter M. *The Wintun Indians of California and Their Neighbors*. Happy Camp, CA: Naturegraph Publishers, 1977.

Myer, Stephen. *End of the Wild*. Cambridge: MIT Press, 2006.

Preston, William. "Serpent in the Garden: Environmental Change in Co-
  lonial California." In *Contested Eden: California Before the Gold Rush*,
  edited by Ramon Gutiérrez and Richard J. Orsi, 260–298. Berkeley:
  University of California Press, 1998.
Sacred Lands Film Project. *Florence Jones and Caleen Sisk: Winnemem
  Healers*. youtube.com/watch?v=9JocJCaBzmc&t=6s. 2015.

Chapter 5. Dad and the Oaks: Slowly Letting Go
of the Family Silence

Anderson, M. Kat, Michael G. Barbour, and Valerie Whitworth. "A World
  of Balance and Plenty: Land, Plants, Animals, and Humans in a
  Pre-European California." In *Contested Eden: California Before the
  Gold Rush*, edited by Ramon Gutiérrez and Richard J. Orsi, 12–47.
  Berkeley: University of California Press, 1998.
Epstein, Paul, and Dan Ferber. *Changing Planet, Changing Health: How the
  Climate Crisis Threatens Our Health and What We Can Do About It.*
  Berkeley: University of California Press, 2011.
Keator, Glenn. *The Life of an Oak: An Intimate Portrait*. Berkeley: Heyday
  Books, 1998.
Logan, William Bryant. *Oak the Frame of Civilization*. New York: W. W.
  Norton, 2005.
Marianchild, Kate. *Secrets of the Oak Woodlands: Plants and Animals
  Among California's Oaks*. Berkeley: Heyday Books, 2014.
Ortiz, Beverly R., as told by Julia F. Parker. *It Will Live Forever: Traditional
  Yosemite Indian Acorn Preparation*. Berkeley: Heyday Books, 1991.
Wohlleben, Peter. *The Hidden Life of Trees: What They Feel, How They
  Communicate—Discoveries from a Secret World*. Vancouver, BC:
  Greystone Books, 2016.
Websites: suddenoakdeath.org; sciencedaily.com.

Chapter 6. My Generation Takes Care of the Ranch

Camp, Charles L., ed. *George C. Yount and His Chronicles of the West:
  Comprising Extracts from His "Memoirs" and from the Orange Clark
  "Narrative."* Denver: Old West Publishing Company, 1966.
Margolin, Malcolm. *The Ohlone Way*. Berkeley: Heyday Books, 1978.

Miranda, Deborah. *Bad Indians: A Tribal Memoir*. Berkeley: Heyday Books, 2013.

Sarris, Greg. "On the 190th Anniversary of the San Rafael Mission." *News from Native California* 21, no. 4 (Summer 2008): 42–47.

Wulf, Andrea. *The Invention of Nature: Alexander von Humboldt's New World*. New York: Vintage Books, 2015.

Websites: The Doctrine of Discovery: indigenousvalues.org; the Land Trust of Napa County: napalandtrust.org.

Chapter 7. Two Waves of Colonizers on the Tulucay Grant

Associated Press. "Report Questions How California schools Managed Lands." *San Diego Union Tribune*, February 2, 2013.

Hastings, Lansford W. *The Emigrants' Guide to Oregon and California*. 1845. Reprint, Carlisle, MA: Applewood Books, 1994.

Lepore, Jill. *The Name of War: King Philip's War and the Origins of American Identity*. New York: Vintage Books, 1998.

McGriff-Payne, Sharon. *John Grider's Century: African Americans in Solano, Napa, and Sonoma Counties from 1845 to 1925*. Bloomington, IN: iUniverse, 2009.

Menefee, C. A. *Historical and Descriptive Sketch Book of Napa, Sonoma, Lake, and Mendocino*. Napa City, CA: Reporter Publishing House, 1873.

Newell, Margaret Ellen. *Brethren by Nature: New England Indians, Colonists, and the Origins of American Slavery*. Ithaca, NY: Cornell University Press, 2015.

Reséndez, Andrés. *The Other Slavery: The Uncovered Story of Indian Enslavement in America*. New York: Houghton Mifflin Harcourt, 2016.

Rose, Viviene Juárez. *Tulucay: The Past Is Father of the Present, Spanish California History and Family Legends, 1837–1973*. Vallejo, CA: Wheeler Printing, Inc., 1974.

Sandos, James. "Between Crucifix and Lance: Indian-White Relations in California, 1769–1848." In *Contested Eden: California Before the Gold Rush*, edited by Ramon A. Guttiérez and Richard J. Orsi, 196–219. Berkeley: University of California Press, 1998.

Silko, Leslie Marmon. *The Turquoise Ledge: A Memoir*. New York: Viking, 2010.

Vallejo, Platon Mariano Guadalupe, M.D. *Memoirs of the Vallejos: New Light on the History, Before and After the "Gringos" Came, Based on Original Documents and Recollections of Dr. Platon M. G. Vallejo* (from *San Francisco Bulletin,* January 26, 1914–February 17, 1914). Fairfield, CA: James Stevenson Publisher, 1994.

Weber, Lin. *Old Napa Valley: The History to 1900.* St. Helena, CA: Wine Ventures Publishing, 1998.

Websites: Genealogy: parkerpress.com; Gordon family in Yolo County: restorerestory.org.

Chapter 8. Manifest Destiny: Letters from the Second Generation After Genocide

Much of this chapter relies on Coombs and Roper family papers—letters, clippings, and an unpublished novel by Frank Leslie Coombs circa 1895.

Brown, Dee. *Bury My Heart at Wounded Knee: An Indian History of the American West.* New York: Holt, Rinehart and Winston, 1970.

Hopkins, Sarah Winnemucca. *Life Among the Piutes. 1883.* Reprint, Bishop CA: Chalfant Press, 1969.

Horsman, Reginald. *Race and Manifest Destiny: The Origins of American Racial Anglo-Saxonism.* Cambridge: Harvard University Press, 1981.

Kroeber, Theodora, and Robert F. Heizer. *Almost Ancestors: The First Californians.* New York: Ballantine Books, 1968.

Lepore, Jill. *The Name of War: King Philip's War and the Origins of American Identity.* New York: Vintage Books, 1999.

Chapter 9. Healing the Deeper Past

Breitwieser, Mitchell. *American Puritanism and the Defense of Mourning: Religion, Grief, and Ethnology in Mary White Rowlandson's Captivity Narrative.* Madison: University of Wisconsin Press, 1990.

Brooks, Lisa. *Our Beloved Kin: A New History of King Philip's War.* New Haven: Yale University Press, 2018.

Coffey, John. *Persecution and Toleration in Protestant New England 1558–1689.* Essex, England: John Pearson Education, Ltd., 2000.

Coombs, William Carey. *The Story of Anthony Coombs and His Descendants.* Amelia, OH, 1913.

Donegan, Kathleen. *Seasons of Misery: Catastrophe and Colonial Settlement in Early America*. Philadelphia: University of Pennsylvania Press, 2014.

Klindienst, Patricia. *The Earth Knows My Name: Food, Culture, and Sustainability in the Gardens of Ethnic Americans*. Boston: Beacon Press, 2000.

Lepore, Jill. *The Name of War: King Philip's War and the Origins of American Identity*. New York: Vintage Books, 1998.

Mann, Barbara Alice. *George Washington's War on Native America*. Lincoln: University of Nebraska Press, 2009.

Mitchell, Sherri. *Sacred Instructions: Indigenous Wisdom for Living Spirit-Based Change*. Berkeley: North Atlantic Books, 2018.

Newell, Margaret Ellen. *Brethren by Nature: New England Indians, Colonists, and the Origins of American Slavery*. Ithaca, NY: Cornell University Press, 2015.

Patchett, Gilbert Gray. *The Saga of the Seven Sisters: Early Pioneer Families of Napa California*. CreateSpace Independent publishing Platform, 2013.

Prechtel, Martín. *The Smell of Rain on Dust: Grief and Praise*. Berkeley: North Atlantic Press, 2015.

Roper, Ella E. *The Ropers of Sterling and Rutland*. East Orange, NJ: Published under the auspices of the Roper Association by Fred H. Colvin, 1904.

Slotkin, Richard. *Regeneration Through Violence: The Mythology of the American Frontier*. Norman: University of Oklahoma Press, 1973.

Williams, Joanne Rigdon. *Ezra Carpenter and Minerva Date Coombs: Their Ancestors and Descendants*. Cottonport, LA: Polyanthos, 1971.

Zinn, Howard. *A People's History of the United States*. New York: Harper & Row, 1980.

Chapter 10. Ceremonies for the Soul Wound

Andreotti, Vanessa. *Deep Adaptation and Climate Justice: 2019: Climate Change and Inequalities*. Filmed in October 2019, Calgary, Alberta, by the Decolonial Futures Collective. Video, 37:49. youtube.com /watch?v=p_TgS_KdaXo.

Duran, Eduardo. Video of Duran's closing keynote remarks: "Forgiving." Filmed in 2013 at Wellbriety conference, Washington, D.C. Video, 50:52. youtube.com/watch?v=D4d2Y3PHJfo.

Easter, Sandra. *Jung and the Ancestors: Beyond Biography, Mending the Ancestral Web.* London and New York: Muswell Hill Press, 2016.

Gustafson, Fred R. *Dancing Between Two Worlds: Jung and the Native American Soul.* New York: Paulist Press, 1997.

Jimmy, Elwood, and Vanessa Andreotti with Sharon Stein. *Towards Braiding.* Guelph, ON: Musagetes Foundation, 2019.

Mitchell, Sherri. *Sacred Instructions: Indigenous Wisdom for Living Spirit-Based Change.* Berkeley: North Atlantic Books, 2018.

Nhat Hanh, Thich. *Creating True Peace.* New York: Free Press, 2003.

———. *Touching the Earth.* Berkeley: Parallax Press, 2004.

Singh, Maanvi. "Native American 'Land Taxes' a Step on the Roadmap for Reparations." *The Guardian*, December 31, 2019. theguardian.com/us-news/2019/dec/31/native-american-land-taxes-reparations?CMP=Share_iOSApp_Other.

Suscol Intertribal Council. *A Brief Look: Historical Trauma and Traditional Healing Project.* September 13, 2019. youtube.com/watch?v=GQVno1c0B20.

Villanueva, Edgar. *Decolonizing Wealth: Indigenous Wisdom to Heal Divides and Restore Balance.* San Francisco: Berrett-Kohler Publishers, 2018.

Website: Vanessa Andreotti and colleagues: decolonialfutures.net.

Genealogical Work Done by or for Family Members

Panttaja, James T. "John Foster Dunlap and Janet Louise Jack, 2008 Edition—Draft." Unpublished, 2007.

Roper, Ella E. *The Ropers of Sterling and Rutland.* East Orange, NJ: Published under the auspices of the Roper Association by Fred H. Colvin, 1904.

Williams, Joanne Rigdon. *Ezra Carpenter and Minerva Date Coombs: Their Ancestors and Descendants.* Cottonport, LA: Polyanthos, 1971.

Index

About the Author

LOUISE DUNLAP is a sixth-generation Californian. In childhood, her passion was wildflowers. As a young adult, she studied medieval English literature. In her working years, she taught writing to undergraduates and grad students in urban and environmental planning, supported writers in advocacy groups, wrote *Undoing the Silence*, and began the journeys into our hidden history that would lead to this book. She honors the spiritual teachings of many traditions and, in 2004, was ordained by Zen master Thich Nhat Hanh into the Order of Interbeing with the name True Silent Teaching.